The Making of an African Christian Ethics

african christian studies series (africs)

This series will make available significant works in the field of African Christian studies, taking into account the many forms of Christianity across the whole continent of Africa. African Christian studies is defined here as any scholarship that relates to themes and issues on the history, nature, identity, character, and place of African Christianity in world Christianity. It also refers to topics that address the continuing search for abundant life for Africans through multiple appeals to African religions and African Christianity in a challenging social context. The books in this series are expected to make significant contributions in historicizing trends in African Christian studies, while shifting the contemporary discourse in these areas from narrow theological concerns to a broader inter-disciplinary engagement with African religio-cultural traditions and Africa's challenging social context.

The series will cater to scholarly and educational texts in the areas of religious studies, theology, mission studies, biblical studies, philosophy, social justice, and other diverse issues current in African Christianity. We define these studies broadly and specifically as primarily focused on new voices, fresh perspectives, new approaches, and historical and cultural analyses that are emerging because of the significant place of African Christianity and African religio-cultural traditions in world Christianity. The series intends to continually fill a gap in African scholarship, especially in the areas of social analysis in African Christian studies, African philosophies, new biblical and narrative hermeneutical approaches to African theologies, and the challenges facing African women in today's Africa and within African Christianity. Other diverse themes in African Traditional Religions; African ecology; African ecclesiology; inter-cultural, inter-ethnic, and inter-religious dialogue; ecumenism; creative inculturation; African theologies of development, reconciliation, globalization, and poverty reduction will also be covered in this series.

SERIES EDITORS
Dr. Stan Chu Ilo (DePaul University, Chicago, USA)
Dr. Esther Acolatse (Duke University, Durham, USA)
Dr. Mwenda Ntarangwi (Calvin College, Grand Rapids, MI, USA)

The Making of an African Christian Ethics: Bénézet Bujo and the Roman Catholic Moral Tradition

WILSON MUOHA MAINA

PICKWICK *Publications* · Eugene, Oregon

THE MAKING OF AN AFRICAN CHRISTIAN ETHICS
Bénézet Bujo and the Roman Catholic Moral Tradition

African Christian Studies series 11

Pickwick
An Imprint of Wipf and Stock Publishers
199 W. 8th Ave., Suite 3
Eugene, OR 97401

www.wipfandstock.com

Paperback ISBN: 978-1-4982-7939-0
Hardcover ISBN: 978-1-4982-7941-3
Ebook ISBN: 978-1-4982-7940-6

Cataloging-in-Publication data:

Names: Maina, Wilson.

Title: The making of an African Christian ethics : Bénézet Bujo and the Roman Catholic moral tradition / Wilson Maina.

African Christian Studies series 11

Description: Eugene, OR: Pickwick Publications, 2016 | Includes bibliographical references.

Identifiers: ISBN 978-1-4982-7939-0 (paperback) | ISBN 978-1-4982-7941-3 (hardcover) | ISBN 978-1-4982-7940-6 (ebook)

Subjects: 1. Theology, Doctrinal—Africa, West 2. Catholic Church—Theology 3. Bénézet Bujo I. Title II. Series

Classification: BX1746.M1 M34 2016 (print) | BX1746.M1 (ebook).

Manufactured in the USA.

Table of Contents

Preface

THIS WORK DEALS WITH Bénézet Bujo's appropriation of the theory of moral autonomy in the making of an African Christian ethics. In the tradition of Catholic moral theology, the moral autonomy debate proceeds from an understanding of the natural law. Natural law, in this context, is understood as pertaining to reason, and thereby an individual human being is seen as having the power of moral self-determination in a concrete situation. I explore Bujo's reflection on the moral autonomy debate, and how he uses this theory in the making of an African Christian ethics, and his critical analysis of natural moral law tradition. My main concern will be the theology of Bujo and the impact of autonomous ethics in his theology.

It may seem ironic and self-contradictory for Bujo, who embodies an African communitarian ethics, to make use of autonomous ethics. However, Bujo does not deny the validity of the natural law as it has continued to develop in the tradition that has its root in the theology and philosophy of Thomas Aquinas. What Bujo will be shown to have done is to rethink the natural law tradition contextually while avoiding the universalistic thinking in the natural law tradition. It is in counter-argument to the universalizing tendency of the theory of natural law that Bujo states: "There is no doubt that the modern person needs moral norms, based on mutual understanding and as binding for all . . . This also means that nobody can consider his philosophically or culturally determined rationality absolute to the point that it could function as a universal criterion, in disregard of other forms of rationality."[1] Bujo argues, therefore, that there is no one way or one philosophy all people should use in the determination of moral norms. He approaches theology from an intercultural perspective that does not claim absoluteness even within the community in which it is established, though it does not exclude dialogue with other communities of communication. It

1. Bujo, *The Ethical Dimension of* Community, preface.

is in this context of the community of communication that Bujo proposes the African palaver as a continuous process in which a community determines its moral norms.

Bujo's theological method is grounded in history. His theology begins with an analysis of an African historical context. This is a theological responsible way of presenting an African Christian ethics. According to Bujo, African history has contributed to the shaping of the way things are today in Africa. He opines that one cannot consider theology in Africa without at the same time thinking about slavery and the slave trade, colonialism, early missionaries, and the advent of African theology. Bujo gives a strong foundation to his theology by emphasizing the indispensability of an African historical perspective. He shows how an African ethics is contextualized in African history. According to Bujo, historical factors that have shaped Africa cannot be ignored in the development of an African Christian ethics.

An African Christian ethics, in the work of Bujo, fits very well in the historical perspective as advocated by the Second Vatican Council. In *Gaudium et Spes*, the council fathers emphatically stated:

> Just as it is in the world's interest to acknowledge the Church as a social reality and a driving force in history, so too the Church is not unaware how much it has profited from the history and development of mankind. It profits from the experiences of past ages, from the progress of the sciences, and from the riches hidden in various cultures, through which greater light is thrown on the nature of man and new avenues to truth are opened up.[2]

It is true, therefore, to say that the theologies developed before and after the Council pay a great deal of attention to history. The theology of Bujo is viewed in this work as part and parcel of the theological trend that recognizes the indispensability of history in theological studies.

Besides African history, Bujo's theology also has its foundation in an African anthropology. According to Bujo, human beings occupy a central place in the understanding of the Africans' moral universe. God and the spiritual world of the ancestors are only understood as they relate to life in the community. African traditional religion(s) are indispensable to the understanding of the moral universe of the African people. African traditional religion(s) are anthropological in the deepest sense of the word. Further, human experience has shaped what the African believes. Those who live near the mountains believe in the God of the mountains, while

2. Flannery, "Church in the Modern World," 946n44.

those near the forest believe in the God of the forest. Jean-Marc Ela refers to the God of the forest as nearer to the people than the God of the heavens.[3] Religious faith is inseparable from human experience. Furthermore, religious faith radically shapes the ethical life of its adherents.[4]

African life is lived in the community. There is no life outside the community. Some African people would say that man is family. Individualism, in an African context, is a failure to contribute to the good of the community. The Gikuyu people of Kenya would say "one who eats alone dies alone." Of course, no one anywhere can host a party where they are also the only guest. The people, as members of the community, determine the community ethos, and therefore the individual is not lost in the group. Bujo demonstrates the indispensability of the community in the African ethics.

Bujo also draws exceedingly from the development of moral theology in the West. The issues he raises from an African perspective are connected to what has been going on in the West. An example of this would be his use of autonomous ethics in the analysis of an African ethics. Despite the fact that Bujo is critical of the natural moral law tradition in the Roman Catholic theology, we cannot separate his theology from this tradition. He is concerned with an African way of theologizing, but to do this he is not limited to an African context. Bujo studied in Europe, where he continues to teach even today. It would be right to say that he is a man of two worlds. He is an African theologian teaching moral theology at Fribourg University in Switzerland.

Bujo is a leading African theologian who studies ethics from an African perspective. In this work, I argue that he uses autonomous ethics as the basis for an African Christian ethics. He has been influenced methodologically by German systematicians like Karl Rahner and J.B. Metz, as well as moralists like Alfons Auer and Franz Böckle, among others.[5] The theological method of Bujo shows that he has been influenced by the theory of the autonomous character of moral reasoning that had its early roots in Germany shortly after Vatican II. From Bujo's work, I explore how

3. Ela, *My Faith as an African*, 26–27.

4. For example, Boyle asks the question "whether religious faith makes a difference in the way the believer perceives moral values, arrives at moral judgments, and executes moral acts" (Boyle, "Faith and Christian Ethics in Rahner and Lonergan," 247).

5. When I emailed Bujo, he confirmed his work has been influenced by German theology as well as by the theologians in Zaire who were his first teachers at Lovanum, Kinshasa. It is important to note that many African theologians have been trained in Europe and, therefore, have been influenced by Western theology.

he develops the idea of moral autonomy as relevant in the making of an African Christian ethics. In this way he contributes to the debate on the autonomous character of Christian ethics.

Bujo's understanding of autonomy goes beyond the notion found in the work of theologians like Alfons Auer, Franz Böckle, and Josef Fuchs. Specifically, he applies the notion of moral autonomy to the community in Africa and not the individual. The idea of palaver grounds Bujo's understanding of autonomy. In this context, "palaver" does not mean unnecessary or meaningless talk. Palaver implies the discussion of an issue in a community where various people gather together, and share perspectives and arrive at the best solution. African palaver does not exclude individual decisions because everybody in the community is represented. Bujo presents an individual person as a member of the community. From the principle, "I am because we are," or "I am because I am known," Bujo shows how indispensable the community is in the understanding of the individual.

Where Western ethicists affirm the dignity of the individual person in moral decisions, Bujo is cautious to show that in an African context the individual is never alone. An individual human being is always with the community, which includes even the dead members, the ancestors. Yet, Bujo is conscious of the moral responsibility of each individual person. Every individual person is not only responsible to oneself but also to the whole community. It would be right to say that Bujo uses the moral autonomy debate to go beyond the same debate. Those opposed to autonomous ethics are the adherents of what is known as *Glaubensethik*, such as Joseph Ratzinger and the biblical scholar Heinz Schürmann.[6] Ratzinger argues the autonomous nature of ethics displaces the role of the magisterium. According to Schürmann, the Bible is an indispensable source of moral teaching and therefore it is possible and necessary to have recourse to it for concrete norms. Bujo makes use of the Bible, and also demonstrates that moral autonomy should proceed not only from a theory of natural moral law, but should also consider an intercultural method as a viable alternative. Where other theologians, like Alfons Auer and Josef Fuchs, begin with the dignity of an individual human being, Bujo begins from the community to show the dignity of each individual human being in an African society. He promotes an understanding of African communitarian ethics.

Further, I argue Bujo's perspective of moral autonomy goes beyond the encyclical *Veritatis Splendor* on the subject of the natural law doctrine.

6. The responses to autonomous ethics and the articulation of faith ethics by Schürmann and Ratzinger can be seen in their book, *The Principles of Christian Morality*.

The Roman Catholic Church's understanding of the natural law is viewed by Bujo as inadequate because of its tendency to universalize and absolutize principles. Bujo proposes that in African ethics, natural law and theories drawn from it should be understood in particular contexts and not absolutized in universal claims. The main criticism that Bujo makes of *Veritatis Splendor* is based on the encyclical's understanding of natural law as universal and essentialist without considering the context of its application. An African ethics, according to Bujo, is founded on the community, and it does not claim absoluteness outside the community. Any moral decision in an African community is contingent upon context and open to the emergence of new insights to provide a better argument. From his understanding of autonomous ethics, Bujo develops an African understanding of moral autonomy. Bujo shifts from the autonomy of the individual, as seen in Auer and Fuchs, to show an individual person as always in a community in an African setting. He especially gives a central place to the African palaver where members of the community met and discussed the issue at hand and decided upon the course of action to take. This clearly distinguishes Bujo from the Western understanding of moral autonomy.

The autonomous ethics debate is useful in doing away with a naive use of faith in African moral theology. Instead of the theory of the natural moral law, Bujo proposes an intercultural approach to moral theology, an approach he holds to be relevant in the study of Christian ethics considering the cultural diversity that exists in the world. An African ethics, in the work of Bujo, refers to the whole endeavor of providing a better understanding and way of living out, in a genuinely Black African context, the realities connected to the Christian faith. Hence, I will also explore how Bujo incorporates liberation ethics into the debate on moral autonomy.

Bujo takes as his foundation the premise that African theology has to begin from an African social context. It is supposed to be a theology that addresses the African people in their cultural context. Although Bujo had written several theological books and journal articles before 1986, his *Afrikanische Theologie in ihrem gesellschaftlichen Kontext* (African Theology in its Social Context) marks a major theological contribution to African theology. In this book Bujo articulated his view of what constitutes African theology. He began this work from a historical perspective of the African continent. He dealt with factors that shaped African history such as colonialism and slave trade, but also positive ones like the early Western missionaries to Africa, and the advent of the first African theologians. Bujo presents an analysis of what constitutes an African world-view and applies this to the understanding of moral theological issues such as marriage and social justice. He begins his theology with the basic premise that Jesus Christ must be understood in the African context as a member of the community. He refers to Jesus as the Proto-Ancestor.

Bujo shows the relevance of the development of moral theology in the Roman Catholic Church in the West to the Christians of Africa. Many elements of the renewal of moral theology, especially after Vatican II, are to be found in the theology of Bujo. These include among others: the use of scripture, the relevance of history, the debate on moral norms, the relevance of social sciences to moral discourse, the theory of natural moral law, and the relation between the theologian and the magisterium. This work, therefore, locates the theology of Bujo in the development of moral theology after the Second Vatican Council.

The theological writings of Bujo are taken analytically and comparatively as the primary sources of this work. This does not exclude reference to the contribution of other theologians in the development of moral theology, and especially on the debate on moral autonomy. Chapter one establishes issues of foundations in an African Christian ethics. Perspectives on African historical and cultural contexts are explored. Chapter two locates an African moral theology, especially in the work of Bujo, in the development of Catholic moral theology after the Second Vatican Council. The call for renewal, which had begun even before the council, is viewed as reflected by some aspects of the theology of Bujo. The renewal movement was concerned with the history of moral norms, the use of Sacred Scripture, the renewed understanding of the natural law, and the view of morality as Christo-centric. Further, chapter three deals with the communitarian ethics in the work of Bujo. Bujo is viewed as reconciling the communal and individual dimensions in African ethics. In chapter four, I analyze Bujo's theology and his writing on liberation ethics in an African context. Jesus, the Proto-Ancestor, is viewed as the Liberator from all the ills that affect Africa. Jesus is understood to revitalize and positively transform African customs. Chapter five critically analyzes the debate about the autonomous character of moral reasoning and argues for relevance of the debate in African ethical reasoning. A variety of perspectives on these ethical debates are explored. Finally, chapter six presents a critical examination of the encyclical *Veritatis Splendor* as a reaction to the debate on the autonomous character of morality.

Acknowledgments

THIS WORK IS DEVELOPED from my doctoral dissertation at Fordham University, New York. While I am responsible for the content of this work and any mistakes therein, I am especially grateful to my mentor, Prof. Thomas Kopfensteiner, and the doctoral committee members, Profs. Leo Lefebure and Daniel Thompson. Their insights helped shape my work then and now. I also appreciate the guidance and assistance by the editors, the reviewers, and the staff at Pickwick Publications and Wipf and Stock Publishers.

Some of the chapters in this work were previously published in the *Journal for the Study of Religions and Ideologies* and *Pacifica*. These journals initially gave permissions for the future development and publication of this work in other sources. I am grateful to their editors and reviewers for the various suggestions in the development of this work.

1

The Foundations of African Christian Theologies: African Traditional Religion(s) and the African Historical and Cultural Contexts

THE HISTORICAL DEVELOPMENT OF African Christian theology requires a critical analysis. In this work, I view an attempt to generalize African people as sharing the same traditional religions and way of life as creating an overly homogenized African people and African Christian theology. The basic premise here is that an African Christian theology appropriates African traditional religions and Christian teachings, and therefore any generalization of African traditional religions constitutes an untenable generalization in African Christian theology. I argue there are many African traditional religions. There is evidence of diversity in language and culture among African people which therefore calls for many African Christian theologies. This chapter avers in a radical way that African history and culture informs theological developments in the continent, and especially theological ethics.

Contemporary Africa has witnessed the birth and development of an African Christian theology. Unfortunately, African theology has remained in its preliminary stages for decades. From a critical-analytical and comparative approach, this work raises questions on the various perspectives taken by some African theologians as the starting point in their work. Theological responses are dialectically analyzed from the perspective of cultural diversity in Africa. Diversity is especially evident through an observation of multiplicity of African languages, and how these leads to many theologies within African Christianity.

An African Christian theology is based on an understanding of the African traditional religion(s) and varied responses to Christian faith and teachings. The (s) in African Traditional Religion(s) caters for two views in the understanding of religion in Africa. One view refers to African religion in the singular and the other view, which I view as more accurate, holds there are many traditional religions in Africa. It is for this reason I deal with the problem of generalization in African traditional religions and the ensuing theological perspective that African theology is one as opposed to many theologies.

This chapter is divided into two parts. Part one explores the meaning of African Christian theology, its diversity, and foundations in African traditional religion(s). African continent is presented as comprised of diverse traditional religions, cultures, and languages, and this is thought to presuppose the development of many theologies and not just one theology. Part two explores an African theology and ethics as informed and shaped by an African historical and cultural setting. The work of Bénézet Bujo is used in part two to show the historical and cultural perspective in African Christian theology.

Part One: African Christian Theology, African Traditional Religion(s), and Cultural Diversity

African Christian theology is informed by a critical analysis of an African cultural context. It bases the Christian teachings, through critical reflection, on African reality that shapes human living in society. Hence, a proper understanding of African traditional religion(s) is necessary in the understanding of the relationship between religion and ethics in Africa.

1. What is African Christian Theology?

African Christian theology is a science or discipline that is responsible for understanding the Christian message in an African social context. The purpose of African Christian theology is to see to it that the message of Christ is expressed in African categories and thought patterns. Bujo expresses the role of African theology as follows: "the inculturation of Christianity, however, should not hide the social relevance of African tradition, but rather challenge the African person to transform his/her world into a better place."[1] African Christian theology is concerned with making Christian doctrine relevant in an African context. To do this, African traditions and customs have to be given their rightful place for it is only in this way that an African can hear the call by Jesus Christ to faith. It is also in this context that Charles Nyamiti wrote:

> Indeed, if African theology is the understanding and presentation of the Christ-event in accordance with African needs and mentality, then African Christologies must have existed since the beginning of evangelization on the Black continent (although mainly in latent, oral, and unsystematic form). Despite their predominantly Western way of theologizing, missionaries were often induced to present Christ's mystery to answer to the problems and ways of thinking of the African people. The people received that message in its Western form according to which it was delivered and also in accordance with their African experience.[2]

To understand how African Christian theology evolved an article by A. Ngindu Mushete is helpful. He distinguishes three currents that typify theology in Africa: missionary theology, so-called African theology, and "black theology" as exemplified in South Africa.[3] He presents the three distinctions as stages in the development of theology concerning Africa. He states; "For one school, the aim of mission work is the *conversion of the infidel*. For a second school it is the *establishing or implanting of the church*. For a third school it is *giving birth to a native church and helping it to grow properly*; this means helping it to assume its proper role and responsibility in communion with Christ and all other local churches."[4] Mushete presents missionary theology as centered around the salvation of souls or the conversion of the infidel. It was developed and defended in particular by the missiological school of Münster. It polarized missionary reflection for several centuries right up to the start of the twentieth century. Mushete holds that missionary theology was "solidly grounded on the adage, *extra ecclesiam (romanam) nulla salus*. The theology centered on the salvation

---

1. Bujo, *The Ethical Dimension of Community,* 19.

2 Nyamiti, "African Christologies Today," 19.

3. Mushete, "The History of Theology in Africa: From Polemics to Critical Irenics," 23.

4. Ibid., 23–24.

of infidels logically led its partisans to wholly disqualify the cultural and religious traditions of African peoples."[5]

The missionary theology of church implantation, according to Mushete, "was solidly ecclesiastical and even ecclesiocentric in its orientation. On the clean slate, or the slate wiped clean, of people without culture or civilization, missionaries were to establish the church as it had been known historically in the West."[6] The goal of mission work was to establish the church where it does not yet exist visibly. It must give stable and perduring organization to the various means of salvation: i.e., the clergy, the laity, religious communities, and Christian forms in general.[7]

Contemporary African Christian theology should not be viewed at the level of missionary theology. It is at the level of critical African theology. This theology should be seen in what Mushete says, that "African" theology attempts to take due account of the Africans to whom the faith is addressed. It takes note of Africa's culture, religion, and civilization. It advocates the right of African Christians to ponder Christianity and its truth in their own terms.[8]

2. African Christian Theology and African Traditional Religion(s)

The correlation of African Christian theology with the African traditional religion(s) leads to a further dimension of the foundation of African ethics and Christian ethics. The focus here is on the inseparable relation between religion and ethics in an African context. Further, I analyze the African world-view that informs the making of an African Christian theology and ethics.

(a) The relation between Religion and Ethics in an African Context

Ethical behavior is very much influenced by people's beliefs as established in their religion. African morality does not escape the fact that it is shaped by the African traditional religion(s). For example, Ukachukwu Manus holds that "the truism that religious outlook and worldviews are symbiotic is very sure in Africa where, more than elsewhere, both realities are

5. Ibid., 24.
6. Ibid., 24–25.
7. Ibid., 25.
8. Ibid., 27.

interdependent and influence each other."[9] The same symbiotic relationship can be said of religion and morality.[10]

    Religion and ethics are inseparable in Africa.[11] This is true not only in Africa but also in other places where religious beliefs can be said to inform the ethical life of its adherents. Laurenti Magesa notes that "morality or ethics is of the very nature of religion."[12] Religion has always to do with human life and experience. Separating religious belief from human activity or ethics is an untenable demarcation. Hans Küng's understanding of religion is helpful in relating religion and ethics. Küng is of the opinion that religion is "a believing view of life, approach to life, way of life, and therefore a fundamental pattern embracing the individual and society, man and the world, through which a person (though only partially conscious of this) sees and experiences, thinks and feels, acts and suffers, everything. It is a transcendentally grounded and immanently operative system of coordinates by which man orients himself intellectually, emotionally, and existentially."[13] It is true, therefore to say that morality is part and parcel of religion. Religious faith can be said to be a motivating factor in good ethical conduct in human beings. According to Mbiti, God is thought to be "the

9. Manus, "African Christologies: The Centre-piece of African Christian Theology," 7.

10. See Häring, "Morality," 113–14. Häring states: "What connection is there between that part of morality which regulates a man's relation to other persons, to the community and to himself, and the religious mystery? It cannot be denied that the claim of moral value and duty is also experienced by human beings who have not yet or not yet fully found their way to faith in a personal God. Phenomenologically—in the realm of experience—morality is not always expressly connected with the 'holy,' with religion. But no explanation of morality is satisfying or leaves its deepest experience intact if it omits or indeed denies the link between religion and morality. In genuine moral experience a human being who is prepared on principle to live according to conscience, is not ultimately dealing with a mere principle or merely concerned with his own fulfillment. He knows that ultimately he is in relation with a Thou who can unconditionally give and demand" (Häring, "Morality," 114).

11. This statement may seem to contradict the understanding of western autonomous debate by putting ethics as somehow determined by religious faith. The intention is not to separate faith and morality but to show that there is an indispensable relationship between the two. See O'Neil's statement: "To be sure, as in the "autonomy school" of moral theology, particular religious narratives may provide laudable motivation, but the norms governing moral conduct (the content of the *humanum*) are logically and semantically independent of distinctive religious attitudes and beliefs" (O'Neil, "African Moral Theology," 137). Further, religious experience is human experience, and human experience can also be religious experience.

12. Magesa, *African* Religion, 2.

13. Ibid., 24. Magesa here quotes from Küng et al., *Christianity and World Religions.*

ultimate guardian of human morality."[14] Most of the time, any religion has to do with the idea of the absolute.

Nevertheless, the relations between religion and morality can be understood more concretely in a transcendental way. Transcendental theological method advocates the claim that a human subject cannot be understood without saying something about the absolute being or God. The idea of the absolute gives human knowing a transcendental perspective of being able to know all that there is. Josef Fuchs, writing on the relation between faith, ethics and law states the following:

> Christian faith acknowledges and recognizes man, his nature, his being a person, his reason, as the creation of God. It understands that humanity, freed from its sinful alienation from God through Jesus Christ, is accepted by the God of Love. God belongs to the specificity of man, whose ultimate dignity thus stems from God. God does not give positive rights and duties to man; rather, man is the image of God and participates therefore in God's providence.[15]

Fuchs, in this context, holds that Christian morality is in the realm of the human being. Human beings have to discover moral norms through reason. This does not exclude God because there is a Christian understanding that God is the source or the creator of all that there is. The created world can be said to acquire a deeper meaning when viewed in connection with God who is its source and sustains it in his providence. Human realization of the moral norms becomes the human participation in God. We can say of Fuchs, that he understands human capacity for realizing ethical norms as inherently given by God. Human rational nature is the distinctive mark of what it means to be human. In this view humanity cannot be understood without having its reference in God. This can be referred to as the transcendental perspective of morality in the theological ethics of Fuchs. This transcendental element in ethics is also evident in African traditional religion(s) where there is a realization of the presence of God (or the sacred) in human beings.

In an African setting, to understand morality, religion is indispensable. Magesa states:

> Consequently, understanding the morality of the African people—that is, their perception of the Holy that demands and

14. Mbiti, *Introduction to African Religion*, 180.
15. Fuchs, *Christian Ethics in a Secular Arena*, 118.

enforces their emotional and behavioral commitment and so gives direction to their lives—requires us to examine the worldview and ethos contained in their religious symbols. Such an exercise will open the door through which we can enter the mind and heart of Africa and truly appreciate the controlling motivation of her values and her people's attitudes.[16]

People have come to know God through their daily experiences. It can be said that it is through the work of creation and probably the order that exists in creation that people have come to believe in God. But limiting experiences such as drought, famine, disease, war, and others can also lead people to postulate the existence of the One who is above all and the one who can conquer all evil. To realize the fullness of humanity, we can say that human persons look towards God.

It is in a worldview where religion and all area of human living are embedded together that Bujo holds that among many African peoples there is no separation between church and state. "The traditional African world-view sees no dichotomy between religion and politics, since the human being does not act in a solely secular manner and without relationship to the religious dimensions even for a single moment."[17] We can, therefore, say that religion reflects peoples' everyday life. Religion and ethics, or even politics permeate each other. It would be impossible, then, to understand ethics separated from religion in an African traditional context, and vice versa. The Gikuyu people of Kenya had a council of elders that combined both religious and "secular" functions in the life of the community.[18] This council of elders is a typical example of the non-separation of the religious and the secular, or religion and ethics. The same elders, who participated in the arbitration of conflict between individuals, were the same people who offered sacrifices to God in time of need. Among the Gikuyu people there was no "career" priesthood but it was a rotating priestly function depending on age and credibility of an individual in a community.

Discussing the African religious heritage, Mbiti is also of the opinion that "religion is found in all areas of human life."[19] He holds the view that

---

16. Magesa, *African Religion*, 4.

17. Bujo, *Ethical Dimension of Community*, 19. See also the statement Meditz notes from Joseph Cardinal Malula: "For our people, the church was the state, and the state was the church" (Meditz, *Zaire: A Country Study*, 114).

18. Kenyatta, *Facing Mount Kenya*, 232.

19. Mbiti, *Introduction to African Religion*, 9.

religion has dominated the thinking of African peoples to such an extent that it has shaped their cultures, their social life, their political organizations and economic activities. We can say, therefore, that religion is closely bound up with the traditional way of African life, while at the same time, this way of life has shaped religion as well.[20] Mbiti further views values and morals as the "part of religion which deals with the ideas that safeguard or uphold the life of the people in their relationship with one another and the world around them."[21] In all these, we can therefore say, there is no separation between religion and ethics in many African communities.

(b) Why do some African Theologians refer to African Theology in the Singular?

The view that a theologian holds on African traditional religion(s) is viewed in this work as shaping the nature of the African Christian theology developed from that perspective. Looking at African traditional religion(s) as all the same is a view not cognizant with the reality one finds in the African continent. For this reason even to argue for a singular African Christian theology is problematic because of the variety in African traditional religions and cultural diversity. Therefore, my objective here is a critical analysis of various understanding of African Christian theology. Diversity in Africa cannot be ignored. Below I consider some perspectives on African traditional religions and how these have shaped African Christian theologies.

(I) THEOLOGICAL DIMENSIONS AND THEIR RELATED VIEWS OF AFRICAN TRADITIONAL RELIGION(S)

The theology of Bujo is shaped in a special way by his understanding of traditional religion in the continent of Africa. Bujo views African religion in the singular. It is for this reason that he writes of an "African ethic." The argument for this view of religion is based on a general view of similarities that can be found in various groups of people in Africa. This is a disputed claim. Some African theologians argue for a plurality of African traditional

---

20. Ibid. Cf. Jassy, who states: "The organization and functioning of traditional society were inseparable from a vision of the world and of religion" (*Basic Community in the African Churches*, 25).

21. Mbiti, *Introduction to African Religion*, 11.

religions. The understanding of African traditional religion(s) has shaped the various approaches African Christian theology has taken up today.

Bujo makes reference of African traditional "religion" and not "religions" in the plural. An example is when he says, "in the first place we must discuss how African religion is the very heart of the traditional society."[22] In his various books he presents one African anthropology and not several anthropologies. He refers to "Africa's anthropocentric ethical system,"[23] and that "the focus of African religion is life."[24] To him, therefore, African peoples have the same or similar ethical and religious system. For this reason, it is my view that Bujo promotes a relational view of religion in an African context.

The view of African traditional religion in the singular is based on the belief that all the different groups of people in Africa have similar or related beliefs, rituals and ways of life. Various examples are cited to support this view which include the belief in a supreme being, the reverence of and belief in the ancestors, and their influence in the life of the community. The danger of applying this approach, viewing the African traditional religion as one, is that of generalization. Taking one element of a particular tribal group and applying it to all other African people does not seem to do justice to the richness of each religion. This approach would be advantageous, if and only if it is backed by extensive research that proves that there are indispensable elements in African traditional religion(s) that are common to all.

The Tanzanian theologian, Laurenti Magesa, also shares Bujo's concept of an African ethical system or an African traditional religion. Making reference to John Mbiti, Magesa holds that "the philosophy underlying religious expression of the African people . . . is a philosophy in the singular."[25] According to Magesa; "the varieties are more those of expression than basic belief. They are much like the varieties of expression we find in any major religion, such as Christianity (in the form of denominations) or Islam, for instance. They may be referred to by different names, such as Roman Catholic, Lutheran, Anglican, Presbyterian, or Baptist in Christianity, or Shia, Sunni, or Sufi in Islam. Nonetheless, they remain Christian or Muslim."[26]

22. Bujo, *African Theology in its Social* Context, 17.

23. Ibid., 35.

24. Ibid., 34.

25. Magesa, *African Religion*, 15.

26. Ibid., 16–17.

Magesa suggests that different denominations can share the same faith but only differ in rituals. He suggests the same of African traditional religion(s) that they differ only in their respective rituals.

Evidently, Magesa shares the same opinion on African religion as Bujo. He is of the opinion that there are shared elements in the religion(s) of the various people of Africa. He states: "Yet to conclude that there is therefore no internal, essential unity in the various expressions of African Religion is to exaggerate."[27] Magesa refers to the tendency of

> [s]ome philosophers, theologians, and students of comparative religion . . . to regard African Religion as a "primal" or "ethnic" religion, thus robbing it of its universal character . . . This attitude also reduces the capacity of African Religion to interact with other religions and to influence and change the world and minimizes its role in conversation with other religions. It becomes a subordinate partner rather than an equal. The study of African religion, from this perspective, then becomes merely a description of appearances instead of a portrayal of a phenomenon with moral power that shapes and directs the lives of millions of people in their relationship with other human beings, the created order, and the Divine.[28]

Magesa even argues that there is a universal element in the African religion. This is especially evident when he refers to some objections that have been leveled against African religion. On the objections to African religion, Magesa writes:

> First, because African Religion has no written scriptures, even some liberal Western scholars of religion have been reluctant to consider it as any more than a "tribal" religion. "World" religions such as Judaism, Islam, or Hinduism all have their own written sources. Western scholars thus could neither conceive nor allow that a religion dependent on oral traditions, such as African Religion is, could be regarded as an equal.[29]

About this objection on the lack of scripture in the African religion, Magesa responds that Judaism existed as an orally based religion for many centuries before its oral story was codified in writing.[30] The other factor of

27. Ibid., 17.
28. Ibid., 19.
29. Ibid., 22.
30. Ibid., 22.

African religion Magesa notes is lack of interest in aggressive proselytizing, like other world religions such as Christianity and Islam.[31]

Theo Sundermeier, a German theologian, who lived for many years among the southern Bantu and Khoisan people in Southern Africa, takes a middle position on the question of African traditional religions. He holds that they are not all the same, though they have some similarities. On the peoples of sub-Saharan Africa, Sundermeier states that "they are not culturally homogenous, yet the difference between the ethnic groups are slighter than between them and the Arabic-speaking peoples of northern Africa."[32] For this reason he concludes that there is no single, all-inclusive name for their religions. Sundermeier makes the following statement:

> It is certainly one thing to start from the primary experience of the southern Bantu and Khoisan peoples . . . and another to adopt the perspective of West African or eastern Sudanese (Nilotic) ethnic groups . . . The more deeply you enter into African spirituality, and understand the ethnic and social basis for the way Africans cope with the world, the more—it seems to me—you are justifying in talking of African religion in the singular . . . One basic structure runs through all African religions, the creation of symbols around people . . . It is this basic pattern which entitles us to examine these religions with regard to their image of humankind.[33]

There is no reason why the argument above could not be made about world religions. They have so many similarities yet they have core elements that distinguish them. In the perspective of Sundermeier, to deny diversity in Africa is to deny the reality on the ground. Hence, an analysis of diversity in Africa is required.

(II) DIVERSITY AMONG AFRICAN PEOPLE AND THEIR WAYS OF LIFE

Similarity and relatedness in the African traditional religions do not exclude the existence of diversity. Nevertheless, those who believe in plurality of African traditional religions hold that Africa as a continent is very diverse. Religions are as many as there are ethnic groups in Africa. To support this view the proponents cite the different ways of life witnessed from one community to the other. Despite the fact that Africa has diverse cultures, it

31. Ibid., 23.

32. Sundermeier, *The Individual and Community in African Traditional Religions*, 34.

33. Ibid., 6–7.

would be unjustifiable to deny that in diversity there is similarity.[34] There are so many elements in which African traditional religion(s) are related to each other. Mbiti demonstrates the idea of similarity and difference when he states:

> The African heritage is rich, but it is not uniform. It has similarities, but there are also differences from time to time, from place to place, and from people to people. Some of this heritage originated on the African soil; it is therefore, genuinely African and indigenous. But some developed through contact with peoples of other countries and continents. African forefathers exported their heritage, or lent it to other peoples of the world; and in return they also learnt something from other peoples.[35]

Although, Mbiti refers to "African Religion" in the singular, he acknowledges that "religion takes on different forms according to different tribal settings."[36] He holds that a person from one setting cannot automatically and immediately adjust himself to or adopt the religious life of other African peoples in a different setting. Mbiti admits to the fact that diversity exists.

Additionally, Alyward Shorter has explained similarities in religion among various groups, through the interaction of people. Shorter maintains that "the study of African oral history has revealed a high degree of interaction between different ethnic groups. This interaction was seldom the result of great conquests or migrations, rather it was a filtering movement of small groups of people, a highly complex process of ebb and flow from every possible direction."[37] We could also take the argument of similarity further by putting forward that similarity does not mean sameness. The

34. Cf. Tanner, who has argued that culture is what distinguishes one society from another. She holds that no two societies share the same culture—culture is what marks the boundary between one society from another. She states: "Though Culture is universal in the sense that all people have one, the anthropological use of the term highlights human diversity. All people have culture but they do not all have the same one. What culture amounts to varies widely with time and place. The fact of 'culture' is common to all; the particular pattern of culture differs among all. Culture therefore comes in the plural; the anthropologist speaks of cultures" (*Theories of Culture*, 26).

35. Mbiti, *Introduction to African Religion*, 3. Cf. Hastings, who states: "The sheer size and range of the Christian churches in Africa today, not to speak of their vitality, can hardly not require the emergence of a whole range of theologies, and equally of liturgies and of spiritualities" (*African Catholicism*, 86).

36. Mbiti, *Introduction to African Religion*, 13.

37. Shorter, *African Christian Theology—Adaptation or Incarnation?* 50.

very fact that two things are similar does not mean that they are the same. The same can be applied to African traditional religion(s), that though they have similarities, it does not mean that they are the same among different ethnic groups.

The position that many theologians take on African theology as homogeneous has its dangers considering the size and the diversity of the continent. Although majority of theologians are aware of the enormousness of the continent, they builds their theology by taking the elements of various ethnic groups that are similar and as determining the basics of African traditional religion(s). It is my view that there are as many African traditional religions as there are ethnic groups in the continent. It would be true to say that a monolithic view of African traditional religion(s) poses the danger of universalizing a few cultural, moral and religious elements to all the peoples of Africa. Some African theologians could also be accused of the same universalizing tendency in Christian churches that they oppose in others. For example, Bujo writes that "Christians cannot avoid paying close attention to the process of globalization precisely because it tends to a *monoculture*, with clear consequences for evangelization. If the good news of Jesus is to *make its home* among every people, it cannot identify itself with one specific culture, not even a global or monoculture."[38]

(III) Many Languages as indicative of Diversity

The idea of the diversity and distinctiveness of each ethnic group is indispensable, if the gospel message is to be meaningful to every ethnic group in Africa. It has to be rooted in that specific group's way of life. I would be opposed to the idea of talking of an African anthropology in the singular.[39] Referring to an African anthropology seems to be a genus that requires clarification by stating the specific difference of each ethnic group of people. An example of a genus would be when Bujo states that the "the human person is himself only in an orientation to the totality of humanity, of history, and of the cosmos."[40] This is a statement that can be said of any human being in the world. Despite the particular cultural and social elements that go into the defining of any particular group of people, Christians cannot

---

38. Bujo, *Foundations of an African Ethic,* xii.

39. Ibid., 1. See also Njoku, *Essays in African Philosophy, Thought & Theology,* 105–24.

40. Bujo, *Foundations of an African Ethic,* 4.

deny the basic human nature that is shared by all.[41] It is for this reason that we can see that theologians like Bujo, though critical of the natural law reasoning, not denying it. Just as the natural moral law reasoning needs to be concretized, so also an African ethnic group needs to think for itself the implications of the Christian message in their daily life. The natural moral law reasoning is a central aspect in the renewal of moral theology in the Roman Catholic Church, especially on the debate on universal moral norms, and it also has influenced the developing of an African Christian ethics.

The point that needs to be noted is that Africa does not have one culture. If we consider a single country like the Democratic Republic of Congo, Meditz records that in Congo "about 250 languages are spoken. French remains the primary language of government, formal economy, and most education. Four indigenous languages also have official status: Kikongo, Tshiluba, Lingala, and Kishwahili."[42] The number of languages reflects the fact that there are as many as over 250 different ethnic groups, mostly Bantu speaking. Of all these ethnic groups the largest Bantu-speaking groups are Luba, Kongo, Mongo, and Lunda. Many languages are a sign of cultural diversity, and the same can be said about the relationship between language and religion. Hence, it is true what Sundermeier says: "Religion and language are closely linked, because faith lives from the fact that truth is put into words."[43] Therefore, it is questionable whether one can say that Africa is culturally or religiously homogeneous.

41. Christians generally hold that there is a commonly shared human nature that is created by God, but some contemporary theologians and philosophers question the very existence of a human nature shared by all. For example, Rorty argues: "The temptation to look for criteria is a species of the more general temptation to think of the world, or the human self, as possessing an intrinsic nature, an essence. That is, it is the result of temptation to privilege some one among the many languages in which we habitually describe the world or ourselves. As long as we think that there is some relation called 'fitting the world' or 'expressing the real nature of the self' which can be possessed or lacked by vocabularies-as-wholes, we shall continue the traditional philosophical search for a criterion to tell us which vocabularies have this desirable feature. But if we could ever become reconciled to the idea that most of reality is indifferent to our descriptions of it, and that the human self is created by the use of a vocabulary rather than being adequately or inadequately expressed in a vocabulary, then we should at last have assimilated what was true in the Romantic idea that truth is made rather than found. What is true about this claim is just that languages are made rather than found, and that truth is a property of linguistic entities, of sentences" (Rorty, *Contingency, Irony, and Solidarity*, 6–7).

42. Meditz, *Zaire*, xxvi.

43. Sundermeier, *Individual and Community*, 22.

Kwame Appiah, a philosopher at Princeton University, is of the opinion that major differences exist among African peoples. His view is that "the peoples of Africa have a good deal less culturally in common than is usually assumed."[44] He capitalizes on the problem of finding a common African language for research and educational purposes. He writes of

> the practical difficulties of developing a modern educational system in a language in which none of the manuals and textbooks have been written; nor should we forget, in the debit column, the less noble possibility that these foreign languages, whose possession had marked the colonial elite, became too precious as marks of status to be given up by the class that inherited the colonial state.[45]

Appiah shows how the use of the languages of the colonizers led to an alienation of traditional African languages. Individual self-identity has shifted from identifying oneself with an African traditional language to an imported foreign language. Appiah adds:

> Yet despite these differences, both Francophone and Anglophone elites not only use the colonial languages as the medium of government but know and often admire the literature of their ex-colonizers, and have chosen to make a modern African literature in European languages. Even after a brutal colonial history and nearly two decades of sustained armed resistance, the decolonization in the mid-seventies of Portuguese Africa left a Lusophone elite writing African laws and literature in Portuguese.[46]

Appiah demonstrates the fact that diversity exists in the African continent as it is attested by the plurality of languages. The very fact that we Africans cannot speak one language says much about our differences. The languages in Africa are as diverse as there are people. "But to find their way out of their own community, and acquire national, let alone international, recognition, most traditional languages—the obvious exception being Swahili—have to be translated. Few black African states have the privilege

44. Appiah, *In My Father's House*, 17.

45. Ibid., 4. The conception of the language issue in Africa is put clearly by Ngugi wa Thiong'o, a renowned Kenyan novelist. Thiong'o wrote: "The choice of language and the use to which language is put is central to a people's definition of themselves in relation to their natural and social environment, indeed in relation to the entire universe. Hence language has always been at the heart of the two contending social forces in the Africa of the twentieth century" (Thiong'o, *Decolonising the Mind*, 4).

46. Appiah, *In My Father's House*, 4.

of corresponding to a single traditional linguistic community.[47] Linguistic differences mark the various ethnic distinctions in the countries of Africa, with the exception of Somalia, "whose people have the same language and traditions but managed, nevertheless, to spend a decade after independence in which their official languages were English, Italian, and Arabic."[48] However, the existence of many African languages does not deny that there are religious and cultural similarities.

The reality of linguistic diversity in Africa has ensured the use of foreign languages in scholarly work. English and French have dominated many African countries as the sole medium of instruction in schools. Hence, Appiah argues; "Together such disparate forces have conspired to ensure that the most important body of writing in sub-Saharan Africa even after independence continues to be in English, French, and Portuguese. For many of its most important cultural purposes, most African intellectuals, south of the Sahara, are what we can call "Europhone."[49] European languages continue up to today to influence the daily lives of the people in Africa. The adoption of European languages has also meant the adoption of foreign cultural practices. According to Appiah:

> This linguistic situation is of most importance in the cultural lives of African intellectuals. It is, of course, of immense consequence to the citizens of African states generally that their ruling elites are advised by and in many cases constituted of europhone intellectuals. But a concern with the relations of "traditions" and "modern" conceptual worlds, with the integration of inherited modes of understanding and newly acquired theories, concepts, and belief, is bound to be of special importance in the lives of those of us who think and write about the future of Africa in terms that are largely borrowed from elsewhere. We may acknowledge that the truth is the property of no culture, that we should take the truths as we find them. But for truths to become the basis of national policy and, more widely, of national life, they must be believed, and whether or not whatever new truths we take from the West

47. Ibid.

48. Ibid. See Wiredu, *Cultural Universals and Particulars*, 45–60. Wiredu argues that there is universalism and particularism in religion from an African perspective. He points out that there is no one way to describe religion in Africa. All African indigenous groups have their particular culture and religion. But there are also points of convergence in religion and culture in Africa. See also Maddox, "African Theology and the Search for the Universal," 25–36.

49. Appiah, *In My Father's House*, 4.

will be believed depends in large measure on how we are able to manage the relations between our conceptual heritage and the ideas that rush at us from worlds elsewhere.[50]

Diversity is not detrimental to the flourishing of Africa as a continent. Shared views ensure that no monolithic view dominates the society. The idea of one culture complementing the other is always a healthy way to boost the wellbeing of a society. Appiah professes not to believe in a homogenous Africa but he is quick to say, "I do believe that Africans can learn from each other, as . . . we can learn from all of human-kind."[51]

Part Two: Doing Theology in an African Historical Context

African Christian theology is a product of discourse in an African context. The work of Bujo is an example of an African theology with its foundation in an African historical and cultural context. Bujo approaches an African Christian ethics from a historical perspective. He gives prominence not only to the African cultural setting but also to the African historical background. He categorizes African history into the major events that have been marked as turning points in the shaping of Africa as we have it today. Among these events, Bujo includes the effect of the trans-Atlantic slave trade, colonization of Africa, the advent of Christian missionaries, and the political independence movements, as well as the birth of African theology. All these events, according to Bujo, are indispensable in an understanding of an African ethics today.

African Christianity requires a theology that goes beyond inculturation. It requires a theology that is not just concerned with adaptation of external cultural elements. Inculturation alone is not enough, but needs a historically conscious method. It is this kind of sound theology that Bujo refers to when he states: "As regards the social significance of an African theology, I am convinced that only a theology, which chooses *African tradition* as its partner in dialogue, will be capable of building a black Christianity which is rooted in the soil, and is consequently full of the promise and vigor of a life in which no African fears to lose his identity."[52] African traditions develop and change through contact with "others." In response

50. Ibid., 4–5.

51. Ibid., 26.

52. Bujo, *African Christian Morality at the Age of Inculturation*, 119. See also Muzorewa, *The Origins and Development of African Theology*, 5–20.

to this interaction, some traditions are already extinct and others replaced. Other traditions have advanced to acquire a more meaningful standing in the community. It would, therefore, not be right to consider an African ethics as stagnant because culture develops.

The other major problem is that of making an African theology that is not addressed to Africans themselves but only answers to foreigners' questions. A theology that does not address itself to the issues affecting Africans but only concerns itself with an apologetic end is irrelevant. This kind of theology does not answer questions coming from the African scene but addresses foreigners in their own philosophical and theological categories. This is what Bujo addresses when he says that "African theology is also in danger of turning itself into an article for export, appreciated only for its exotic appeal. Many of our black theologians are much better known overseas than at home, and indeed one may meet them at sundry international conferences, but never run into them in the bush. Studies in African theology are *by preference being published overseas*, and mainly sold to a Western clientele."[53] The same could also be said of the concern to address "outsiders" in synods and conferences that have been held in foreign Western cities to discuss what theology fits in an African context. It is noteworthy what Bujo says of the African Synod that ". . .it is to be deplored that the document *Lineamenta* for the African Synod was prepared entirely in Rome without paying much attention to the real problems that affect the continent."[54]

An African Christian ethics should be concretely founded in an African historical-cultural setting. The aim of such an ethic should be the improvement of Christian or human living in Africa. The main concern would be to ask ourselves in which way can Jesus Christ be an African among the Africans according to their own religious experience. This is true of Bujo when he states:

> It is still pertinent today to ask ourselves who Christ is and what impact he has on the African who does not need to change culture in order to be called a child of God . . . to establish the reign of Christ in Africa means to start from the most basic elements of black culture in order to revitalize modern life. It is essential, in

53. Bujo, *African Christian Morality at the Age of Inculturation*, 124. See also O'Neil's article "African Moral Theology," 123, where he makes reference to p'Bitek when O'Neil states: "Okot p'Bitek warned us against the hubris of trimming African wisdom to fit Western scholarly prejudices." This is from Okot p'Bitek's book, *African Religion in Western Scholarship*.

54. Bujo, *African Theology in Its Social Context*, 10.

fact, that the impact of a truly inculturated Christianity should be made plainly manifest to the African who has been and still is prey to injustice, disease and other social evils.[55]

To address the question of Africanization of the Christian faith, Bujo analyzes a variety of tendencies in African theology today: One dwells exclusively on the African cultural heritage. It is, however, only one aspect of a genuinely African theology and it ignores the contemporary African context. The other one, according to Bujo, is the true African theology that is concerned with the question of understanding the faith or incarnating the message of Christ today. Bujo's concern for an African historical context makes his approach relevant.[56]

Further, Bujo analyzes the above-mentioned African historical events and their impact on an African Christian ethics. I examine those events under the following subheadings: (1) Slavery; (2) Colonization and the coming of the early missionaries to Africa; (3) the advent of African theology.

1. Devastation of Africa through Slavery

It is impossible to understand African theology without considering Africa's contact with the west. Africa's history has some positive aspects while some despicable evils like slave trade are inseparable from Africa's past. Slavery represents an extreme exploitation of Africa. Unfortunately, the element of control over Africa has continued unabated through globalization in the market economy as well as through political manipulation. Bujo says that "besides the loss of human potential and without considering the physical and moral sufferings of slavery, the colonial period initiated and ruthlessly carried out a large scale exploitation of Africa's natural resources. Modern economic practices ensure that this domination continues unabated. The transfer of capital towards the North is just one aspect of this unpleasant reality. This fact should be taken into account whenever the Third World's, and particularly Africa's, over-indebtedness is mentioned. Mature reflection will lead us to discover that it is the North that is in debt to Africa."[57] The same can be said of Africa's economy which is dictated by the World Bank and the International Monetary Fund. Bujo agrees with the fact that integral development of Africa goes beyond economic concerns but also

55. Ibid., 11–12.

56. Ibid.

57. Ibid., 9.

incorporates religio-cultural factors. Hence, Bujo writes that "Africa's material poverty is deeply rooted in anthropological pauperization . . . in fact, the African's culture and religion have been utterly ignored by the colonizing powers who used the African as an object of no value for which any substitute could be found."[58] Hence, the liberation ethical issues are of major concern in contemporary African theology. An African Christian theology, then, uses African history as its starting point in the endeavor of conceiving Christian faith and general human living. This history also includes colonization and the work of the early missionaries.

(2) Colonization of Africa and the advent of Early Missionaries to Africa

In the name of civilization, Africa has been alienated from her cultural background. Missionary and colonial movements were meant to be civilizing tools. The myth of the "primitive" had to be propagated as a justification for domination of Africa during the colonial and foreign missionary period. They found functioning societies in which people lived reasonably prosperous and happy lives. Bujo shows how the African religion is the very heart of the traditional society, and how colonization and missionary activity together often upset the delicate balance between the basic elements of the old clans and tribes.[59] Despite the fact that African traditional religion(s) are irreplaceable, Bujo argues the colonial governments and some early missionaries saw "nothing in Africa which really deserved the name 'human.'"[60]

Bujo sums up that the establishment of colonies in Africa was motivated by the self-interest of European governments. The colonizers came to Africa to benefit from the unexploited resources.[61] The approach of the colonizers was to destroy the cultural practices of the people and then impose their way of life on the Africans. According to Bujo "various means were used by the colonizers to subdue the Africans which can be grouped under three headings: the drawing of frontiers, the manipulation of traditional chiefs, the attitude to traditional religion."[62]

58. Ibid. Cf. Martey, *African Theology: Inculturation and Liberation*, 7–35.

59. Bujo, *African Theology in Its Social Context*, 17.

60. Ibid., 39.

61. Ibid.

62. Ibid., 40. See Isichei, *A History of Christianity in Africa*. Isichei states: "It has been

Africa was divided among European powers in the Berlin conference of 1884. Without a clear knowledge of what the European nations were dividing, they each took a piece of Africa depending on the stories they had heard from early explorers. Each nation had a vested interest in the resources they would get from Africa. They did not care what the boundaries meant for the inhabitants of Africa. Consequently, they divided families, clans, and tribes into different nationalities that existed nowhere else before. The frontiers were without considering ethnic distribution of the people, or customary law.

Unfortunately, the church followed the same boundaries as the colonial governments. Having divided Africa, the naming spree followed. The Europeans gave new names to geographical features like mountains and rivers, and invented names for new "nations." After the sub-division of Africa among European powers, the "civilizing" mission that followed was a radical attempt to replace African traditional customs with European ones. To do this, African traditional religion(s) were at times prohibited by law or discouraged as primitive practices. It is in this view that Appiah also wrote:

> Colonial authority sought to stigmatize our traditional religious beliefs, and we conspired in this fiction by concealing our disregard for much of European Christianity in those "syncretisms" . . . the colonial state established a legal system whose patent lack of correspondence with the values of the colonized threatened not those values but the colonial legal system.[63]

Bujo also mentions that the traditional religion was discouraged, polygamy outlawed, art stolen, and ultimately Africa robbed of its culture. It is in this context that Appiah observers, "for, though the picture is a good deal too complex for convenient summary, it is broadly true that the French colonial policy was one of assimilation—of turning 'savage' Africans into 'evolved' black Frenchmen and women—while British colonial policy was a good deal less interested in making the black Anglo-Saxons."[64] All these colonial

---

suggested that both mission and imperialism rest on the same postulate: the superiority of one's own culture to that of the other" (92). Compare with the statement by Mugambi, *African Christian Theology*, who has observed: "Although each missionary society had its own policies, objectives and approaches, in the colonial situation the early missionaries did not make it too obvious to their prospective African converts that they were not one with colonial authorities and that Christian missionaries and the colonial authorities were complementary agents of European civilization" (40–41).

63. Appiah, *In My Father's House*, 8.

64. Ibid., 3–4. cf. Hopkins, *Black Theology USA and South Africa*, 7–31.

practices effected such a tremendous alienation in the lives of the African people that today many people still struggle to understand what is African and what is foreign in their modern cultural and social practices.

Being unconcerned with the traditional African way of life was not only the problem of the colonizers, but also one that affected the missionaries. Bujo views "the measures against African rituals and customs were executed by the colonial government with the full co-operation of the missionaries of the Catholic Church. These were deeply marked with the Roman spirit, which took it for granted that the catechism used in the Roman West was entirely suitable for Africa, and considered that in the work of evangelization the emphasis must be on stamping out savage and immoral customs."[65] Many missionaries had a crusade of their own, fighting what they regarded were corrupt practices such as polygamy and witchcraft, not to mention the changing of names.

Unfortunately, some foreign missionaries identified themselves with their governments and not the people they had come to evangelize. This was also true of colonial governments. On this Bujo states that "governments sometimes refused to admit missionaries who were not of the same nationality as the colonial power."[66] Some colonial governments considered missionaries as part of their civil servants. The colonial endeavor had three arms: government, mission, commerce, and all had to work together. These compromised the task that missionaries had come to accomplish.

Further, Bujo, as it will evidently emerge in the following section, situates the beginning of African theology to a period earlier than 1960, but does not deny the connection between African theology and the political independence movements. This is also comparable to Manus's view. Although Manus historically locates African theology later than its starting point, it is true that he connects African theology to the movement for political liberation in various parts of Africa. He states that "African theology is born in sub-Saharan Africa during the decade when most African nations were struggling for political independence and freedom from colonial rule (1960–1970)."[67]

---

65. Bujo, *African Theology in Its Social Context*, 44–45.

66. Ibid., 43.

67. Manus, "African Christologies," 9.

3. *African Christian Theology as a reaction to Cultural Alienation*

From the above it is understandable why Bujo views African Christian theology as a reaction of African Christians to the alienation of their culture.
Bujo argues that the "contemporary African theology arose out of the feeling of black people that they had not been taken sufficiently seriously by
white people, including missionaries. African theology is a reaction."[68] This
is also true in what Robert Schreiter says in the foreword of Bujo's book.
According to Schreiter, "modern African theology began in 1956 with
the publication of *Les Prêtres noirs s'interrogent*. In that volume a group of
young African theologians raised questions about how theology was being
done in Africa and whether or not things could be different—both theologizing in a more genuinely African way and dealing with topics important
to Africans."[69] African theology, therefore, becomes a call to recognition
of African traditional religion(s) as valid religion. It is a realization that
an African way of life provides a rich soil for the Christian message. In
connection with the foregoing, Bujo states the position of African authors
and theologians as an understanding that "to attack the African religious
system is to condemn all those human beings who live by it, and to deprive
them, not only of their natural dynamism, but of their very identity."[70]

Accordingly, Bujo holds that the consciousness of African authors
began with the movement known as "negritude." Of the "negritude" movement, Bujo states that "it was foreshadowed at the end of the nineteenth
century with the Negro slaves in the USA and in the "pan-Negro" ideas
of people such as W.E.B. Dubois (1897), but the real founding fathers of
Negritude were three Africans who were studying at the Sorbonne in Paris
in the 1930's: Léopold Sédar Senghor, Aimé Césaire and Léon Contran
Damas. The movement had its origins in the experience of racial discrimination which, while, it was less brutal in France than in the United States,
was still effective enough to arouse the resentment of the African students
in Paris . . . Negritude is a kind of an act of faith in Africa, in its past and in
its destiny."[71] It was in this context that Senghor could state that "no political liberation without cultural liberation."[72]

68. Bujo, *African Theology in Its Social Context*, 49.

69. Schreiter, foreword to *African Theology in Its Social Context*, 5.

70. Bujo, *African Theology in Its Social Context*, 49–50.

71. Ibid., 50.

72. Ibid., 51.

Surprisingly enough, Bujo admits the fact that the reaction of the theologians began with a European missionary priest. He writes that:

> The real starting-point of African theology came from a European Franciscan missionary in the Belgian Congo, Placide Tempels. His great effort was to try and understand the African cultural heritage so as to be able the better to announce to the people of Africa the Good News of Jesus Christ. His classical study, "*La Philosophie bantoue*"(Elizabethville, 1945), analyzed the fundamental elements of the African cultural tradition in order to get at the thought-categories and the religion of the people of Africa. One of his most important findings was that the focus of the whole African religion and world-view generally was vital force, or "life-force". Tempels went so far as to claim that for the African "to be" was the same as "to have life-force.[73]

Tempels adopted the Swahili, "Jamaa," as a way of understanding the Christian community. "Jamaa" has in fact much the same sense as the old word "ecclesia." It means an assembly of the people. Tempels said that "Jamaa" is a vital religious experience of the church as a living community of priests and people.[74] From Tempels' work, it is true to say that African theology is not isolated from the rest of the world nor is it an exclusive theology. The contact of Africa with the western world had its positive elements. And hence, the question of who is an African theologian goes beyond race, color or even religion.

From the above, we can say that the birth of African theology came about from a need of an African understanding of Christianity. It is an attempt at contextualizing the gospel of Jesus Christ. In this perspective, African theology becomes an expression of a need of the people of Africa. Living their Christian life does not constitute abrogating one's identity as an African. If African theology came about as an expression of a need, then we can say that it began with the people not the theologian. Bujo makes an analysis of how African theologians came about and their approach to theology in Africa. African Christian theology is characterized by its use of the African culture, the Bible, and the Christian tradition. Therefore, we can say that the first African Christian theologians were the first African converts to Christianity in their attempt to understand the Christian doctrine in their cultural milieu.

73. Ibid. See also Tempels, *Bantu Philosophy*, 21.
74. Bujo, *African Theology in Its Social Context*, 58.

African theology began from a historical context, and has created its own history today. Like any other theology, African theology has always been on the move. Bujo makes reference to the major works that have had a great impact in the development of African theology. In his book, *"African Theology in Its Social Context,"* Bujo begins by making a historical survey. He also traces the development of African theology to Vincent Mulago who wrote a thesis entitled, "Life unity among the Bashi, Banyarwanda and Barundi" in 1956. He also makes note of Alexis Kagame's *La Philosophie Bantu-Rwandaise* (Brussels, 1956), as an important contribution in the beginnings of African theology. The historical list cannot be complete without mentioning the group of African priests that published *Les Prêtres Noirs s'interrogent* (Paris, 1956). Of these priests, Bujo says that "they amounted to no more than preparatory steps towards this goal."[75]

Africa is a big continent. Bujo makes references of developments of African theology from one geographical location to the next. This further expounds his original thesis of the similarities of the cultural and religious practices in Africa. He makes reference to theologians in the French-speaking Africa as well as in the so-called English-speaking Africa. To describe some parts of Africa as Anglophone and others as Franco-phone is to take an element of colonialism into the description of Africa. This description is inescapable since Africa cannot deny her past.

Consequently, Bujo makes reference to the event that took place in January 29, 1960, at the Faculty of Catholic Theology in the University of Lovanium in Kinshasa, a debate between Alfred Vanneste, the Dean, and Tharcisse Tshibangu, then a student, later auxiliary bishop of Kinshasa. This was followed by a report of the proceedings which was published in the *Revue du Clergé Africain,* and the term "African theology" was still so new that people only dared to use it in inverted commas.[76] Bujo notes:

> Tshibangu called his talk, *Vers une théologie de couleur africaine?* (Towards a theology with an African slant). He maintained that Africa must have an African Church. Africanization was not simply a matter of personnel, of having African bishops and lay leaders; nor was it enough to adapt the liturgy, and to reform parish and pastoral structures. Thought must be given to an "African

75. Ibid., 59.
76. Ibid.

theology." African studies and African theology must go hand in hand.[77]

Further, Bujo analyzes the event of 1960 at Kinshasa: "Tshibangu proposes certain elements which could serve as guiding principles for an African theology. He mentions life-force, symbolism and intuition as key factors in Africa's vision of reality."[78] The other side of this debate was represented by Vanneste who gave a response to Tshibangu. On African theology, Vanneste could not see that it was useful to try to use primitive concepts that were frankly magical in inspiration. Adaptation should mean rising to a higher level, not descending to a lower level. Vanneste wondered whether it was really possible "for Western-educated Africans to revert to primitive conceptions which they had in fact outgrown."[79] It is good to note that Vanneste makes reference of "Western-educated Africans" as not able to revert to their African traditions. We can ask here whether education is the means for uprooting a person from the environment in which he/she was brought up, or whether education means the understanding of oneself from the environment of one's upbringing. At this early time in African theology, Tshibangu had made an early contribution. Bujo suggests that because Tshibangu became a bishop he did not go beyond the level of posing the question.[80]

As time progressed from the initial stage of African theology, the move now was towards a renewed African theology. Bujo points out the contribution of other theologians in the 1960s and the 1970s. Among the theologians in this time he mentions John S. Mbiti and Charles Nyamiti. He views theologians during this period as concerned with reconciling theology and African tradition. He states that "Mbiti's special effort was to try and compare African concepts with the biblical message. The effort was admirable, but it cannot be said that the attempt to incarnate Christianity in the African context was a success."[81] He views Charles Nyamiti as more ambitious than Mbiti. On Nyamiti, Bujo states the following; "He tries to state in systematic fashion the Catholic dogmatic tradition in terms of African tradition, drawing on ethnological material. Unlike V. Mulago, Nyamiti goes beyond simple anthropology into genuine theological research. He

77. Ibid., 60.
78. Ibid.
79. Ibid., 61.
80. Ibid.
81. Ibid., 67.

calls on other African theologians too to transcend a mere preliminary clearing of the ground and at long last to proceed to tackle the propositions of theology itself."[82]

According to Bujo, the criticism of Nyamiti is that he wants to fashion African theology on the model of the European speculative tradition.[83] In this perspective, an authentic African Christian theology must take account of African tradition, the Bible and Fathers of the Church. He writes, "our guide in the construction of an African theology must be, apart from African tradition, the Bible and the Fathers of the Church. They must be the light which will show up the limitations and the inadequacies of any theological system, however brilliant."[84] From the on-going discussion, we can surmise that Bujo is also methodologically similar to the path that western theology has taken. It is my view that Bujo's theology fits in the development of theology after the Second Vatican Council in the Roman Catholic Church.

Conclusion

In this chapter, a conclusion is drawn that an African Christian theology and ethics is inseparable from the historical factors that continually contribute in shaping contemporary Africa. The impact of these historical events cannot be understood without paying attention to an African anthropology, belief in the ancestors, and even the concept of God in an African cultural setting.

By now it is evident that for Christianity to take root in Africa, African traditional religion(s) should act like the Old Testament to the coming of Jesus Christ in the New Testament. African traditional religions can also be viewed as an "old testament" preparing for the coming to Africa of the New Testament, the Christian doctrines. To do away with the beliefs and the worldviews of a people means that there is no starting point for dialogue. Without making reference to the cultures and traditions present in African peoples, there is no *status quo* for the gospel in Africa. Any attempt to evangelize without taking due consideration to the people's traditions becomes a kind of an imposition, or for that matter an imperialism. For Christianity to avoid being viewed as foreign, there is need for the gospel to dialogue with

82. Ibid., 67.
83. Ibid., 67–68.
84. Ibid., 68.

its hearers and in their perspectives. This also applies to Christian ethics. An African ethical perspective can also express the Christian ethical directives. Christian ethics should not be seen as doing away with African ethics but as confirming and promoting them as well. This will be discussed later in this work.

The view that any theologian takes on African traditional religion(s) shapes the direction one takes in African Christian theology. There are those who take African traditional religions as all related and similar to each other. To them there is an African theology in the singular. To those that recognize the element of diversity in Africa, there are many ways of doing theology in the continent depending with where one is located. An uncritical assertion of viewing African traditional religion(s) in the singular leads to untenable generalization.

2

The Call for Renewal of Moral Theology by the Second Vatican Council and the Development of African Moral Theology

MORAL THEOLOGY IN THE Roman Catholic Church after the Second Vatican Council (1962–1965) has adopted diverse methods in variety of cultural-historical contexts. There has been a renewed interest in Sacred Scriptures, the person of Jesus Christ, and an acknowledgment of the reality of diversity. A historical and philosophical consciousness informs the renewal of moral theology and also the centrality of the sources of theology such as Sacred Scripture, Christology, and church tradition. However, the debate on the relation between faith ethics and autonomous ethics has also generated controversies among moral theologians coming after Vatican II.

The development of African moral theology is also in the perspective of the call for renewal of moral theology by the Second Vatican Council in the Roman Catholic Church. The work of the African moral theologian, Bénézet Bujo, fits into the category referred in this work as African moral theology. Bujo's work contains elements of the renewal of moral theology which preceded the Council and was also called for by the Council. Renewal elements evident in African moral theology, especially in the work of Bujo, include among others, the use of Sacred Scripture, a historical consciousness, and an analysis of the theory of the natural moral law. African moral theology is representative of the diversity of the theologies coming after the Vatican II Council.

It is therefore necessary to analyze the understanding and the place of history in the renewal movement affecting moral theology. A major emphasis within the renewal movement is the realization of the Christocentric nature of moral theology. In a special way the focus here will be the use of history and Christology in an African moral theology especially in the work of Bujo. The theology of Bujo will be seen to reflect renewal elements called for by the Council.

To understand the historical context calls for an evaluation of theological developments before the Second Vatican Council. The work of theologians whose work reflects the spirit of the renewal movement before and after the Council is studied here. In addition, the engagement with the natural moral law tradition is presented as an element of the renewal in moral theology. Finally, African moral theology is understood to have risen within the context of the renewal called for by Vatican II. The renewal elements in the work of Bujo are also analyzed in this work.

Part One: Vatican Council II and the Call for Renewal in Moral Theology

The renewal movement in Roman Catholic moral theology began long before the Second Vatican Council. To understand what renewal meant, I provide a brief excursus on moral theology before the Council. It is imperative to have some knowledge of the manuals of moral theology before Vatican II in order that one may get a glimpse of what renewal meant. For this reason, I describe in this chapter the theology of the manuals and the theological/pastoral need they were supposed to address. Without considering the Thomistic revival in the Roman Catholic Church, it is impossible to understand moral theology before the Vatican II Council. For the preceding reason, I analyze neo-Thomism, neo-scholasticism, and ultimately transcendental Thomism that crowned the renewal movement before the Council.

A. The Shaping of Moral Theology before Vatican II

Theological studies, after the encyclical *Aeterni Patris* of 1879, were very much influenced by the works of St. Thomas Aquinas. Transcendental Thomism, as evidenced in the work of Karl Rahner and Bernard Lonergan, is also a good example of the theology before and after the Second Vatican

Council. *Nouvelle theologie* is another example of the theologies in the process of the renewal of moral theology before the Vatican Council II.

i. Emergence of the Manuals of Moral Theology

Manuals were developed in the context of the Counter-Reformation. Moral theology was viewed as a form of pastoral or ministerial reflection. John Gallagher says that "the intellectual context of moral theology was the seminary, not the monastery, nor the university."[1] Manuals were meant to assist in the preparation of future priests. "The manuals viewed moral issues from the perspective of the individual Christian and the moral requirements incumbent upon him or her, not from the wider, more comprehensive perspective of Christian philosophy or modern papal thought."[2]

The manuals from 1540–1650 were a product of the Council of Trent. The Council of Trent was responsible for the founding of the seminary system. The major work of the seminaries was the formation of the future confessors. Penitents were required to confess all their mortal sins "specifically and particularly" in order that the priest might impose an equitable penance.[3]

The manuals from 1879 to the 1960s had a neo-Thomist orientation. The encyclical, *Aeterni Patris* of 1879 by Leo XIII, made the work of Thomas Aquinas the official theology and philosophy in the Roman Catholic Church. The manuals were also influenced by the new code of canon law (1917). They were intended to provide the theological basis for a pastoral ministry focused on the sacraments.[4] McCool "proposed as central to the theological vision of the neo-Thomists: first, the proper distinction between nature and grace, faith and reason, body and soul, philosophy and theology; second, the unifying theological theme of St. Thomas: the idea of God, considered in his inner being and his exterior creative and redemptive work."[5] Manuals of moral theology had a legalistic outlook towards

---

1. Gallagher, *Time Past, Time Future*, 30. Cf. Slater, *A Manual of Moral Theology*, 1:163–232.

2. Gallagher, *Time Past, Time Future*, 30–31. See also Ford and Kelly, *Contemporary Moral Theology*, 1:3–18. Cf. Dirks, "How Can I Know What God Wants of Me," 81.

3. Gallagher, *Time Past, Time Future*, 33.

4. Ibid., 37. Cf. Connell, *Outlines of Moral Theology*, 27–37.

5. Gallagher, *Time Past, Time Future*, 49.

morality; "Moral obligation as portrayed by the manualists arose primarily as a function of the law."[6]

The manuals of moral theology were an inadequate way to tackle moral issues because of their legalistic nature. Their legalistic and generalized view of moral issues did not meet the needs of the diverse nature of the Church. There was an urgent need for renewal in moral theology, a renewal that would address itself to the spirit of the time.

ii. Thomistic Revival

Renewal in moral theology did not take place instantaneously, but it was a gradual process that was underway in the church for a long time. Although the Thomistic revival is generally viewed as influencing the formation of the manuals, I argue that this was also an essential component of the renewal. The renewal of moral theology, or even the formation of moral theology as a discipline, is a historical fact in which one stage of development is founded in the former stage.

Leo XIII's *Aeterni Patris* gave rise to two distinguishable movements: neo-Thomism and neo-scholasticism. Transcendental Thomism should be viewed in the context of neo-Scholasticism. Neo-Thomism was involved with the interpretation of the writings of Thomas Aquinas and required a specific understanding of the relationships and distinctions between nature and grace, faith and reason, philosophy and theology, body and soul. From the nineteenth century onwards, neo-Thomism was the dominant position of many Jesuits and Dominicans. It was also supported by the papacies of Leo XIII, Pius X, and Pius XII, and for this reason remained dominant for over a 100 years.[7]

On the other hand, neo-scholasticism interpreted *Aeterni Patris* as requiring not just a return to the writings of St. Thomas but also to medieval scholastic philosophy and theology generally. The neo-scholastics studied the works of Bonaventure, William of Auxerre, and the Victorines, among other medieval scholastics. Vincent MacNamara describes neo-Scholasticism as "the name given to the late nineteenth- and early twentieth-century movement in theology which took its inspiration from medieval

6. Ibid., 77. Cf. Davis, *Moral and Pastoral Theology*, 1:11–41.

7. Gallagher, *Time Past, Time Future*, 151–52. Cf. McHugh and Callan, *Moral Theology*, vol. 1. From Thomas Aquinas, McHugh and Callan states: "The natural law is defined theologically as a participation of the eternal law in man" (100).

scholasticism."[8] Neo-Scholasticism had some influence in the manuals of moral theology used in the training of priests. Further, MacNamara says that "Neo-Scholasticism was a very settled system in which there were clear and unquestioned ideas about the meaning and norm of morality, the source of moral obligation and the relations between morality and God. It was predominantly a natural law morality and not the most distinguished account of natural law. In the forties and fifties many theologians began to question this conception of morality."[9]

The major constructive essays of Rahner (Spirit in the World) and of Lonergan (Insight) need to be understood as emerging from within the dynamics of neo-Scholasticism. Rahner and Lonergan were influenced by the early *nouvelle theologie* theologians, Rousselot and Maréchal. *Spirit in the World* and *Insight* were the result of the *nouvelle theologie's* emphasis on understanding (*intellectus*) rather than reason (*ratio*). The theological works of Rahner and Lonergan covers the period before and after Vatican II. Lonergan highlighted the importance of experience in theological method. The writings of the later Lonergan, unlike those of Rahner, generally did not address specific doctrinal issues, but rather focused on the development of an adequate theological method. Transcendental Thomism was an effort to establish a response to Immanuel Kant's philosophy in a manner consistent with the thought of Aquinas.[10]

Of great significance here is Rahner's contribution in moral theology. In the theology of Rahner, moral theology is viewed in the context of systematic theology. John Boyle makes this point clear when he writes:

> In addition to revealed moral commands, however, Rahner has in many places defended the validity of the natural law. He writes of an a posteriori natural law and also of an a priori natural law. A transcendental method is needed to discover those elements of human nature, which are truly immutable. Moreover, since "nature" is a theological *Restbegriff* which can be known only with the aid of revelation, reason unassisted by grace cannot truly know what "nature" is. However, it should be noted that Rahner's notion of anonymous grace makes it all but impossible in practice to distinguish reason assisted by grace from reason without it. There is in the concrete order no purely "natural" man. Thus the neat but

---

8. MacNamara, *Faith and* Ethics, 9.

9. Ibid., 3.

10. Gallagher, *Time Past, Time Future*, 152–54.

abstract distinctions between faith and reason found, for instance, in the documents of Vatican I has been considered muddled.[11]

We can therefore make an observation that the development of moral theology is evident from the works of neo-Thomists to neo-scholasticism, climaxing in the work of transcendental Thomists. The same renewal or developmental aspect of moral theology is evident in the *nouvelle theologie* theologians.

iii. *Nouvelle Theologie*

Even before the Second Vatican Council, it is evident that Catholic theology needed to address the issues arising from contemporary philosophy, and particularly the significance of history.[12] *Nouvelle theologie* was not limited to moral theology alone. *Nouvelle theologie* was a post-war theology that emphasized the necessity of returning to the sources of theology; scripture, the fathers, and the medieval authors. *Nouvelle theologie* theologians were historians and exegetes. Two schools associated with *nouvelle theologie* were the Dominican House of Studies, Le Saulchoir, in which Marie-Dominique Chenu and Yves Congar were the principle figures. On the other school associated with *nouvelle theologie*, Gallagher states:

> Henri de Lubac and Jean Danielou provided much of the inspiration for the Jesuit Seminary at Fourviere; their colleagues included Yves de Montcheuil and Pierre Teilhard de Chardin. The name, *nouvelle theologie*, given to this movement was first sarcastically applied to it by Reginald Garrigou-Lagrange in his 1946 essay entitled, *"La nouvelle theologie, ou-va-elle?"* (The New Theology, Where is it Going?[13]

Humani Generis was the official magisterial reaction to the *nouvelle theologie*. The Church's magisterium saw *nouvelle theologie* as promoting false irenicism (that we can express Catholic tradition in a way consistent with modern modes of thought) and dogmatic relativism.[14] According to Gallagher: "*Humani Generis* (August 12, 1950) had an impact on the *nouvelle theologie* similar to that which Pius X's *Pascendi Dominici Gregis*

---

11. Boyle, "Faith and Christian Ethics in Rahner and Lonergan," 252.

12. Gallagher, *Time Past, Time Future*, 141.

13. Ibid., 143.

14. Ibid., 149.

had had on Modernism. Both encyclicals brought to an end much of the innovative theological speculation within Roman Catholicism which was construed by the papal magisterium as inconsistent with the tradition. Pius XII was quite clear that the tradition to be taught in the schools and seminaries was the teaching of Thomas Aquinas."[15]

B. Patterns in Renewal

The renewal of moral theology since Vatican II led to multifarious theological approaches. The patterns of renewal are themselves as diverse as the theologians of the twentieth century. Before Vatican II, the Scholastic method made its contribution through analysis of the moral life of individuals toward their final end and intermediate means chosen to that end; the analysis of the moral agent into body and soul, and the intellect, will, and other faculties; the analysis of the moral act into object, circumstances, and goal; and, of course, the analysis of morality itself into objective and subjective within an overall distinction between the natural and supernatural. Recent moral theology has attempted to recover or reclaim the living unity which links and subsumes all this into an intelligible whole.[16] It can be characterized as the shift from "faculty" morality (speech, or procreation) to a morality that is concerned with the totality of the human person. Of special note would be the application of the principle of totality in medico-moral theory, now called bio-ethics.

Since renewal in moral theology has taken many diverse ways, it is, therefore, necessary to analyze the meaning of the renewal called for by Vatican II and the patterns moral theology has taken ever since.

i. The Second Vatican Council and the Call for Renewal
in Moral Theology

The most important statement on the call to renewal of moral theology in the Vatican II documents occurred when the Council Fathers stated:

> In like manner the other theological subjects should be renewed through a more vivid contact with the Mystery of Christ and the history of salvation. Special care should be given to the perfecting of moral theology. Its scientific presentation should draw

15. Ibid.

16. Mahoney, *The Making of Moral* Theology, 310.

more fully on the teaching of Holy Scripture and should throw light upon the exalted vocation of the faithful in Christ and their obligation to bring forth fruit in charity for the life of the world.[17]

In the preceding statement, the Council Fathers summarized what was to be done in moral theology, and of course what some theologians had done long before the Council. It is imperative to note that the main aspects of renewal that the Council reiterated included the emphasis on the mystery of Christ, the history of salvation, the scientific nature of moral theology drawing from the Sacred Scriptures, and the vocation of the faithful in the world. The bishops read the signs of the times. The Church had to be involved in the life of the world. The relevance of the mystery of Christ in the transformation of the world is a notable emphasis of the Second Vatican Council.[18]

Vatican II was responding to the crisis in the world at the time. On the need for change in the presentation of the teachings, John Kobler is instructive by stating that "Scholasticism, while long on theoretical concepts, is short on the practical psychological techniques needed to work within human consciousness and influence attitudinal change."[19] The Church was looking for ways to become relevant to the people of the time. Referring to Pope John XXIII's reasons for calling the Council, Kobler adds: "Rather, in a critical global situation he was looking for ways to make his religious truths work more effectively at all levels so that men would be able to comprehend

17. "Training of Priests," in Flannery, ed., *Vatican Council II*, 720n16. See also Collins, *Christian Morality*. Collins notes: "The Council's call for the more thorough nourishment of moral theology by scriptural teaching in order to 'show the nobility of the Christian vocation of the faithful and their obligation to bring forth fruit in charity' implied a radical recasting of moral theology. Rather than focus on sin, moral theology was to focus on charity. Rather than focus on acts, it was to focus on vocation. The Council's call was a radical renewal of moral theology. It was an appeal for moral theology to be renewed by means of a fresh contact with the scriptural roots of the Christian tradition" (3).

18. See Fuchs's statement: "The Council believed that before all else it should remind Christians of the fact that their morality is based on the person of Christ who came into this world. It may sound strange to many people, perhaps to many Christians and Catholics, that in reality, and not only as some seemingly pious thought, their day-by-day morals and the morality of the whole of life, should be centered in Christ" (Fuchs, "The Christian Morality of Vatican II, 57).

19. Kobler, *Vatican II and Phenomenology*, 70. See also the statement by Bujo: "The Christian message encounters every human person in that person's historical, social and cultural situation and environment, and does not compel him or her to abandon his or her identity" (Bujo, *African Christian Morality at the Age of Inculturation*, 103).

them in human, everyday terms. Hence, he called a *pastoral* council."[20] We can, therefore, conclude that the Council was addressing itself to the long overdue needs of the people of God at the time.

ii. Renewal Patterns

The Council's call for renewal of moral theology has taken different theological directions among different theologians. The response of the Roman Catholic Church has been critical to the various ways of doing theology since the Second Vatican Council. To show the pattern of renewal, I refer to John Mahoney, who makes a major contribution in his book, *The Making of Moral Theology: A Study of the Roman Catholic Tradition.* Mahoney puts forth the major elements that have been instrumental in the history of the development of moral theology.

The pattern in renewal can be characterized with the theological use of Scripture in moral theology. The Church has over the years maintained that she is the sole custodian of the Word of God. To show the Council's emphasis on scripture and renewal in moral theology, Mahoney quotes the following statement from the Council documents:

> The church safeguards the deposit of God's word, from which religious and moral principles are drawn. But it does not always have a ready answer to individual questions, and it wishes to combine the light of revelation with the experience of everyone in order to illuminate the road on which humanity has recently set out.[21]

A point to note besides the necessity of using scripture, in this statement, is the council's recognition of the contribution individual members in the church can make through their experiences. There is a realization that scripture does not provide ready-made answers to moral questions but that human reasoning is irreplaceable in moral discernment.

The theological works of Josef Fuchs, Bernard Häring, and Fritz Tillman are good examples of renewal of moral theology. The contribution of Fuchs in "Human Values and Christian Morality" shows the role of faith in moral theology. Häring and Tillman represent the Christocentric tradition. They view moral theology as a science, and show how it is related to other sciences and other branches of theology. Häring and Tillman represent also

20. Ibid., 168.

21. Mahoney, *Making of Moral Theology*, 303. *Gaudium et Spes* (GS), §33, in *Vatican II Documents.*

the change from moral theology as devotional writing addressed to laity to systematic moral theology.[22] Most important is the fact that renewal in moral theology has also meant renewal in methodology and the way in which we approach specific moral issues, such as those in sexual and medical ethics, modern warfare, amassing of nuclear weaponry, world poverty, and the imbalanced access to and use of the earth's resources.[23]

Notable in the renewal movement is the concern expressed about moral absolutes. For many renewal moral theologians and especially among the "revisionists," every human act has to be considered in a perspective that is whole, considering all the circumstances and concrete factors that come to qualify the act. The influence of St. Thomas Aquinas is remarkable in the development and renewal of moral theology. Aquinas taught that the primary precepts of natural law are completely unchangeable, but not the secondary precepts deriving from them. Mahoney makes the preceding clear when he writes: "It appears to be the case that for Aquinas these secondary precepts would include the Judeo-Christian Ten Commandments, and that he would consider these generally binding, but not invariably so in practice, and this because of particular factors or circumstances in reality."[24] Further, Mahoney adds that "a more indirect attack on the citadel of moral absolutes, however, involves cutting off their supply line with human nature and arguing that if nature can and does change, either in general or specific instances, then natural law conclusions claiming to originate in nature must themselves also change accordingly."[25]

Mahoney demonstrates in a very vivid way the importance, for the renewal moral theologians, of considering the morality of individual actions not just in themselves, but as they enter into a total continuity and pattern of an individual's moral history and life. Notably, the renewal has been characterized by the shift from human nature to the more comprehensive concept of person as the basis for objective moral criteria.[26] Renewal moral theologians can be characterized also by their interpretation of the natural moral law.

The understanding of the natural law in terms of reason has also led to an understanding of the inherently social nature of the human person. The

22. Mahoney, *Making of Moral Theology*, 306–7.

23. Ibid., 307–8.

24. Ibid., 313–14.

25. Ibid., 314.

26. Ibid., 318.

theory of moral autonomy should be seen in the context of the understanding of the natural law. Natural law has come to be qualified as exemplified in the human person and reason. A human being is capable of concretely applying natural law in individual decisions in concrete cases. For this reason the autonomous ethics debate can be seen as the outcome of continuing reflection on the natural law tradition.[27]

Another feature finding expression in the renewal of the subject requested by the Bishops of the Vatican Council is the realization of diversity in the Roman Catholic Church. Despite the universal nature of the Church there are differences in her members from region to region. These differences could be cultural, social, or historical. The Church is believed to be one, holy, catholic and apostolic. The oneness of the Church and its diversity can be seen in terms of viewing the whole in different ways. It is in this context that Mahoney writes that "it is not, then, in liturgy, or in moral theology, a matter of 'mere terminology,' but of the underlying objective diversity of cultural and historical resources and heritages of which different languages are so many living repositories and expressions . . . the simple fact that moral theology is now beginning to be conducted in a diversity of languages is a feature whose cultural significances and full implications have not begun to be realized."[28] There is in the Church the diversity of moral and human experience.

Mahoney argues that diversity is unavoidable just as the fact that we cannot do away with the development and changing of language. He makes reference to Rahner that some norms of Christian living are relevant to a particular age, and with change in time become irrelevant. This is historical change that affects all human beings on earth. An example illustrating historical change would be the medieval law in the Catholic Church forbidding usury.

Traditional moral theology was concerned with universals and law, and anything else was seen as an exception to the rule. The recovery of the mystery of God through different human concrete experiences has demonstrated the true nature of diversity among peoples and nations. In relation to the preceding claim, Mahoney says "it is the mystery of God which earths all theology and at the same time makes theological pluralism unavoidable."[29]

27. Ibid.
28. Ibid., 323–24.
29. Ibid., 337. Cf. McCool, *From Unity to Pluralism.* Also see Dubay, "The State of

From the renewal "the primary task of moral theology, according to the letter and spirit of the council, must be to explain that man is called personally in Christ by a personal God."[30] Moral theology with Vatican II came to be seen as faith put into effect in moral specificity.

iii. Diversity in Moral Theology after Vatican II

Vatican II's call for renewal had a great impact on moral theology. It initiated a new impetus in the exploration of the methodologies moral theology was to take henceforth. This is evident in the work of the various theologians and their work coming after the Council. Some of these theologians are referred to in this study.

Theology after the Second Vatican Council was characterized by diversity. There was a recognition that theology can be done in various ways. No one way of theological study was the perfect one. Theological truth was no longer in the hands of one group in the Church. Mahoney expresses this trend clearly when he states the following:

> The recognition of diversity between individual and groups—not simply in their behavior and not simply in some particular attitudes, but more generally in the way in which they perceive and interpret the whole of reality or large sectors of it—underlies the growing awareness of pluralism in society, which for the Christian often takes the form of exploring how to live and commend the Christian view of life in a pluralist society . . . pluralism acknowledges a plurality of coexisting philosophies or theologies of life, and a variety of value-clusters as espoused by different individuals or groups and operative simultaneously in society, without attempting to evaluate them or their correspondence to "reality" or to the truth.[31]

Hence, change in renewal of moral theology is viewed as a move from Thomism and Augustianism to pluralism. Even before the Council, Pius XII referred to "open questions" the church had not yet pronounced on doctrinal solutions. The plurality that came with the renewal of moral theology favored diversity in methodology on moral issues. The choice was not between deductive and inductive approaches to morality but an

---

Moral Theology," 482–506.

30. Mahoney, *Making of Moral Theology*, 339.

31. Ibid., 330. See also Schreiter, "The Impact of Vatican II," 158–172.

intercultural approach that appreciates various cultures and different historical contexts. Questions arose on how much attention is to be accorded to the *apriori* over against the *posteriori*, or to intellectual considerations alone over against respect for the data of experience and the significance of moral insight or intuition arising from such experience.[32]

There is no one way of doing theological studies after the Second Vatican Council. Gallagher says of some theologians: "Although there are affinities in Curran's writings to positions taken by Häring, and in Fuchs and McCormick to the theology of Rahner, these authors do not in any way constitute a new school of theology. On the contrary, they exemplify the plurality of theologies which form the contemporary environment."[33] Gallagher characterizes the diversity after Vatican II in a special way in the theology of the revisionists. The revisionists, according to Gallagher, are theologians who have "attempted in one manner or another to revise, to bring up to date the moral theology which dominated the discipline in the years of their seminary and graduate education."[34] On the differences in revisionist theologians, Gallagher states:

> For Louis Janssens and others it has meant a more adequate understanding of the writings of St. Thomas Aquinas. For Häring and indirectly Curran, revisionist theology has meant not only the further development of insights originally developed by the Tübingen theologians, but also the employment of the philosophy of Max Scheler and H. Richard Niebuhr. Schüller and McCormick have clearly attempted to distinguish their positions from that of neo-Thomism.[35]

The term "revisionist" has come to be seen to be too weak to represent all theologians associated with the renewal of moral theology after Vatican II. The situation has been filled with diversity. It is, as Gallagher comments, because changes continue to abound that the term "revisionist" has been seen as limiting. There are more diverse theologies. To cite a few examples: "Häring's introduction of concepts such as invitation and response, conversion, and the following of Christ provides a significantly different

---

32. Mahoney, *Making of Moral Theology*, 332.

33. Gallagher, *Time Past, Time Future*, 203. See also Curran, "Absolute Norms in Moral Theology," 139–73.

34. Gallagher, *Time Past, Time Future*, 204.

35. Ibid.

orientation in terms of the cure of souls."[36] In Bernard Häring; "The theo-
centric ethic of neo-Thomism is replaced by a Christo-centric ethic,"[37]
while "Rahner's theology constitutes a major alternative to neo-Thomist
moral theology."[38] The major contribution of Karl Rahner was "to relocate
the topics associated with moral theology into a systematic theology and,
within that context, to elaborate a theological anthropology."[39]

The understanding of human subjectivity in the theology of Rahner
makes a special contribution in the understanding of Christian ethics.
"Rahner's critical natural law theory rests upon the *apriori* conditions of
human personhood, which establish specific guides to human action."[40]
Every individual is understood as unique, and irreplaceable in his or her
transcendental experience of God. The human subject is open to God or
has a capacity to know God personally. Hence, in the theology of Rahner
"the material will of God to which the individual must respond is not a deduction from a universal norm, but rather an individual or existential norm
unique to the person to whom it is addressed. Rahner's formal existential
ethic focuses on the coming-to-be of the unique, individual person."[41]
Rahner puts forth the conditions of possibility for the individual to develop
into a moral subject.

Bruno Schüller blends philosophy and theology and uses a Rahnerian
notion of nature and grace; moreover, a "considerable dependence upon
contemporary philosophy clearly distinguishes his position from that of
the neo-Thomist manualists."[42] He is a critic of neo-Thomist manuals of
moral theology. Gallagher makes an observation that the opening chapter
of his [Schüller's] "*Gesetz und Freiheit*" is an examination of the manualists'
presentation of divine law. Schüller holds that traditional manuals contain
nothing which could not be found in philosophical ethics and church law.
Schüller is highly critical of the conception of law as static, as unchanged
in whatever ethical or salvation-historical context humankind might find

---

36. Ibid., 204–5.

37. Ibid., 205.

38. Ibid., 207.

39. Ibid.

40. Ibid. Gallagher makes reference to Bresnahan, "Rahner's ethics: Critical Natural Law Theory in Relation to Contemporary Ethical Methodology," 41.

41. Gallagher, *Time Past, Time Future*, 209.

42. Ibid., 212.

itself.[43] He has attempted to develop an autonomous theistic ethic. According to Schüller, "creatureliness and independence (freedom) are the necessary conditions for morality and moral obligation."[44]

Further, a shift in moral methodology is also observable in the work of Charles Curran: "His explicitly theological contributions to contemporary moral theology involve his use of the responsibility/relationality ethical model and the theological methodology which he employs."[45] In his responsibility/relationality model, Curran can be viewed as providing an alternative to teleology and deontology. He does not think there is a specifically Christian ethic. In connection with the revisionist moral theologians, Richard McCormick formulated five premises assumed by the majority of Catholic moral theologians: the primacy of charity, the essential interiority of law in the New Covenant, the existence of the natural law, the relationship of the natural law to gospel morality, and the rejection of moralism.[46]

In addition, liberation theology is also among the plurality of theologies after the Council. The current situation in the Roman Catholic Church can be characterized as one of moral pluralism. As an example of this moral pluralism, Mahoney states that "the major debate in contemporary social morality which best exemplifies the tension of methodology and the growing phenomenon of moral pluralism in the church—the whole powerful current of liberation theology."[47] Liberation theology has its origins in the social and political conditions which individuals find themselves. Liberation theology makes situations of poverty, alienation, and oppression methodologically significant. In liberation theology, orthodoxy goes together with orthopraxis. The theological works of Gustavo Gutiérrez, Archbishop Oscar Romero and the emphasis on the preferential option for the poor in Latin America and Africa are vivid representation of theological pluralism after the Council. With the plurality in theologies especially in the Roman Catholic Church, new opportunities are presented to the magisterium on how to present her teachings in changed historical circumstances in the universal body of Christ.

From the preceding, it is evident that there is no one way of studying theology after the Second Vatican Council. Theological methods are as

43. Ibid., 209–10.
44. Ibid., 211.
45. Ibid., 217.
46. Ibid., 214–15.
47. Ibid., 332–33.

diverse as there are theologians. The development and interpretation of the natural moral law is a good example of diversity in moral theology after the Vatican II Council. Diversity is a good element that should be embraced by all.

Natural Moral Law

In the debate concerning the natural moral law theory, one question summarizes the concern of many moral theologians: whether nature is morally normative. The view held by many theologians is based on the understanding that nature as such is not normative, but it is human reason that interprets nature to formulate moral norms. Central to the natural law tradition are varieties of perspectives on human nature and the possibility of realizing moral norms based on the interpretation of human nature. Contemporary scholarship mostly views the natural law as focusing more on the human person who interprets nature through the faculty of reason.

The revival of the theology and philosophy of St. Thomas Aquinas, sparked especially by Pope Leo XIII's *Aeterni Patris* in 1879, and the subsequent development of scholasticism, saw the revival in the understanding of the natural moral law and other related theories. The theory of autonomous ethics is also as a result of the development of the theory of natural moral law. Aquinas is famous for his analysis of the natural moral law in the *Summa Theologiae*.[48] There is also an influence of the natural law tradition in the development of an African Catholic moral theology.[49]

Making reference to Cicero, John Macquarrie affirms that according to this theory, natural law has a universal dimension through its foundation in human nature. He cites Cicero's remarks on the natural law:

> There is indeed a true law, right reason, agreeing with nature, diffused among all men, unchanging, everlasting . . . It is not allowed to alter this law or to derogate from it, nor can it be repealed. We cannot be released from this law, either by the magistrate or the people, nor is any person required to explain or interpret it. Nor is it one law at Rome and another at Athens, one law today and

48. Aquinas's treatise on law is in *Summa Theologiae*, I-II, Q. 90–105; see Baumgarth, eds., *Saint Thomas Aquinas: On Law, Morality, and Politics*, 11–135. Also, Pegis, *Introduction to St. Thomas Aquinas, The Summa Theologica; The Summa Contra Gentiles*, 609–50.

49. For example, Bénézet Bujo wrote his dissertation and habilitation on St. Thomas Aquinas. He published his dissertation as *Moralautonomie und Normenfindung bei Thomas von Aquino*, while his habilitation was published as *Die Begründung des Sittlichen*.

another hereafter; but the same law, everlasting and unchangeable, will bind all nations at all times; and there will be one common lord and ruler of all men, even God, the framer and proposer of this law.[50]

From the above passage, Cicero presents the natural moral law as universal and immutable. From Thomas Aquinas, Macquarrie holds that natural law has to do with reason. Human reason participates in eternal reason. He states that "among all others, the rational creature is subject to divine providence in a more excellent way, in so far as it itself partakes of a share of providence, by being provident both for itself and others. Therefore it has a share of the eternal reason, whereby it has natural inclination to its proper act and end; and this participation of the eternal law in the rational creature is called the 'natural law.'"[51] An understanding of the natural law in terms of reason makes it possible to avoid the equivocation of natural law to nature. Nature is not normative but requires interpretation which can only be done through reason. Macquarrie has presented the various views on the natural law as follows: "The natural law is said to be unwritten; it is not invented by men but discovered by them; it is a kind of tendency rather than a code; it has a constancy or even immutability."[52] Macquarrie does not defend either of these assertions. He qualifies the natural law not as a written law but as a tendency. Tendency can mean here a capacity to discern what is morally right or wrong from nature or creation by human beings.

Johannes Gründel presents the natural law as moral knowledge drawn from the human experience of God's creation. Among Catholics, Gründel holds that the natural law is understood in the context of moral law dealing with human relations. In this context, natural law stipulates a "moral obligation which can be determined in the form of norms for the minimum standard of moral behavior and also enforceable as law."[53] Gründel views this as a legalistic view. He states that "man finds the law of his moral action primarily in the truth of God's creation—in the nature and essence of things. Thus the philosophical axiom *agere sequitur esse* comes into play. The 'ought' is founded on the 'is.' The principle only implies, to begin with,

---

50. Cicero, *De Republica* 3.22–23 (trans. Salmond, *Jurisprudence*, 28). Macquarrie, "Rethinking Natural Law," 130.

51. Macquarrie, "Rethinking Natural Law," 130. *Summa Theologiae*, II-I, 91, 2, 750.

52. Macquarrie, "Rethinking Natural Law," 131.

53. Gründel, "Natural Law (Moral)," 157.

a close connection between being and obligation, ontology and ethics. Being valid also for the realm of grace—every gift bestowed by God on man becomes a task."[54]

The natural law debate is an analysis of human nature and by extension how human beings should live and relate to each other, God, and the created order. The human person is the central focus in the understanding of the natural law. Gründel's perspective is comparable to Bruno Schüller's. According to Schüller, "Catholic natural law doctrine answers that obligation is grounded in being. In grasping what he is, man also grasps what he is to become by his free self-determination. In man every gift is also a task."[55] Therefore for Schüller, natural law is a capacity for moral self-criticism in all people. He represents a wave in the understanding of the natural not just from an ontological perspective, where natural law is seen in terms of the nature of being, but a deeper understanding of the natural law as made possible by the human subject. Schüller has a Rahnerian understanding of grace and nature, where the two are viewed as inseparable.

Schüller describes the natural law as follows:

> From the side of the knowing subject natural law can be defined as the complexus of all those moral (and legal) norms of behavior knowable to man by reason independently of God's revelation. For without access to revelation man can only rely on the natural humanity of mankind for the validity and meaning of moral commands. Opposed to this is the *lex gratiae* or those divine commands which refer to the Christian in so far as he is a "new creation" in Christ. This *lex gratiae* is only knowable by faith.[56]

Additionally, William Hordern presents natural law as based upon the human experience with reality. "Natural law is no longer seen as being based upon the ultimate metaphysical nature of reality. Rather it is based upon the human's experience of the world and other persons in it."[57] In Hordern, a shift occurs in the understanding of natural law in terms of nature to the understanding of natural law in terms of the human person. This is also evident in Joseph Arntz who distinguishes the understanding of the natural law in the teaching of the Stoa and that of Thomas Aquinas. He states that the Stoa emphasized nature while Aquinas laid emphasis on

54. Ibid., 157.
55. Schüller, "Can Moral Theology Ignore Natural Law?," 97.
56. Ibid., 94.
57. Hordern, "Natural Law," 393.

man. According to the Stoa, the opposition between nature and reason is eliminated by the immanence of the *Logos*, while for St. Thomas the contrast is bridged by reason, human reason. For Aquinas it is the "*naturaliter cognitum*" that matters. For us, so many centuries later in the history of philosophy, this opposition already shows the seed of the priority of the object over the priority of the subject.[58]

Development in the understanding of natural law has been a movement from a merely metaphysical or ontological perspective to one that pays a great deal of attention to the human person. It is a shift from morality based on the structure of being to a moral understanding where the human person is at the center. "Hence natural law is not a heteronomous morality but the structure of moral order which is assigned by God to man in creation and imposed on him as the goal of self-fulfillment."[59] Natural law is an internal law. Some have conceived the natural law as concerned with the basic goods which perfect human nature and dependent on tradition as well as context.[60] However, for Aquinas, no created good can be a human person's ultimate end.[61]

From Franz Böckle's reading of Thomas Aquinas, natural moral law does not refer to a natural moral code, or a collection of extant norms. He states that "In Thomas Aquinas' own words, the natural moral law is 'participation (by rational being) in eternal reason, whereby the being possesses natural inclinations to the actions and the objective which are appropriate to his existence' (S. Th. I.II., q. 91, a. 2)."[62] Hence, we can say that natural moral law implies the human person's inherent capacity to know what is morally good or bad.

The shift from the understanding of natural moral law in terms of nature to that of the human subject is clearest in the theology of Karl Rahner. Rahner's theological method is commonly referred to as the turn to the subject. James Bresnahan, in his analysis of Karl Rahner's ethics, indicates that in Rahner natural law has to do with the human subject. On Rahner's theology, Bresnahan states the following:

58. Arntz, "Natural Law and its History," 27.

59. Gründel, 157. See also Häring, "Dynamism and Continuity in a Personalistic Approach to Natural Law," 199–231.

60. Boyle, "Natural Law and the Ethics of Traditions," 158.

61. McInerny, *Ethica* Thomistica, 30.

62. Böckle, "Nature as the basis of Morality," 394.

Rahner's ontology offers a way to understand the nature and the conditions of possibility of that unavoidable reference [human subject]; as will be seen, his ontology attempts to construct an understanding both of the *content* of that unavoidable reference and also of the *method* for an ongoing elaboration of that content. Rahner's metaphysical answer to the question of the normatively human treats what traditional Thomism calls "constitutive principles of being"—such as "essence" or "nature" in natural law—differently than do the larger number of exponents of that tradition. It is the self-conscious "spirit in the world", the self-disposing "person in the world", or subjectivity, in a Kantian sense, that one seeks to subject to explanatory understanding by talk of "constitutive principles of being (emphasis mine).[63]

Rahner's theology is a critique of the theory of the natural moral law as presented in the traditional theology in the Roman Catholic Church. For example, Bresnahan summarizes Rahner's contribution to ethics with the following statement:

Rahner's critical metaphysics or ontology provides a starting point from which he criticizes pre-Kantian Scholastics because their conception of nature was excessively objective. By that Rahner means that human nature was treated as if it were not decisively different from what it meant by nature in infrahuman entities (such as animals). "Nature" is "essence" considered precisely in relation to characteristic activity of the being.[64]

All things have nature, which is determined by essence and existence, but human beings distinctively have subjectivity which consists of conscious self-possession (knowing) and self-disposal (freedom). Rahner insisted that human nature should not be equated with the nature of other beings such as animals and inanimate beings. In Rahner, the focus is on the human subjectivity that makes knowledge possible. Hence, Bresnahan sums up moral normativity in Rahner's theological method as follows; "To act against nature means, in some degree according to the character of the action, to effect the self-destruction of the actor as conscious and free in his action and thus to diminish the personal, whether in the individual actor or in a human grouping. It is to exclude meaning because one destroys being itself."[65]

63. Bresnahan, "Rahner's Ethics," 39–40.
64. Ibid., 40.
65. Ibid., 47.

Why Natural Law?

Natural law has developed in the Roman Catholic moral theology as a possible way to understand the human personality and the ethical demands that go with it. From a Christian perspective, a good understanding of the human person makes it possible to understand the place of Jesus Christ in human existence. Thomas Aquinas understood the natural law as participation in the eternal law by the rational creatures. From Aquinas, therefore, the natural law provides an avenue for understanding the Christian faith without any contradiction whatsoever. In natural moral law, there is a possibility for human beings to give a human response to the call to faith in Jesus Christ. It is only when a person makes a choice in following Christ that one is said to be a responsible disciple.

The Natural law demonstrates the place of Christians in the world with other people. Macquarrie makes the following note: "Indeed, I believe that a viable account of natural law could make a vital contribution toward solving three major problems—the linking of Christian and non-Christian morals, the shape of a contemporary Christian ethic, and the relation between faith and morals."[66] We could also add to Macquarrie's list, the fact that the natural law unites all world religions in so far as their members share human reason. Further, religious dialogue can only take place through an acknowledgement of the other as a rational human being.

The religion of Christianity is not opposed to being human, but on the contrary it is understood as a way of life to realize one's humanity and its implications. Christianity embraces what it means to be human and teaches ways to bring humanity to its perfection. It is as Macquarrie notes:

> Christianity, I wish to assert, is not a separate moral system, and its goals and values are not fundamentally different from those that all moral striving has in view. Yet it cannot be denied that there are some ways in which the Christian ethic differs from non-Christian ethics. It seems to me that the differences have to do with the different ways in which the several groups or traditions perceive the goals that are implicit in all moral striving, and the means to these goals; or with the different ways in which they understand and engage in the moral obligations laid upon all; or with the different

---

66. Macquarrie, "Rethinking Natural Law," 121. See also Hughes, *Authority in Morals,* 26–63.

degrees of explicitness to which the idea of an authentic humanity has emerged in the several traditions.[67]

Is Jesus Christ and the gospel not morally normative? Why look outside? Are there no explicit moral answers in the gospels? Natural law reasoning is a way of reflecting on the moral implication of being human and also of being Christian. Christianity does not contain in its doctrine answers to all situations that confronts a believer in Christ in everyday life. Christianity provides principles that act as guidelines in human decision-making. Schüller's statement is instructive on the gospel of Jesus Christ and its normativity:

> Because Jesus did not leave a code of prescriptions for every possible situation in life. They looked first to the words of Jesus, but very soon found situation demanding moral judgment which went beyond Jesus' commands. In 1 Cor 7 Paul rejects divorce saying, "I give charge, not I but the Lord." Then concerning mixed marriage he says, "to the rest I say, not the Lord."[68]

In diverse historical contexts such as in Africa, the gospel has also to dialogue with culture if meaningful ethical understanding is to be acquired. People have always to look in the cultural milieu for answers to their ethical questions.

Christians live in the world. Being in the world, Christians experience contingencies like everybody else. Theo Beemer argues that Christians should think of themselves as part of the world. He writes the following: "When the church talks about God's will as the norm of human conduct, this is seen by many either as superfluous statement as what we already know as good and worth pursuing, a belated confirmation, or as an attempt at breaking through what is experienced by all and setting Christians apart from the rest of mankind as a group of better informed initiates."[69] Beemer also presents the salvific power of Christ as encompassing all of creation. He writes:

> The proclamation concerning Christ shows forth creation as incarnation and redemption. Hence all ethics is of necessity a Christian ethic, and human ethic is in fact a Christian ethic. The result is that we only practice a truly Christian ethic when we constantly

67. Macquarrie, "Rethinking Natural Law," 126.

68. Schüller, 95.

69. Beemer, "The Interpretation of Moral Theology," 62.

and consistently recognize man's autonomy, and recognize it effectively. In the unfolding of this thesis the essential intersubjectivity of all human action displays the shape of God's presence in the world. Thus human inter-subjectivity becomes communion with God.[70]

In Christian theology, Beemer views Christology as the hermeneutic of ethics. Christology provides to the human person what was hidden from the foundation of the world.[71]

From the above, it is justifiable to say that Christians are part of the society in which they live. The work of Aquinas shows he was involved with social and political issues of his day: "[H]e was optimistic and generous, capable of living in the middle between the universe and the reign of God."[72] Christians are called, like everybody else, to participate in making societal life better. Richard McCormick, among other moral theologians, has suggested that through the theory of the natural moral law, Christians can participate with non-Christians in the making of public policy. The Christian churches are not just simply influence to their societies but help in the formation of consciences and hence indirectly influence policy making.[73] The work of Archbishop Desmond Tutu in bringing to an end the South African Apartheid is also a good example of Christian life in society. Natural law can be said to be the meeting point where all people come together regardless of religion, gender, or race. All people in leading a good life use reason as a guide to their actions.

Bujo's Critique of the Natural Moral Law

Bénézet Bujo raises the question of the relevance of the natural moral law reasoning as it pertains to Africa. He incorporates the natural law thinking into an African ethics, even while the same has also been used to condemn some African lifestyles as contrary to human dignity. An example is the Christian condemnation of polygamy and marriage by stages.[74] Bujo proposes an intercultural method to go hand in hand with the natural moral law reasoning. Bujo is a contemporary moral theologian and his work fits

70. Ibid., 65.
71. Ibid., 66.
72. O'Meara, *Thomas Aquinas*, 35.
73. McCormick, *Notes on Moral Theology 1965 through 1980*, 3.
74. Bujo, *The Ethical Dimension of Community*, 29–35.

into the category of the renewal of moral theology coming after the Second Vatican Council. The preceding is notable in Bujo's analysis of the natural moral law reasoning in Africa.

In his work, Bujo engages and acknowledges the validity of the theory of natural law. However, he clarifies that there are other moral theories besides the natural law tradition. According to Bujo, "the natural law model, which is based on one particular philosophy, is one among many models of ethical reflection. The ethos of Old Testament takes a different path, and natural-law ethics begins with the attempt to understand and systematize this biblical concept, a procedure already adopted by Thomas Aquinas."[75] Bujo makes a positive contribution by insisting that the theory of the natural law argumentation is not the only way to determine morality. This may sound as an obvious thing to say but the natural law theory has been extolled for years, especially in the Roman Catholic Church, as the proper context for debate regarding moral norms, birth-control, among others. In this regard, natural law is held as indispensable. We can never deny the role of reason in theology or any human transaction or science, but we must acknowledge that human beings can use reason differently to reach the same or different conclusions. Bujo's intercultural approach to moral issues can also not afford to be devoid of reason or natural moral law argumentation. Bujo's model of theologizing makes a contribution by his emphasis on culture and historical context. In this way, Bujo opposes the false universalism of the natural law tradition.

Bujo is critical of the way the natural law has been presented as absolute and without taking due consideration of a cultural-historical context. For example, when the natural law is used by the Church to condemn artificial insemination (by anonymous donor), Bujo suggests that the doctrine could be more effective if the idea that there is no anonymity in African society were used to decipher the same teaching. Bujo is critical of the way church documents meant for westerners are presented without the concern of an African context. The example he gives is the Instruction *Donum Vitae* of the *Roman Congregation for the Doctrine of the Faith* (1987), of which he says, "[T]his document does not move beyond the framework of traditional doctrine of the natural law,"[76] while making claims for universal validity. Also noteworthy, Bujo says of the encyclical *Humanae vitae*, that

75. Bujo, *Foundations of an African Ethic*, 12.

76. Ibid., 17. See also Rahner, *Theological Investigations*, vol. 14. Rahner holds that norms of Christian living develop from one particular age to the next (14).

it would have "found a readier hearing if it addressed the ethical attitude in Africa, oriented toward the community, instead of giving the central position to *natura*."[77] According to Bujo, reason "must integrate its own given nature in such a way that the human person can act responsibly."[78] It is sinful to act against reason.

Natural law argumentation has been used to condemn whatever is customarily different from some church teachings. Bujo says that natural law was used to cast suspicion on many African forms of marriage such as marriage by stages and polygamy. African marriage is a process that involves the whole community.[79] Bujo suggests dialogue between ecclesiastical moral theology, based on natural law and African moral theology, based on the community. He says that this is possible through the Thomistic distinction between *ius naturale* and *ius gentium*. He states: "The *ius naturale* speaks of the existing state of affairs as something that has assumed a fixed, stable form; but the *ius gentium* points to the elaboration of the *ius naturale* in terms of the goal at which a specific context and society consciously aim."[80]

Bujo's criticism of the natural moral law reasoning does not mean he is opposed to it. He is critical of a generalized view of the natural law that does not address itself to the context of a particular people. He affirms the natural law, and also criticizes it when he states:

> The emphasis here on the norms' claim to validity and on the reciprocal and universal justification of these norms does not in the least mean that one abandons content; but practical reason both transcends context and is immanent to context . . . The fact that practical reason both transcends context and is immanent to context indicates however, that various contexts correct and supplement one another.[81]

In judging any moral action we have to ask ourselves how the action was done, by whom, and according to what rationality this is established and asserted.[82] Further, Bujo argues: "When, for example, the encyclical *Veritatis Splendor* says that *praecepta negativa* are valid *semper et pro*

77. Bujo, *Foundations of an African Ethic*, 17.
78. Ibid., 18.
79. Ibid.
80. Ibid., 19.
81. Ibid., 23.
82. Ibid., 22.

semper, it will be necessary, . . . to find a contextual solution to some questions that ought to be investigated."[83] From all these it is true to say that context is indispensable in the consideration of moral norms. The question on universal moral norms, can therefore, be raised when the issue of the context is focused. Bujo refers to Böckle on this when he states: "Franz Böckle is one of those who hold that we live in a contingent world, where contingent goods so compete with one another that we are able to recognize the absolute *bonum* only in the contingent *bona*."[84] Bujo proposes that the preceding can be used in the dialogue between African ethics and the doctrine of natural law. Natural law has to be thought of and applied in an African context.

Nevertheless, Bujo argues that an African ethics is broader than a natural moral law ethics. He comments that "whereas the natural-law argumentation proceeds in a rational and abstract manner, African ethical justification also includes a narrative dimension, which allows one to question an excessively idealistic theory and to put it to the test by means of an example. The natural-law argumentation gives the impression of looking for the absolute 'ultimate justification,' whereas African ethics is content with a less ambitious goal—not an absolute 'ultimate justification' but only an 'ultimate justification' until a better argument turns up."[85] In an African setting, Bujo is of the opinion that "the theories with universal claims must be brought down to earth by particular practices which concretize the universal; more than this, they must also expose themselves to questioning and demonstrate their worth."[86]

The main question that Bujo raises here is on the presentation of the natural moral law as universal and absolute. It is clear that Bujo emphasizes context and the cultural aspect in the understanding of Christian moral demands in an African ethics. The issue on the natural law and the cultural implications is further developed below where its limits are debated.

Limitations of the Natural Law

Bujo is not the first one to raise questions on the universality of the natural law. He acknowledges that Aquinas had pointed out the limitation of

83. Ibid., 21.
84. Ibid., 22.
85. Ibid.
86. Ibid., 23.

human beings to realize the natural law fully. Aquinas was very much aware of the general limitation of reason in relation to the knowledge of truth. Bujo writes:

> Not only does Thomas argue in some places along lines other than the natural law; he also clearly recognizes the boundaries of reason—first because reason needs a long time until it can clearly recognize some truths, and also because, even where the truth can be known, it is sometimes an object of dispute among specialists; in some cases, only a minority of persons can recognize the truth. This leads Thomas to postulate the necessity of divine revelation, which allows the human being to know in a manner genuinely free of error.[87]

Jean Porter also acknowledges that there are limits in the realization of the natural law. She refers to ST I-II q. 94 a. 4, to show that Aquinas realized that natural law is not the same in practical rectitude or truth for all people but only in the general principles. On Thomas Aquinas, Porter states: "[H]e is aware of the need to qualify and extend the basic norms of the natural law at the level of socially sustained reflection, as well as at the level of individual decision."[88]

Historically, the natural moral law has been used to show how objective and sometimes how absolute moral norms are regardless of the context of the moral agent. Considering the universality of the natural law, moral reasoning proceeds from a deductive or inductive method to arrive at moral norms. A deductive or inductive method is an inadequate way to deal with issues in a morally responsible way. We have always to consider the intention, the circumstances, and the object of the moral agent. On the natural law and deductive method, Joseph Arntz states the following: "[P]urely deductive procedure ends up by turning natural law into positive law. It means that this indefinite perpetuation of analysis and deduction has lost touch with concrete reality. In spite of the realistic start of this system the reality becomes unreal to it because it rests on ideas. That an idea should spring from experience seems unrealistic to one who relies exclusively on ideas."[89]

The other problem of taking the natural moral law uncritically is holding it to be immutable or unchangeable. It is, therefore, necessary to

87. Ibid., 13.
88. Porter, *Moral Action and Christian Ethics*, 99.
89. Arntz, "Natural Law and Its History," 28.

emphasize that the natural law is not a written code of conduct. Natural law is an unfinished project, meaning that human beings in natural moral law reasoning have to make decisions continually. What Bresnahan writes is helpful in understanding the nature of natural law in morality. He states:

> [I]t must be stressed that normative content in critical natural law cannot be given a more important place than the process of dialectical reflection by which this normative content is constantly renewed. The ideal of this approach is an ever renewed critical perspective rather than the establishment of some kind of immutable code. One's own limited worldview, the unavoidable starting point of each effort to rethink the relationship of concrete matters for decision to the fundamental conditions of possibility for free decision itself, is to be submitted over and over again to disciplined reflection. And, this hermeneutical task is to be part of the very process of reflecting on matters of normative content in ethics.[90]

People change and develop over time. If the natural moral law has to do with human beings, it also has to develop. For example, if the argument that made the church in the past to condemn usury was based on a law derived from the natural law, that law changed. We can say that natural law is realized in time and thereby a development in its understanding is inevitable. Joseph Arntz warns us of the danger of the way we conceive the natural law. He says

> a solution would be to adopt neither the Stoa nor St. Thomas without qualification. If the starting point is an unchangeable nature, then all that is left is a change in our knowledge of this unchangeable fact. If we start, with St. Thomas, with the *prima principia*, then the development is simply the history of their explication or unfolding. But this history cannot touch these *prima principia* in themselves.[91]

Further, Arntz suggests that "we must return to the origin of these first principles, and approach them not at the level of reflection, but at the level of the evidence which precedes all reflection, and which is only expressed in judgment."[92]

The objection to an arbitrary conception of the natural law regardless of time and place is the realization that we live in a culturally diverse world.

90. Bresnahan, "Rahner's Ethics," 43.

91. Arntz, "Natural Law and Its History," 28.

92. Ibid.

A responsible natural moral law reasoning should always be attentive to the people's history and cultural settings. According to Arntz:

> The question is to find something which will help us to understand the factual multiplicity of cultures. These are always the realization of human possibilities which emerge from a specific view of man. But the principle must also be able to explain—although this is not my concern here—that some cultures show an endless repetitive pattern while others develop and reach a ceiling above which they cannot rise.[93]

It is also necessary to emphasize that the natural law is not a written code of conduct. Natural law is an unfinished project, meaning that human beings in natural moral law reasoning have to make decisions continually.

Notably, the most distinguishing factor in the renewal of moral theology, before and after the Second Vatican Council, is the development of the debate on the theory of the natural moral law. From the theologians studied above, it is evident that the natural moral law has been developing in various ways. Bujo emphasizes that moral reasoning always takes place in human beings who are in a concrete cultural and historical context. Context is indispensable in the natural moral law theory. Historically, the natural moral law has conceivably been developing. African Christian ethics, especially in the Catholic tradition, is also part of the development in the natural moral law reasoning. The study of the natural moral law theory in the work of St. Thomas Aquinas and the historical development of this tradition provides a useful method in addressing contemporary moral issues. The African moral theology as developed by Bujo is also part of this theological diversity after Vatican II.

Part Two: African Moral Theology in the Light of the Vatican II Council

African moral theology as developed by Bujo and others reflects in a very clear way the aspects of the renewal of moral theology, such as the use of Sacred Scripture and the realization of the relevance of culture and history, as called for by Vatican II. To show the nature of post-Vatican II theology,

93. Ibid., 29. Cf. Lottin, *Morale Fondamentale*. Lottin holds: "Certains énoncés de la loi naturelle sont donc incomplets et, en un sens, faux; mais la loi naturelle, en elle-même ou, si l'on veut, adéquatement formulée, est immuable et ne comporte aucune exception" (126).

I make an analysis of the use of the Sacred Scriptures and history in the making of an African ethics. The work of the African moral theologian, Bénézet Bujo, is taken as a case study of some perspectives in African moral theology. Just as in the work of "revisionists," a historical consciousness in the theology of Bujo is realized in the way he uses Christology. For Bujo, like any other renewal moral theologian, Christian ethics is essentially Christocentric.

A. The Use of Sacred Scripture in the Theology of Bujo

In his works Bujo makes use of Sacred Scripture despite the fact that he has not made known the method he employs. However, an analysis of the basic way in which Bujo uses Sacred Scripture and his theological focus indicates he fits in the methodology of renewal moral theologians. It is important to re-emphasize here that there is no one way to classify renewal moral theologians, or even the so-called "revisionists" in that they are all as diverse as their names suggest.

Bujo uses Scripture so much to show that what is in the Bible does not contradict whatever is reasonable in human thinking.[94] He has argued that some biblical teachings can be realized through sound human reasoning. Although he does not deny the Bible is God's self-disclosure, there is an affirmation in his work that everything has its source from God, including human reason. God created man and woman in his own image (Gen 1:26–27).

Hence, it is necessary to examine further the use of Scripture in Bujo's African theological ethics. Scripture will be seen to enhance or serve as the source of some theological teachings, if not all. Human history and reason will be seen in Bujo's theology as non-contradictory with God's revelation in the Bible. However, the use of Scripture in moral theology will be dealt with in another forum especially in an analysis of how the encyclical, *Veritatis Splendor*, employs Scripture to respond to the various issues raised by contemporary moral theologians.

---

94. On the use of Sacred Scripture in African theology, Hastings states: "True theology, then, is not even ideally to be measured by the standard of a pure interpretation of *scriptura sola*. It is rather a wrestling between revelation and something else, some part of the contemporary praxis of humankind, and what is required is a double fidelity" (Hastings, *African Catholicism*, 83).

B. Historicity as a Necessary Dimension of the Meeting with Faith

The Christian message is always lived in a concrete historical location. Just as Jesus himself proclaimed the message of the kingdom of God in first-century Palestine, so also Christian life is to be proclaimed in an African cultural setting. Paying attention to historical and cultural setting is in accordance with Vatican II as I have shown in the preceding section. Bujo argues that the Church's intent today should be to present "to Africans a Christ who is as close to them as he can possibly be, and who is interested in their traditional culture, to the extent that this culture contributes to the development of the whole human being."[95]

Bujo uses the Old Testament and the history of the early church to show how indispensable history is in Christian living. He maintains that "the man who comes into contact with the faith is necessarily situated, and cannot be understood, nor can exist, separated from his former history."[96] Who we are and what our culture is determines how we respond to the gospel of Jesus Christ. Historicity is a necessary dimension of the meeting with faith. Understanding a cultural setting is, therefore, important not only to theological study but also in everyday living of Christian life. Bujo says,

> In the meeting with the message of faith, in the coming of Christianity, man must in no way renounce his cultural identity, and the "Gospel" in the broadest meaning of the term, as message of faith has no right to lose its *proprium*. When Christianity meets a people, the following elements must be kept in mind: the Gospel, the tradition of Christianity, the local culture, the social changes in that culture, and the superstructure of powers that transcend regions and localities. It has become trite to say that each people and each era has its own experience of faith, so that plurality, far from being an impoverishment, widens the horizon of the Gospel experience.[97]

An African ethics, as Bujo argues, takes into consideration African culture and history. This requires understanding the African world-view other than through the lens of imported foreign cultural and philosophical theories. It is true that Christianity has always been bound by classical philosophy, but we cannot equate Christianity to classical philosophy or

95. Bujo, *African Christian Morality at the Age of Inculturation.* 39. See also Martey, *African Theology*, 63–86.

96. Bujo, "Can Morality be Christian in Africa," 10.

97. Ibid., 11.

culture. The gospel can be understood as transcending any particular cultural or philosophical outlook but is also immanent to the same. Christianity has historically found expression in all cultures of the world and taken root in different concrete historical situations. It is in this context that we can understand Bujo's statement that:

> Indeed, if man is a historical-cultural being, and if he can exist only in such a relationship, the ethical values which he has to realize enter equally the line of the historico-cultural context of each one, of each people and of each epoch. Thus the moral way of acting of a Christian cannot be written only by having recourse to the pre-evangelical tradition; but neither can it be seized only from the point of view of evangelical or post-evangelical tradition. It is all this at the same time.[98]

To study theology in an African context, then, requires one to be attentive to the culture of the people. Bujo's approach is representative of a culturally sensitive method in theology. He makes the following observation:

> Concretely for the black African, one needs to study not only his tradition with all its beauty, ugliness, strength and weaknesses, but also this tradition confronted with the often brutal reality of colonialism, with imported Christianity, and with political independence which in many places have been subjected to neo-colonialism. Finally, the meeting with Christianity is relevant for the black African only if one takes seriously this bundle of realities. But then the theologian will necessarily be led to distinguish between authentically black African traditions which are still alive, latent traditions, and those which have already fallen into disuse. Then he needs to sort out carefully the traditions, which are worthy of being carried on, and those which need to be brought back from latency or oblivion. To put it in another way, this means that the traditions must be studied in their nakedness for this is how faith surprises them in order to assume them in the incarnational *kenosis*.[99]

Bujo shows the importance of a historical-cultural approach in the study of an African ethics. He gives concrete examples of the cultural elements assumed by faith beginning with the Old Testament. He points out that there are traces of cultural elements in the ethos of the Old Testament.

98. Ibid. See how South African theology was shaped by the fight against apartheid in Hopkins, *Black Theology*, 93–97.

99. Bujo, "Can Morality be Christian in Africa?" 11.

"Old Testament exegetes have shown sufficiently how the majority of the customs and practices of the people of Israel were a heritage common to several peoples in the Ancient East."[100] This is in line with the renewal of moral theology called for by Vatican II, especially in Bujo's use of scripture, history, and an appreciation of culture in ethics. Further, Bujo adds:

> The precepts and laws according to which people of Israel were already living before the theophany of Sinai, that is, the obligations which ruled Israel before the meeting with Yahweh, were placed under the immediate authority of God, by the formula of auto presentation which is found in Exodus 20, 1–2 and Deuteronomy 5, 6. It is because Yahweh is Yahweh, that is, he who liberated Israel and who will continue to accompany her and make her future, that henceforth whoever loves him will avoid whatever displeases this benefactor God in customs and morality in general. Faith in Yahweh becomes from then on, a criterion of selection for moral action.[101]

The historical-cultural element is also evident in the Psalms. Bujo makes reference to Psalm 2 which marks a ceremony of coronation and anointing. He views this Psalm as a reflection of the old politico-monarchical period of Israel. It concerns an important mandate that Yahweh entrusts to his elected King. This king henceforth gathers in himself the hope the people put in Yahweh as liberator of his people. That is expressed by the power the king possesses to destroy those forces opposed to him which are also the enemies of God.[102] This historical consciousness is also present in the prophetic literature. The song of the servant of God in Isaiah 52:13–53:12, is different from Psalm 2 although it has some similarities. "It is the differences resulting from different human and religious experiences which should, above all, be emphasized."[103]

Bujo's reflection on Isaiah 42:3 views it as a text referring to some experience of suffering. Accordingly, this text,

> inevitably suggests solidarity, and further, identification, with the weak and oppressed. It is no triumphant conquering king who appears in this text. The historical background to this teaching on suffering is found, according to several exegetes, in the fall of

100. Ibid., 12.

101. Ibid.

102. Ibid., 13.

103. Ibid.

Jerusalem, which reawakened awareness of a national catastrophe. This historical experience of catastrophe has been confronted with faith in God, who remains faithful to his people in spite of a dehumanizing situation. God seems to suffer with his people.[104]

The integration of suffering with faith and the deepening of faith in God were possible only on the basis of historical facts in human experiences.

Traces of cultural elements are also present in the ethos of the New Testament. Bujo holds that the ethical concept of Jesus can be recognized in his public ministry and his message about the kingdom of God:

> The kingdom of God which Jesus proclaims is an eschatological kingdom which is extremely important for the ethical behavior of the believer. The reign and the kingdom of God which Jesus proclaims challenge the believer in a radical way to decide now, in this eon, for God. This is possible only through an uncompromising *metanoia*.[105]

Bujo categorically notes that Jesus' aim in proclaiming the kingdom of God "is not the stipulation of norms, but rather the gathering together of Israel."[106] The message of Jesus required a practical application in people's lives. Bujo is of the opinion that "the final consequence of the proclamation of Jesus is to bring us to reflect on the concrete action of man; but Jesus did not want to build an ethical and social system."[107] Even the Sermon on the Mount does not provide concrete ethical norms. The Sermon on the Mount can be applied in a number of ways such as promotion of peace and disarmament but it "should not be too quickly interpreted as containing concrete ethical norms of Jesus."[108] In the Gospels, the aim of Jesus was not to come to decree ethical norms for society. According to Bujo, one cannot find anywhere in Jesus' teachings a program for social reform. For this reason we should not look for moral norms to elaborate an economic ethics in the Gospels (Luke 12:13–14). There are so many things that Jesus did not teach. For example, Bujo says that "Jesus did not preach a movement of emancipation of women even though a consequence of his teaching was to favor the dignity of woman."[109] The fact that Jesus did not teach on a

104. Ibid.
105. Ibid., 14.
106. Ibid.
107. Ibid., 15.
108. Ibid.
109. Ibid., 16.

particular subject does not mean that his teaching cannot be applied to that issue. The teaching of Jesus is foundational to all Christian moral teaching. This is why Bujo states that "the eschatological message of Jesus which culminates in the proclamation of the Kingdom of God is a fundamental orientation for the moral behavior of the Christian."[110]

Further, Bujo attributes a historical-cultural setting to the ethical concept of the early Church. Referring to baptism in the early church, Bujo states:

> the Lord who bought and acquired the neophyte at the price of his own blood attests by baptism that the newly baptized is marked "with the seal of ownership." He assures him "of obtaining all the graces of salvation," so that the baptized person no longer belongs to himself. He passes to a new life.[111]

Bujo insists that the language of baptism as an appropriation of a person is taken from the buying and selling of slaves in ancient times. This language introduced a fundamental Christian anthropology which was to have unheard-of consequences for the Christian being and which would necessarily have repercussions upon the ethical actions of the believer. In Pauline literature, new being in Christ through faith and baptism influences the way the Christian lives. "This brings us to the famous problem of the Indicative and Imperative in St. Paul . . . in Romans 6, Paul reminds us that by baptism the Christian dies and is buried and resurrected with Christ. By Baptism one dies to sin in order to live for God in Jesus Christ."[112] Pauline theology is necessary if one is to understand the theology of the sacrament of baptism and the new life in Christ through baptism. "To be baptized in the name of Christ means to become an integral member of his body. So he who lives in debauchery prostitutes the body of Christ! We see here how, because of the Christic reality, the Christian must have a new understanding of the body and how this must affect his attitude to his body."[113]

An African Christian ethics, like the early Christian church, must be historically conscious if it is to address the Christian faithful in Africa. Just as Paul follows the argument based on the experience of the "new-being-in-Christ," so also we in Africa have to express our Christian faith in our own language, and thereby the Christian obligation. In the African church,

110. Ibid.
111. Ibid., 11.
112. Ibid.
113. Ibid., 17–18.

the status should be Christian and African. From this perspective we can talk of an African Christianity and an African ethics. Bujo clarifies, "The second attitude which is possible in the determination of the behavior of the believer in the light of his Christian status is the dialogue and confrontation with a pre-existing ethos in view of reaching a compromise."[114] 1 Cor 8, which takes "the weak into consideration is situative, applies to a particular community, in a clearly determined epoch and culture. The norm found here could not claim a universalization, which could make it valid in all situations where such a problem no longer exists or never existed. But this case is a model which indicates to us how faith has to take into account concrete events and circumstances."[115]

The best example, often quoted, of faith and culture coming together is the Council of Jerusalem. The dialogue between the Christian gospel and the African culture is compared by Bujo to the Council of Jerusalem. "The Council of Jerusalem is a model which shows clearly how the community of believers should proceed in creating norms. All parties must be listened to attentively. Moreover, faith must not necessarily brutalize or destroy the elements of the pre-existing tradition. In a pluralist community the law of agape must take priority to save *Koinonia* which would otherwise run the risk of crumbling."[116]

The ethical concept of the early church is an ethic marked by its time, indebted to the cultural and religious inheritance of both the earlier and the contemporary period of the proclamation of the Christian gospel. What Christianity did was to throw new light on them and gave them a new base. Bujo makes reference to the following Pauline understanding of the Christian community:

> We know how the concepts of "virtuous" (Phil. 4:8), of "honorable," of "shameful" (Phil. 4:8; Col. 3:18; Eph. 5:4, 5, 12) have their origin in the Stoic philosophy. Especially in reading Col.3, 18–4, 1, we know that Paul made use of the moral precepts given by contemporary philosophy, adding to these words "in the Lord." That no doubt gives a new orientation but remains anchored in the culture and the concepts of the time. And Paul does not invite to social revolution; on the contrary, he asks his readers to keep to the pre-established order (for example in 1 Cor. 7:17–24; 1 Thess.

114. Ibid., 18. Cf. Njoku, *Essays in African Philosophy*: "Language is a carrier of meaning, visions and culture of a people" (90).

115. Bujo, "Can Morality be Christian in Africa?," 18.

116. Ibid., 19.

3:12; Rom. 13:1–7). Paul's concept concerning women is only too well known and incontestably reflects the customs of his time (for example, 1 Cor. 11:2–16). But even the numerous cases of slavery did not drive the apostle to make himself the voice of the voiceless to try to overthrow the existing system . . . It is true that the epistle to Philemon teaches a master how to treat a slave in Christ.[117]

From a perspective concerned with meaning and relevance, Bujo raises the important issue of the communicability of the morality proclaimed by faith. He advocates that moral theology should not only use scriptural texts but should also reasonably apply all Christian doctrine in concrete contexts. "Since the Second Vatican Council many efforts have been made to provide a biblical foundation for morality; moral theology's task is to go beyond the biblical texts and even beyond exegesis, for it cannot be satisfied with repeating exegetical affirmations in the manner of a recitation, but it has to interpret exegetical affirmation for a world always in evolution."[118] Bujo uses the natural moral law theory to show that morality has to do with what is human, and therefore, what is reasonable. Accordingly, Bujo cautions that

> moral theology cannot be satisfied with paranetic theory, but its role is to develop an argumentative system. If we neglect this last aspect, we risk falling into a biblicism blind to true human values which can only destroy real humanity, as we see in the case of South African racism which does not hesitate to call on the biblical text: "Each one is to stay before God in the state in which you were called" (1 Cor. 7:24).[119]

In the preceding we can see the importance of ethical hermeneutics as called for by Bujo. He holds that an ethical hermeneutic is necessary if we are to understand Christian morality in a historically reasonable way. He argues the use of reason is evident in the New Testament by giving the following examples: "'Lk. 23:31: if this is what is done to green wood, what will be done when the wood is dry?' Mark 2:27 says, concerning the Sabbath, 'The Sabbath was made for man, not man for the Sabbath.' And in Mark 8:36 Jesus says: 'What does it profit a man to gain the whole world, at the cost of his life?' . . . Lk. 10:7 and Mt. 20:23 uses an existential argument

117. Ibid.
118. Ibid., 20.
119. Ibid.

that all may easily grasp: 'The laborer deserves his pay.'"[120] Bujo gives Rom 1:19–20 as certainly one of the clearest arguments in favor of reason: *Reason is the place of communication with God.*[121]

Reason also needs to be contextualized otherwise we would fall into the danger of a false universalism. One thing can be applicable in one place and not in another. This is true of Christian morality for it is not to be conceived only in the abstract. Human experience is irreplaceable in Christian living. "[M]orality on the Christian level becomes a reality lived and normative reality only when the message enters concrete dialogue with man to whom it is addressed and if it respects man. This means that in morality we have to avoid eschatologism and supernaturalism just as we have to distrust positivism and naturalism. To quote a biblical text or to enunciate a principle, even in the name of the natural law, is not enough for that to be considered as a norm valid for all time."[122]

C. Jesus as Proto-Ancestor in African Ethics

I have noted previously that renewal in moral theology has in a particular way involved the uncovering or "recovering" of its Christocentric nature. Further, I wish to show that an African ethics is Christocentric. In the renewal of moral theology, before and after the Second Vatican Council, Christian morality has since been viewed as Christocentric. Bujo's work reflects the renewal trend of viewing moral theology as centered in Jesus Christ.

Bujo proposes that Jesus Christ in an African ethics is to be viewed as the Proto-Ancestor. He suggests that for Christian morality to be African, Jesus has to be seen as an African with the Africans. Jesus becomes a member of an African community that assumes his teaching as a Proto-Ancestor or an ancestor in a prominent way. Viewing Jesus as the Proto-Ancestor "gives him a position on a transcendental level, where he is the one upon

---

120. Ibid., 21.

121. Ibid. Cf. Mieth, "Universal Values or a Specific Ethic?," 147–153. Mieth argues that Catholic moral theology is universal because "its starting point is universally accessible reason" (147).

122. Bujo, "Can Morality be Christian in Africa?," 22. Cf. Vähäkangas, *In Search of Foundation for African Catholicism*, where the idea of an African Christian theological understanding of ancestorship is seen as the evidence of the success of the comparative method (171–79).

whom existential power and the life of all ancestors depend."[123] In an African community "Jesus Christ is thus the life-giving proto-force of the whole black ethos."[124] On Jesus as Proto-Ancestor, Bujo states:

> The term "ancestor" can only be applied to Jesus in an analogical, or eminent way, since to treat him otherwise would be to make of him only one founding ancestor among many. That is why the title "Proto-Ancestor" is reserved to Jesus. This signifies that Jesus did not only realize the authentic ideal of the God-fearing African ancestors, but also infinitely transcended that ideal and brought it to new completion.[125]

Just as St. Paul and the rest of the New Testament used the Jewish and Greek cultures of their time, so also do Africans understand the Christian message in their culture. Making reference to the New Testament, Bujo states that "in Paul we have only to recall the Christology of the 'first Adam—second Adam' (1 Cor. 15:20 and Rom. 5:12ff), and also the ecclesiology of Jesus Christ as Head of the Body (Col. 1:15), and as 'the first-born from the dead' (1:18, and also 1 Cor. 15:20 again)."[126] The same cultural element is present in "Johanine Christology, a view of Jesus Christ transcending all created life, and from whom all life is derived, is even more explicit."[127] The use of scripture, in an African historical context, by Bujo is evident enough to show how well he fits in the renewal movement and the Second Vatican Council.

Bujo holds the black-African ethos is compatible with the Christian message. He is concerned with how to present Jesus in an African context. Jesus should not be viewed as an outsider in an African context but as a member of the community. He proposes that "Jesus Christ is not certainly just one great ancestor among others. I propose to call him the "Proto-Ancestor". This does not situate him in the biological line, but places him on the transcendental level, where he is the one from whom the existential strength and life of the ancestors flow, but at the same time he is put on the level of the model; it is not merely sufficient to copy the example of this model; the Proto-Ancestor invites his followers to vital creativity. Thus Jesus

---

123. Bujo, *African Christian Morality at the Age of Inculturation*, 104.

124. Ibid. See also Bujo, "A Christocentric Ethic for Black Africa," 143–46.

125. Bujo, *African Theology in Its Social Context*, 80.

126. Bujo, *African Christian Morality at the Age of Inculturation*, 104.

127. Ibid.

Christ is the vital proto-force of the whole black ethos."[128] In Africa today, Jesus has to be understood as a prominent member of the community. In referring to Jesus as the Proto-Ancestor, there is a deep meaning conceived in the life of the African people.[129] As seen before, "the remembering and reenactment of the deeds of ancestors and elders is a memorial-narrative act of salvation designed to secure total community, both before and after death, with all good and benevolent ancestors."[130]

Undoubtedly, Bujo maintains that Christian morality is Christocentric. He states that "the person of Jesus Christ and the community of the church are two of the fundamentals of Christian faith."[131] In an African cultural setting, the theology of ancestors is the starting-point for a new Christology. He presents the first Christians in the early church as a typical example of how Christianity takes over a people's culture as a means for the expression of its teachings. He says the first Christians gave Jesus titles borrowed from their contemporary culture. The task today is to let the Christian message be expressed in a language with which people can identify. Bujo says that "Christian thinkers today are striving to recover the genuinely human dimension of Jesus so that his message may really meet modern people and modern problems, instead of being wrapped in some ancient and often incomprehensible metaphysical idiom."[132]

Bujo makes it evident that it is possible to think of the public ministry, passion and death of Jesus in an African context. The words of Jesus as an ancestor are of paramount importance. Bujo compares the power of the word of Jesus to the last words of a dying person in an African family. He says; "These words are words of life, setting the seal on the experiences and example of one who, while withdrawing from the community, yet truly lives on with it, along with the other ancestors. The final event in the life of a dying person is normative for those he or she is leaving behind."[133] On

128. Bujo, "Can Morality be Christian in Africa?," 23–24.

129. Bujo, *African Theology in Its Social Context*, 77.

130. Ibid., 78. See also Nyamiti, "African Christologies Today," 3–23. Nyamiti analyzes African Christologies as twofold: (i) those that begin with the New Testament and later connect to African traditions; (ii) those that begin with African traditions and only move to the New Testament after establishing a foundation in African traditions (ibid., 3).

131. Bujo, *African Theology in Its Social Context*, 75.

132. Ibid., 76. Cf. Magesa, "Christ's Spirit as Empowerment of the Church-as-Family," 19–35.

133. Bujo, *African Theology in Its Social Context*, 79.

Jesus' ministry, suffering, death and resurrection, and its understanding in an African worldview, Bujo has written the following:

> All that Jesus did was concentrated on the imminent Rule of God as message of salvation; from that kingdom all his acts, teaching and causes derive their meaning. It was for this same kingdom-message that Jesus died, and it was from this that his death derived its saving meaning. Through his death Jesus became the means of salvation. His resurrection also belongs essentially to the same message. It was only the Easter faith that finally made clear what was the relationship between Jesus and his God. Through the resurrection of Jesus, God brought into being a new creation, a creation which infinitely transcended the first creation, including the world of the African ancestors. Jesus Christ is the ultimate embodiment of all the virtues of the ancestors, the realization of the salvation for which they yearned.[134]

Furthermore, in Jesus, an African ethics can only be meaningful if it emphasizes interiority. Jesus in his public ministry emphasized conversion of the heart to God. A Christian ethics, especially in Africa, has to have as its reference center in the interior of the human being. Morality has to have a personal character. Moral values or norms have to be internalized, and it is only then we can have human moral agency or responsibility. Bujo makes it clear:

> Jesus insisted that the root of the matter was to be found in one's own heart. Conversion of heart: that alone can dispose men and women to receive life in its fullness. It is conversion that frees a person from the bonds of egotism and opens that person to the kingdom of God wherein alone can be found true dignity. It is from this point of view that we must read the radical demands of the Sermon on the Mount. They are concerned with the relationship between human beings and envisage the total humanizing of the world in the service of the Father.[135]

One may question the relevance of viewing Jesus as the Proto-Ancestor. Is it a borrowed framework? Proto-Ancestor is "ancestor grammar" drawn from an African understanding of human life and its connection to the spiritual world. The most important fact is that "ancestor grammar," as used by Bujo, is christologically tuned in the sense that it begins with humanity.

134. Ibid., 81.
135. Ibid., 88.

Bujo's Christology is contextualized in an existential situation. "Theology can only speak of God in human terms, and Jesus himself described God in terms drawn from human experience. The legitimacy of such discourse is mythical essence, to be spoken of in abstract terms, without any footing in history. Any such abstract Christology would be meaningless and would constitute an argument against the Christian faith."[136] We can see in Bujo some influence of the theology of Rahner. Bujo states:

> To borrow the words of Karl Rahner, in the incarnation God really assumed humanity in a decisive way. In uttering God's Word, which became our flesh, God immersed himself in the "void" of "godlessness" and "sin", so that henceforth it is impossible for us, if we wish to meet God, to ignore the man Jesus. Not to acknowledge the man Jesus is also not to acknowledge humans at all.91

In a contextual way, Bujo presents the African traditions, just as the Old Testament in Christian thought, are fulfilled in the New Testament. Like the Old Testament, African traditional religion(s) is/are fulfilled in the person of Jesus Christ. Hence, we can also argue from the preceding perspective that African culture is viewed as also fulfilled in Jesus. Jesus, in an African Christian setting, becomes the realization of African humanity, while at the same time in Bujo's perspective, "Jesus corrects and completes the traditional morality of Africa."[137] Faith in Jesus also opens a new horizon to African traditional religion(s). Bujo holds that the moral perspective is no longer limited to my clan, my elders, my friends, but it extends to the whole human race. He states:

> [W]e need firstly a fundamental moral theology which starts from the experiences and reflections of people in Africa, faced with the event and coming of Jesus Christ. Such a moral theology opens the way to the development of a practical ethic by which the Africans will feel themselves really challenged. This new ethic will no longer be limited to the customs of the ancestors but will also have the difficult task of addressing the modern problems of development.[138]

136. Ibid., 80.
137. Ibid., 88.
138. Ibid., 92.

Bujo uses Christology not only as a foundation to fundamental moral theology, but also as a stepping-stone to developing a theology of liberation in Africa. In his theology, orthodoxy is inseparable from orthopraxis.

Jesus Christ becomes the answer to the human question. He transforms the way humanity is understood. Bujo categorically states that "a reading of the gospel shows that the positive elements in African anthropocentrism are thoroughly endorsed in the person of Jesus Christ. African hospitality and sense of family; African care for the elderly, the orphaned, the unfortunate: all these things are taken up by Jesus and brought to completion."[139] The search for salvation in the African people gets its meaning and fulfillment in Jesus Christ. The human experience of God among Africans is fully realized in Jesus. "From now on, Jesus makes his own all the striving of the ancestors after righteousness and all their history, in such a way that these have now become a meeting-place with the God of salvation."[140]

Conclusion

African (Christian) moral theology is centered in the faith in Jesus Christ. Jesus is viewed as a member of a community in Africa. He is the Proto-Ancestor, an ancestor in a prominent way. African moral theology is shaped by Christology. Further, Jesus is seen as offering answers or solutions to human questions of daily living. African moral theology fits in the Second Vatican Council's call for renewal. The renewal elements referred to in the first section of this essay are confirmed in the second section where African moral theology is viewed as raising similar issues such as the use of Sacred Scripture and moral reasoning informed by an African historical and cultural context. Nevertheless, the scholarly task which remains is to promote further development in African moral theology that addresses constantly changing African cultural contexts.

139. Ibid., 88.
140. Ibid., 83.

3

African Communitarian Ethics in the
Theological Work of Bénézet Bujo

THE COMMUNITY AND INDIVIDUAL dimensions of morality are problematic especially in communitarian ethics. Bénézet Bujo's work is presented here as a way to reconcile the individual and communal aspects in African communitarian ethics. The central role of the community in shaping an African ethics, from Bujo's perspective, does not in any way negate the sanctity and inviolability of the individual person as a moral agent. African palaver is not useless talk but an inclusive moral discernment process in a community. From a critical study of Bujo's African Christian ethics, I evaluate the relevance of his work in contemporary African contexts while also questioning the historical context and the cultural homogeneity presumed. Further, African communitarian ethics is viewed as a viable alternative to western subjectivist ethics and ethical theories applied in Christian ethics.

The work of Bujo is an analysis of African communitarian ethics from the perspective of Christian ethics. Born in the Democratic Republic of Congo (formerly Zaire) and currently teaching at the University of Fribourg in Switzerland, Bujo is an African moral theologian whose work focuses on developing an African Christian ethics that is informed by culture and history. It is a search for an authentically African ethics different from western moral theories, and especially the natural law tradition of western moral thinking. That tradition, as developed from Thomas Aquinas, takes human nature or reason as a capacity for distinguishing between what is morally good and to be done, and what is evil and to be avoided. The emphasis in

African communitarian ethics, on the other hand, while also appealing to moral reasoning, lies upon relationship as the determinant factor in the development of moral norms.

This study examines the communal and the individual dimensions in African ethics as represented in the work of Bujo. Any ethical system in Africa will have the community as its centre, since it is the community that makes individuality possible. In an African traditional setting there is no individual human being without the community; the community is a "communion" of individuals. In particular, Bujo presents the idea of the palaver, a coming together for moral deliberation, as a moral norm-finding process in which the individual and the community interact in dialogue. Taking account of the way in which community shapes moral reasoning in an African context, I propose to set out, analyze and critically assess the communitarian ethics of Bénézet Bujo as offering an alternative to the emphasis upon individual moral autonomy in Christian and western ethics..

I. The Community Dimension in African Moral Reasoning

Contemporary African societies have undergone various cultural and social changes. Africa's encounter with the West led to the introduction of western education and culture. Today, people in many African urban centers have embraced some western individualism and social practices. Despite all these changes, Bujo claims that African communitarianism is still a major factor in African societies and has suggested it as a possible foundation for an African theological ethics. According to Bujo, thought in an African community is inclusive. He affirms that "Africans do not think in 'either/or,' but rather in 'both/and' categories."[1] Moral reasoning is a process in which an individual makes rational decisions concerning morality without forgetting that one is a member of a community. Individual morality affects the well-being (flourishing) of a community in an African ethic. It is this line of thinking that is decisive for Bujo: "For Black Africa, it is not the Cartesian *cogito ergo sum* ("I think, therefore I am") but an existential *cognatus sum, ergo sumus* ("I am known, therefore we are") that is decisive."[2] This can also

1. Bujo, *Foundations of an African Ethic*, 1.

2. Ibid., 4. See also by Bujo, *Utamadunisho na Kanisa La Mazingira* [*Inculturation and Basic Christian Communities*]. Writing in Kiswahili language, Bujo states: "Africans very much emphasize people's coming together in a meeting. There is the family meeting, elders meeting, relatives meeting, tribal meetings, etc. What does the word accomplish in a meeting? In a meeting everybody is allowed to express and explain oneself. A meeting

be clarified in the common African maxim: "I am, because we are; and since we are, therefore I am."[3]

Reclaiming the lost centrality of community living provides a good foundation not only to theological ethics but also to other areas of theology such as inter-religious dialogue, ecumenism, ecclesiology, sacraments, and pastoral ministry, among others. An individual in an African traditional setting is always in communion with the community. An African community is made up of individual human beings who communicate with each other. This communication is present in all areas of daily living. For example, Nwaka Egbulem states the following on the Zairean liturgy of the Eucharist: "[I]nvocation of the saints and ancestors is made to establish a unity between the already triumphant church and the pilgrim church. It also seeks to obtain spiritual support for the living members who gather for worship. The invocation reveals the belief that the dead are not strangers to the present assembly of worship."[4] And furthermore, "by opening the celebration with the invocation of saints and ancestors, the Zairean Mass identifies the Christian assembly as the meeting place between the Creator, the ancestors, and the living."[5]

Nevertheless, the emphasis on community in African ethics should not be construed as replacing individual responsibility in moral decision-making and action. This work primarily deals with Bujo's attempt to reconcile individual ethical responsibility and community ethical dimension. An emphasis on community ethics requires a balance or protection of individual moral autonomy. The protection of individual autonomy or self-determination is the basis of the human rights endeavor after the Second World War. For example, the United Nations Declaration on Human Rights was meant to protect individual persons from organizations such as those of state and religion.[6] It is in this context of the community that the

---

is a time of seeing whether the word we 'ate' was chewed well so as to bring out fullness of life, uniting people" (9; my translation).

3. Mbiti, *African Religions and Philosophy*, 106; cf. also Sundermeier, *The Individual and Community in African Traditional Religions*, 17.

4. Egbulem, *The Power of Africentric Celebrations*, 58.

5. Ibid., 59.

6. Gewirth, *Human* Rights, 4. Gewirth argues human rights protect conditions necessary for human (moral) actions. See also Little, "Religion, Human Rights, and Secularism," 256. Little suggests that human rights charters constrain religions and societies by imposing basic universal, individual, and group protections.

indispensability of the individual human being in moral discernment is to be emphasized.

II. The Individual and/or the Community—Understanding Individuality in Community

Human beings are social beings, born into families, groups, tribes, clans, towns, cities, or countries. In an African context, there is no individuality without the community. In his writing Bujo seeks to develop an understanding of the individuality of a person in an African morality, where the individual and communal dimensions are inseparable. He argues that an African person, whose acting and thinking is always in solidarity and almost identical with his or her tribal community, is nonetheless able to make an ethical, responsible decision, as an individual.[7] From this perspective personal freedom is possible but as Bujo acknowledges "too much emphasis on the interests of the clan can obscure individual freedom and individual rights."[8]

In ethical thought generally, the rational and free nature of the individual human person is conceived as the ground of human morality, and Bujo somehow also shares this view. Individuality implies that one is capable of moral decisions. It means that one is not an object but a subject who acts in a responsible way. In an African context, individuality is expressed from the moment of birth in the ritual of name-giving. Each family member is given a unique name. This name characterizes personal and ontological reality. But especially in an African context individuality means acting with the other since "the community . . . enables the self-realization of the individual."[9] Furthermore, decisions made by one person can have an effect on other people in a community.

Communitarian ethics raises the question of whether it is possible to have an autonomous ethics or individual moral autonomy.[10] A communitarian ethics implies that a particular community shapes its moral norms. Is it possible to have a communitarian ethics without at the same time recognizing the individual person as a moral agent? Without individual

---

7. Bujo, *African Christian Morality at the Age of Inculturation*, 95.

8. Bujo, *African Theology in Its Social Context*, 35.

9. Bujo, *The Ethical Dimension of* Community, 28.

10. Auer's book *Autonome Moral und christlicher Glaube* led to the development of the debate on moral autonomy in Roman Catholic moral theology.

persons who can make morally responsible decisions it seems impossible to have ethics at all, let alone a communitarian ethics. Bujo argues that the individual in an African communitarian ethic is at the center of the determination of moral norms. It is not possible to answer the question of who comes first, the individual or a community, in an African communitarian ethic, since one presupposes the other.

The fact that individuality is inseparable from the communitarian nature of human existence in an African society implies that every person has to contribute to the well-being of the community. An ideal community consists of free individual persons who act as moral agents. Accordingly, Bujo states, "In the traditional setting, individuals could not be free unless they first contributed to the freedom of the whole community and vice versa."[11] Further, he suggests that "the individual is always bound to reflect on what is beneficial to herself or himself and to the whole community, and on what leads to participation in the eschatological communion, and what does not."[12] He compares African communitarian ethics with Christian ethics:

> The relationship between African "communitarian" and individual responsibility has immense implications for Christian ethics. On the one hand, Christians make very personal decisions before God. But on the other, they should not do so without regard for the faith community. The Christian is bound together with the Mystical Body. A good work is an important building-block of this Mystical Body.[13]

In a practical way, moral good or evil in a communitarian ethics is determined by whether a particular decision and action contributes positively to the life of the individual and the community. This extends not only to external actions but also to the level of intention, since morality, in a specific way, is both an internal and external act.[14] From Bujo's perspective, an individual person in an African society is required to fully interiorize the ethical demands of the community. These ethical demands include the integration of the ancestral norms by every member. To achieve this

---

11. Bujo, *African Theology in Its Social Context*, 7. Cf. Ozankom, "Oscar Bimwenyi," 95–106.

12. Bujo, *African Christian Morality at the Age of Inculturation*, 97.

13. Bujo, "Solidarity and Freedom: Christian Ethic in Africa," 49.

14. Cf. Janssens, "Teleology and Proportionality," 102.

integration, taboos and even witchcraft have often a protective function for ethical norms.

An example is provided by the rites of initiation among many African peoples. Initiation is a form of education aimed at the integration of moral norms in a community. Bujo's analysis of African moral norms is similar to the one held by Laurenti Magesa, another African moral theologian. Referring to rites of initiation in Africa, Magesa notes, "The proverbs, riddles, songs, and dances, as well as other sources of ancestral wisdom used in this period, exude moral guidance."[15] The rites of passage are words associated with the socialization of the young and this learning process continues through life by means of the occasional songs which help to communicate and perpetuate the traditional understanding of the world and people's attitudes towards it. These rites promote and confirm individual responsibility in community. Noting that the initiates are taught the absolute value of life, Magesa adds, "The phase of formal instruction stresses five areas of ethical concern in the life of the individual and society: religion, the mystery of life and death, domestic and social virtues, sex and sexuality, and forms of self-identity."[16] All these promote moral living in the community but do not exclude individual decisions through which one chooses what to do in various contexts.

To the charge that African morality is merely concerned with physical and external acts, Bujo responds by stating that "a deeper insight into African life shows that this is not so, but rather that he (an African person) has a deeply embodied moral consciousness."[17] He emphasizes the irreplaceable role of conscience, maintaining that "taboos are an important step in the formation of the moral conscience. Their function is to lead people to the formation and the interiorization of ethical norms."[18] Community moral norms, then, do not replace the individual interiority and interiorization of the same norms. "Good and evil proceed from the interior of man. That is why, for example, an enemy who crosses his neighbor's field can cause a

---

15. Magesa, *African* Religion, 97.

16. Ibid. African initiation rites described here compare to the Christian rites of initiation, which include the sacraments of baptism, eucharist, and confirmation. In an African Christian setting, recall of the traditional rites of initiation can be used to promote an in-depth understanding and living of the sacraments.

17. Bujo, *African Christian Morality at the Age of Inculturation*, 98.

18. Bujo, "Can Morality Be Christian in Africa?," 10. Cf. Fuchs, "Conscience and Conscientious Fidelity," 108–24.

bad harvest, for his intention is bad."[19] It is therefore possible to talk of interiority in African ethic: "For the blacks also, good and evil arise from the *interior of the human being*. An evil look at somebody is held to be capable of harming or even killing a person. Likewise, someone pointing his finger maliciously at a neighbor does harm to him."[20] In African ethics, then, just as an in Christian ethics, the intention is just as important as the act itself.

Bujo's emphasis on individual morality as internalization of community ethical norms does leave some questions unanswered. For example, can an individual person through a judgment of conscience differ with community moral requirements? Is it possible to uphold freedom of conscience in individual persons while maintaining community obligations as primary?

III. The Flourishing of The Community and its Relation to Individual Morality

Too great a stress upon community life can raise concerns in regard to individual moral autonomy. Bujo has to show that the communitarian nature of African morality does not mean ending up with a scenario where the individual can be sacrificed for the sake of the nation or ethnic group. While stressing that "members of the clan have a duty to contribute to the growth of the clan by doing good," and also that "the evil committed by one member can diminish the life of the whole clan"[21] Bujo also has to emphasize the community contribution to the well-being of an individual person. The relationship between the community and individual persons in it must be reciprocal.

The members of an African community include the living and the living dead, the ancestors. From this conception of life in the community,

19. Bujo, "Can Morality Be Christian in Africa?," 9.

20. Bujo, *African Christian Morality at the Age of Inculturation*, 98. Cf. Berg, "Culture, Christianity, and Witchcraft in a West African Context," 45–62. Berg states: "Various scholars have noted a lack of acceptance for personal sin within the African Christian context. This may be due to a fundamental difference between Christianity and traditional African religious systems. Christianity acknowledges personal responsibility for sin, whereas traditional African beliefs externalize the origin of bad occurrences. M. C. Kirwen disagrees. He believes that African traditional religious systems maintain personal responsibility for immoral or evil activities" (57). Also see Kirwen, *The Missionary and the* Diviner, 53.

21. Bujo, *African Christian Morality at the Age of Inculturation*, 7. See also Muya, "Bénézet Bujo," 107–49.

Bujo writes: "Not only does what happens to the living concern them but our attitudes and acts can strengthen or diminish the life of the dead. Negatively, our acts can be an offence to our ancestors."[22] This distinctive cultural emphasis, however, should not obscure the principle that the wellbeing of the community of the living should be the primary concern in an African ethics, especially on issues of life preservation.

Reconciling individuality and communal existence is not as straightforward as Bujo sometimes makes out it to be. Individuality implies uniqueness and separateness, while community living implies "the loss or lessening" of individuality. Community as in "communion" implies a joining of lives or an understanding that people are described through relationships rather than in solitary existence. According to Bujo, the community aspect of morality does not deny individual moral responsibility but affirms it. For example:

> For many black Africans, the giving of a name is not only a rite of defense and protection; but it bears an action, a message, and holds a program of life which each one has to realize individually and not by proxy . . . the name indicates the historicity of each one in his singularity and in his incommunicable and unrepeatable uniqueness.[23]

We can certainly say that in the African understanding, there is no individual without the community and there is no community without individual human persons. Hence, it is understandable when Theo Sundermeier says "The relationship of the human being to the community goes further than community life. It involves interdependence: people, animals and environment exchange their strength, and are in a relationship of osmosis."[24] Every person is supposed to contribute to the well-being and the maintenance of these relationships. A well founded theology of the ecology or environment can be based on this understanding of relationship between human beings among themselves and their environment as a whole. It is only by contributing to this harmonious co-existence that a human person realizes the fullness of being human. Sundermeier sums this up when he writes: "As a deliberate antithesis to Descartes and to existentialism, J. V. Taylor produced the formula; *'participio ergo sum'*—I participate, therefore I am."[25]

22. Bujo, "Can Morality Be Christian in Africa?," 8.

23. Ibid. 9.

24. Sundermeir, *The Individual and Community in African Traditional Religions*, 18.

25. Ibid., 19. Cf. Isichei on contextual nature of inculturation: "A practical problem in

IV. The Possibility of Individual Freedom in an African Community Ethic

The extent to which the community shapes human living in an African context raises the problem, as pointed out previously, of whether individual personal freedom is possible. Bujo presents moral responsibility in individual persons as flowing from their obligation to the community. In his work the question of whether individual persons go through the process of ethical decision-making seems not to be adequately addressed. The community, from this perspective, has already laid down moral norms on what is to be done and what is to be avoided. Bujo has argued that in an African setting, individual freedom is a reality but it is not absolute. He is of the opinion that sometimes the individual has to obey the dictates of the community without being convinced. Bujo states:

> Individual conscience is not the last chance without a common listening to each other; the "conscience" of the community might eventually be the last instance for individual action, because one does not feel cheated by the community . . . If an action is embedded in the community of the living and of the dead, and is at least implicitly a common decision, then everybody has to have a share in the heroic deeds as well as in the past guilt of the clan community—the ancestors included. In this way conscience becomes a "memory conscience," which does not only have a claim on one's individual freedom, but is rather a form of conscience, which assumes responsibility for an individual's own decisions as well as those of the community.[26]

There is however the danger of conformity for the sake of doing what the community requires. Somehow, if this understanding of conscience and freedom were taken to the extreme uncurbed, individual autonomy would seem to be at risk.

---

the indigenization of liturgy lies in the fact that this must necessarily take place in terms of a specific language and culture, and is not easy to apply to the polyglot cities" (Isichei, *A History of Christianity in* Africa, 331).

26. Bujo, *The Ethical Dimension of Community*, 75–76. Bujo's view of ethics as measured by the communal good contrasts with Immanuel Kant's categorical imperative: "[N]othing is left but the conformity of actions as such with universal law, which alone is to serve the will as its principle, that is, *I ought never to act except in such a way that I could also will that my maxim should become a universal law*" (Kant, *Groundwork of the Metaphysics of Morals*, 14–15). According to Kant, the source of ethics is the human subject with capacity for moral deliberation.

However, the point to keep in mind, according to Bujo, is that the community facilitates the possibility of individual freedom. "The individual has to contribute to communal freedom. One is free only if one's becoming free promotes freedom within the community. Therefore, one does not become free outside the community but within it and through it."[27] To argue against individual personal freedom seems to remove the foundation of morality. Although Bujo gives prevalence to community than to individual freedom, it is imperative for any ethical theory to emphasize the inviolability of individual freedom and thereby individual human dignity. Community does not exist in the abstract, but through the individual persons who are constituent members.

In addition, Bujo also realizes the problem connected with a communal replacement of personal individual freedom. He has suggested the factor that ensures that individual freedom is not abolished by the community, or vice versa, as dialogue between members of the community. It is in the context of dialogue that Bujo has written that "it is important in this model of palaver that everybody's word be accompanied by the critical words of others, so that the power of the word may not be misused."[28] This also shows that there are no abstract norms but that there is always a need for moral decision-making in a particular context.[29] There are no moral decisions ready-made.

It is in Bujo's analysis of individual freedom and its relation to the community, that he further asks and answers the question: "What then is conscience from an African perspective? It is about talking with and listening to one another."[30] In this context of dialogue in moral decision-making, the power of the word is seen as promoting the life of all people in the community. Fullness of life is realized in community.[31]

After showing how individual freedom relates to the community, Bujo can be seen to be moving towards a communitarian—ecclesial model of conscience. He says that: "If the traditional doctrine of conscience is analyzed in greater detail, then it becomes apparent that the inter-subjective dimension is implicitly present."[32] Further, Bujo holds: "The individual

27. Bujo, *The Ethical Dimension of Community*, 74.

28. Ibid., 77.

29. Cf. Arntz, "Natural Law and its History," 39–57.

30. Bujo, *The Ethical Dimension of Community*, 78.

31. Ibid., 79.

32. Ibid., 80.

Church member is moved by the Holy Spirit for the sake of all and is obliged to place the given gift at the service of his neighbor."[33] He makes references to the view of St. Thomas Aquinas that an individual can correct even the highest authority in the church, if an error exists.[34] Bujo clearly shows that the community and the individual are mutually related. The individual human person has freedom in the community. The community provides an enabling environment for individual self-determination. Hence, the individual and the community are part and parcel of the same whole.

V. Palaver as a Way of Recovering Individual and Communal Moral Norms

To highlight the moral agency of individual persons in community, Bujo presents palaver as a participatory dialogical process. Palaver is viewed as a discernment process leading to the formulation of communal moral norms through active participation of individual persons. Moral norms embody moral values to be realized in human conduct. My concern here is not to enter into the debate on the objectivity or subjectivity of moral norms, or even about negative or positive moral norms, but to evaluate how Bujo views moral norms in an African context.[35]

Moral norms are viewed by Bujo as realized in an African setting through dialogue between members of the community. So conceived, moral norms do not claim any finality or absoluteness; they are always open to new development or improvement, a process which, for Bujo, takes place in palaver. Palaver is a dialogue in the decision-making process where issues of importance affecting the community are discussed. It is not superfluous talk but an efficient institutionalization of communicative action. Palaver addresses people's existential interests, often to the smallest detail. It requires people to share their experiences and also to refer to the entire history of the clan community.[36]

In a concrete way, the concept of palaver in an African context points to the dynamic dialogue between a people and their culture. Moral norms are realized through palaver but they are always open to change. The

33. Ibid., 80–81.

34. Ibid., 81.

35. For an analysis of moral norms, see Gula, *What are They Saying about Moral Norms?* See also Walter, "The Foundation and Formulations of Norms," 125–54.

36. Bujo, *The Ethical Dimension of Community*, 36.

Nigerian novelist, Chinua Achebe, also presents African peoples as continually in dialogue with their culture, and hence their culture is always evolving into new ways of living. Achebe describes the dynamic nature of palaver as follows:

> So while the African intellectual was busy displaying the past culture of Africa, the troubled peoples of Africa were already creating new revolutionary cultures which took into account their present conditions. As long as people are changing, their culture will be changing. The only place where culture is static, and exists independently of people, is the museum, and this is not an African institution.[37]

Similarly, Bujo presents palaver as a practical way in moral decision-making. Palaver is a kind of a moral clearing-ground where a community or an individual consults one another on ethical issues. Bujo indicates palaver takes place "not only at the macro-ethical level, but also and with the same intensity at the micro-ethical level."[38] The palaver-community "as an 'ideal community of communication' is not only cultivated where a general ethical principle affects the well-being of the people as a whole, but also where individual action makes traditional rules uncertain in view of a new context of life."[39]

Palaver opens up in a community the possibility of creating a new tradition.[40] Norms can be and have to be found in a communal manner—hence free of domination and in dialogue. Bujo holds that the African palaver model is close to the European approach called the "ethics of discourse."[41] He refers in this connection to Karl-Otto Apel's "ethics of discourse" as the "ethics of solidary responsibility of all those who are able to argue, on all problems that can be discussed."[42] Communicative ethics or ethics of discourse, according to Seyla Benhabib, derive from modern

37. Lindfors, et al., eds., "Interview with Chinua Achebe," 5–6.

38. Bujo, *The Ethical Dimension of Community*, 36.

39. Ibid.

40. Ibid., 36–37. Palaver can also be applicable to interreligious dialogue. For example, see Bediako, "Christian Witness in the Public Sphere," 118–32. He writes, "[T]he long tradition of hospitality and tolerance that African primal religions have maintained in their meeting with the missionary religions of Christianity and Islam must qualify them to contribute substantially to the quest for inter-religious dialogue and harmony" (123).

41. Bujo, *The Ethical Dimension of Community*, 37.

42. Ibid.

theories of autonomy and of the social contract, as articulated by John Locke, Jean Jacques Rousseau, and in particular by Immanuel Kant. Valid norms are conceived only as a result of engaging in certain argumentative practices and achieving the people's consent. From Apel, Benhabib refers to these argumentative practices as an "ideal community of communication" (*die ideale Kommunikationsgemeinschaft*) and from Habermas as "practical discourses."[43] In an ethics of discourse, as well as in an African palaver, there is a concern of equality of chances for all partners. In the ethics of discourse, only those able to argue reasonably participate, and it is these that care for the interests of all illiterate or uneducated people or those who are not yet intellectually mature.[44]

However, Bujo distinguishes an African ethic from discourse ethics. Of an African ethic, he says "the human being does not become human by *cogito* (thinking) but by *relatio* (relationship) and *cognatio* (kinship). As noted above, the fundamental principle of this ethics is not *cogito ergo sum* (I think, so I am), but rather, *cognatus sum ergo sum* (I am related, so I am)."[45] In the African palaver, the relationship is not basically about thought or theory, but about human beings and their well-being. African palaver is concerned basically with fostering good human relations, a priority to which all ethical norms should adhere. The rightness or the wrongness of an ethical decision depends on how much it fosters the common good.[46]

Bujo also distinguishes the African community ethic from the ethics of discourse on the level of involvement in the making of moral norms. In an African palaver all people are involved, while in the ethics of discourse a few select elite and professionals participate. "The ethics of discourse refers to the real process of coming to mutual understanding within an unlimited "ideal" community of communication, as sole instance of legitimization

---

43. Benhabib, "Afterword: Communicative Ethics and Current Controversies in Practical Philosophy," 330–31.

44. Bujo, *The Ethical Dimension of Community*, 40.

45. Ibid., 54.

46. On the common good and personal good, see Novak, *Free Persons and the Common Good.* Novak presents a Christian understanding of personal good and communal good as one. He states, "God is the universal common good not only of humans but of all created things" (30). Cf. Hollenbach, *The Common Good and Christian Ethics,* where he argues that shared humanity is a basis for global values and human rights (219).

where every participant who is able to discuss is convinced that his statements are valid and can be generalized."[47]

Bujo is critical of such ethics of discourse because of its attempt to provide solid foundations for universal norms and deontological validity. He suggests that the ethics of discourse ignores the conflict between "objective and subjective" which is common in traditional morality. Further, Bujo argues that by concentrating on "right" or "wrong," the ethical model of discourse strives to avoid the "naturalistic" as well as the "ethnocentric fallacy." Hence, he views the ethics of discourse as an ethics of rules which moves around what is morally right.[48] For him, the power of moral judgment is never explicit from the start; consequently, it cannot be bound to a "catalogue of rules," even if this were to be a voluminous catalogue. The reason is that moral power of judgment is essentially based on *phronesis* (prudence).[49]

In terms of participation in the norm-making process, Bujo is also critical of the selective representation involved in the discourse ethics. It is only the elite that participates in the ethics of discourse. He states: "The discourse ethics seems to be elite-oriented and discriminatory since only reason matters. One can only discuss with those who are capable of arguing rationally. In this way, the ethics of discourse remains loyal to the Western tradition of *cogito*, which seeks to define the human person solely through reason."[50] In the preceding, Bujo is critical of Karl-Otto Apel's basic premise which is as follows: "We now can again ascertain that we, in serious argumentation, together with a *meaning-claim* and a *truth-claim*, also presupposes a morally relevant rightness-claim tied up with our acts of argumentation as acts of communication."[51] In Apel's discourse ethics there is an element of morality that is pre-given, just as language is shared by various people.

Despite Bujo's critical analysis of the ethics of discourse, he shares Apel's view that people are always in a particular context (a community of communication). In this his ethical thought has some connection also with that of Hans-Georg Gadamer, who holds that human understanding

47. Bujo, *The Ethical Dimension of Community*, 49.

48. Ibid.

49. Ibid., 50.

50. Ibid., 55.

51. Apel, *The Response of Discourse Ethics to the Moral Challenge of the Human Situation as Such and Especially Today*, 71

and experience of the world are language-bound.[52] According to Seyla Benhabib, Gadamer in his work turned to Aristotle's model of *phronesis* as a form of contextually embedded and situationally sensitive judgment of particulars and practical reason.[53] Hence, Bujo's African ethics, also shares with Apel and Gadamer, the view that human understanding takes place in a historical context.

Whereas, however, the ethics of discourse adopts *phronesis*, which is concerned with the "good life" and prefers the factual *status quo*, Bujo has put forward palaver as an alternate ethical process providing an open way for the improvement of moral norms. In offering a continuous engagement with ethical issues affecting a community palaver meets the need to provide a critical interpretation of the existing law and of the given situation.[54]

In addition, Bujo applies palaver to an African Christian ethic by calling for dialogue among African Christians in order that ethical norms may be formulated from their day-to-day decisions. This ensures that moral norms are not dictated from outside the community but from within. Palaver, according to Bujo, should foster in African Christianity a spirit of working to eliminate alienating situations of oppression and suffering caused by poverty and disease. In the context of solidarity with the poor and suffering, as part of Christian memory of the passion, death, and resurrection of Jesus Christ, palaver aligns itself with the liberation method in Christian theology.[55]

The process of finding authority and ethical norms in the context of palaver as advocated by Bujo rests in the way people conduct their lives from day to day. The method thus offers a model for ethical argumentation in a multi-cultural world. He writes:

> Traditions and cultures are the *prima instrumenta laboris* (the primary working instruments), which provoke argumentation and which facilitate understanding among all cultures. Whenever something is regarded as the product of a given culture and seeks universality, it must not enforce its claim of validity without

52. Gadamer, "The Universality of the Hermeneutical Problem," 157–58.

53. Benhabib, "Afterword," 333.

54. Bujo, *The Ethical Dimension of Community*, 51–52. The ethics of discourse as presented by Bujo seems to miss here what Gadamer called the historical importance (or effective history) a person attaches to any instance in the process of interpretation. In palaver, there also could be a problem of domination or preference for some particular moral opinion. See Gadamer, "Truth and Method," 206–7.

55. Bujo, *The Ethical Dimension of Community*, 41.

dialogue with other contexts and peoples. Universal validity has to be proven by confrontation with other people's forms of thought. If one takes dialogue and discussion with other traditions seriously, then universalization can only be achieved in a contextual way.[56]

While this intercultural theological method advocated by Bujo incorporates natural moral law reasoning, he is concerned that moral arguments drawn from the theory of the natural law reasoning be immanent to a cultural context, avoiding untenable universalization of moral norms.[57] He notes that "The model of Aristotelico-Thomistic morality depends on the principle of 'a good life' (*eu zên*)," St. Thomas summing this up with the basic principle: "Good is to be done and striven after, evil is to be avoided" (*bonum est faciendum et prosequendum, et* malum *vitandum*).[58] But, since natural law reasoning presupposes universality in moral reasoning, the synchronization of such reasoning with a cultural context creates some tension. Bujo, however, is highly critical of monolithic views in ethics where one way of thinking dominates the whole world in ethical matters. He maintains that there are several ethical models that have equal validity alongside western or classical-based ethical systems. Bujo, as indicated, presents palaver as such an alternate model, one in which a communal and dialogue-oriented dimension will replace a universalized and deontological ethics, and even the one-sided Western emphasis on the *cogito*. In a multicultural and polycentric world, Bujo has argued for diversity in ethical approaches.[59]

Critique and Evaluation

This study has so far presented an African ethics, seen in the work of Bénézet Bujo, as one where life in community is paramount, where human persons realize themselves as individuals through the community, and where individuality finds expression through the palaver. In the palaver differing views on community life are reconciled and individuals are given an opportunity to participate in the process of moral discernment. However, it should be pointed out that in many African communities today the historical context presumed by Bujo's palaver is one of yesteryear. Many

56. Ibid., 52–53.

57. Ibid., 43.

58. Ibid. 44.

59. Ibid., 57.

contemporary African communities do not have the cultural and social structures presupposed in his work. Historical change brought about especially through western education and civilization has led to the introduction of an individualism previously absent in Africa. This is especially evident in major African cities today. For example, a visit to Nairobi city in Kenya presents one with a metropolitan perspective common to cities elsewhere in the world.

Apart from historical variance, Bujo's work also fails to acknowledge diversity in traditional African communities. African ethnic groups differ through independent languages (not just dialects), culture, and history. For example, the Maasai people of East Africa are completely distinct in their way of life from the Gikuyu people of the same region. The theological method of Bujo has generalized view of the African people as a whole, leading him to posit an African ethics in the singular instead of recognizing a plurality of ethical systems, as would seem to be required by the size of the African continent and the diversity of its multiple ethnic groups.[60] On this point, Bujo's work falls into the category of many African scholars who argue for a singular African theology or philosophy.

Further, Bujo does not indicate how palaver addresses the exclusion of women in decision-making in many African traditional communities. Historically, it is known that councils of elders in many African ethnic groups were constituted of men, with women considered not fit to participate. Contemporary African women scholars, theologians especially, have raised concern over issues of equality, inclusiveness, and participation in African societies.[61] Bujo has not shown how palaver ethical theory deals with gender discrimination and other cultural practices affecting women in African communities.

On a more positive note, although Bujo limits palaver within the confines of a particular community, in contemporary Africa it should be extended beyond the confines of a single community or ethnic group to

60. See the statement by Isichei: "African Christendom, like Africa in general, is divided by language barriers. Indeed, one of the most lasting and pernicious results of colonialism is its division of Africa into English-, French-, and Portuguese-speaking countries. These divisions go deeper than language" (Isichei, *A History of Christianity in Africa*, 332).

61. Gender equality is one of the key issues raised in the work of the so-called "The Circle of Concerned African Women Theologians," such as Amoah, ed., *Where God Reigns*; and also Oduyoye, ed., *Transforming Power*. Isichei also notes that women are a majority in African churches but are excluded in governing structures (*A History of Christianity in Africa*, 333).

address relations between the various groups that constitute African nations. It is a method that can be used to promote peace and harmony with others outside any immediate African community. Dialogue (palaver) between warring ethnic groups could serve to resolve the internal conflicts which have caused horrendous suffering in so many African countries.

To conclude, African communitarian ethics provides an alternate moral theory. It highlights the community's role in the development of its moral norms. An individual human person, though a moral person in an African traditional context, is inseparable from the community. The moral process is ultimately a communal affair. This community dimension in ethics is an important aspect that African ethics as presented in this work can offer to other ethical systems such as the western subjectivist ethics. African ethics can also act as a corrective to the natural moral law tradition as well as help bring renewal to Christian ethics as developed in various western traditions. Toward this end, the practice of palaver, contrary to a governing or teaching authority handing out universalized moral prescriptions or dictates from above, grounds the source of moral norms from below by promoting peoples' participation in the process. Palaver thereby promotes an understanding of the developing or open nature of moral norms, counteracting claims to moral absoluteness. In this respect, Bujo's work can be said to make a contribution not only to African ethics but also to ethics in general.

4

An African Christian Ethics is a Liberation Ethic in the Theology of Bénézet Bujo

AN AUTHENTIC AFRICAN CHRISTIAN ethics is concerned with issues of human wellbeing in a community. Bujo links African theology to issues in liberation theology. For this reason, I examine the similarities between an African Christian ethics and the Latin American liberation theology. This work relates the theology of Bujo to some ideas from other authors on the transforming aspects of Christian theology today. On these aspects, I formulate some liberation ethical issues that need to be addressed in an African ethics.[1] From a consideration of the problems that bedevil Africa today, it is my view that any theology cannot be complete without being concerned with how it can contribute in making human living better. Hence, I argue that Christian ethics in an African context should be a liberation ethics. Consequently, African theology and particularly the theology of Bujo will be viewed as leading to praxis. The important issue viewed as of utmost importance concerns the impact of theology on the

1. The article by Brackley and Schubeck is helpful here to show how liberation theology became connected with moral theology in Latin America. They hold that liberation theology in Latin America has played a great role in shaping Latin American moral theology. According to Brackley and Schubeck, the influence of liberation theology is evident in method and content of moral theology, and how moral theology deals with issues in bioethics, ecology, cultural transformation, feminist ethics, human rights, and economy. The same connection can be made between liberation theology and moral theology in African theology (see Brackley and Schubeck, "Moral Theology in Latin America," 124–25).

everyday life of the people. Further, this work explores how fundamental moral theology as developed by Bujo links up to a theology of liberation in an African context.

This chapter begins by showing that an African liberation Christian ethics has a foundation in an African Christology. The social-economic problems affecting African people today are viewed as resulting from the problem of cultural alienation. Salvation history is viewed as a history of liberation in Africa, and God is understood as the God of the poor. Further, the celebration of the Sacrament of the Eucharist is viewed as an expression of solidarity in an African community. An African community ethics is applied as a means of understanding democracy. Finally, the role of an African Christian ethics is located in the formulation and protection of human rights in an African context.

i. Jesus, The Proto-Ancestor, is the Liberator

A genuine African Christian ethics has as its foundation a sound African Christology: the teaching, the ministry, the death, and the resurrection of Jesus Christ. An example of a christological approach to ethics is evident in the work of Bujo who has argued that Jesus Christ has to be viewed as the Proto-Ancestor in an Africa context. He has noted: "To develop a viable Christian "orthopraxis," adapted to the African mentality, it seems to me that it is a matter of urgency to work out a moral theology centered on Jesus Christ as Proto-Ancestor."[2] Jesus, presented by Bujo as the Proto-Ancestor, is understood as one that is concerned with giving life in its fullness in an African context. As the Proto-Ancestor, Jesus is the liberator who redeems people from dehumanizing situations such as those caused by poverty and war. In an African context the salvific act of Jesus gains a deeper meaning when it is considered in reference to the concrete historical context.

Just as the African ancestors transmitted life to their descendants, so also Jesus, the Proto-Ancestor, in the theology of Bujo, transmits life in its fullness in African Christianity. The concern here encompasses all the aspects of the daily life of all the Christians. It is not just the profession of the Christian faith but it is translating that faith into action. Bujo argues:

> If Jesus Christ is Proto-Ancestor, source of life and happiness,
> our task is to bring to realization in our lives the memory of his
> passion, death and resurrection, making of that saving event the

2. Bujo, *African Theology in Its Social Context*, 87.

criterion for judging all human conduct . . . This consecration is the goal of the absolute commitment of Jesus of Nazareth to the restoration of human dignity. He vigorously defended the rights of the weak, of women, of children, and identified himself with outcasts and sinners.[3]

The idea of memory gains prominence in the concern of the liberation of the marginalized. Memory calls for solidarity with the poor and the oppressed. There is a concern for the integral wellbeing of all human beings. Bujo borrows the idea of memory from Johann Metz and Gustavo Gutiérrez, among others. He observes that "the goal is an anamnestic solidarity with those oppressed and defeated ones, who now create a place and community of communication. It is hoped that the victors will not indifferently live at the expense of those victims and exploited so that their happiness would be established on the "expropriation of the dead."[4]

Additionally, African ancestral worship is not restricted to the victims of history. It is meant to keep in memory the history of the people and this way be integrated into the solidarity of the offspring. In an African setting, Bujo argues one's identity can only be found without contradiction by not forgetting the forefathers.[5] He connects an African traditional ethics with Christian ethics which he presents as a model of an African ethics based on Christology. In this model Jesus is presented as the Proto-Ancestor who liberates his people from suffering. "The Proto-Ancestor's testament thus challenges his posterity to work relentlessly to get rid of any inhumanities."[6] The Christian community modeling itself on Christ has a responsibility to make better the lives of its members, and thereby becoming a community of caring and compassion. Bujo states:

> If Christ is Proto-Ancestor, source of life and fulfillment, our human conduct must model itself on, re-enact the memory of his passion, death and resurrection . . . His cross finalizes his deep commitment to restoring human dignity, for he had defended the weak (women, children) and identified with sinners and outcasts, and his cures showed his concern for human, earthly life at all levels.[7]

3. Ibid.

4. Bujo, *The Ethical Dimension of Community*, 30.

5. Ibid. 30–31.

6. Bujo, "A Christocentric Ethic for Black Africa," 145.

7. Ibid., 144.

The example of Jesus Christ in his public ministry and his passion, death, and resurrection has to be taken up by those who believe in him. Becoming like Christ in an African context means identifying ourselves with the poor and the suffering, and in this way seeking solutions to the dehumanizing conditions. It is in the eradication of poverty and all forms of suffering that Bujo holds that the "Christ-event thus becomes both *memoria liberationis* and *subversionis*, both liberating and subversive—both humanizing and purifying—for black African ethos."[8]

As in the theology of Metz, Bujo clearly insists that the Christ-event has to "revolutionize history and create a new heaven and a new earth."[9] We cannot proclaim the gospel and not be concerned with the everyday lives of the hearers of the good news. The situation in Africa has been one of alienation and deprivation through poverty and sub-standard living conditions. There is the danger of romanticizing African traditional religion and not doing anything about the social welfare of the people of Africa today. Hence, an African theology has liberation as its major perspective. Liberation theology is a reaction to traditional Roman Catholic theology. Liberation theology viewed the poor as absent in the mainstream theological systems. According to Bujo:

> liberation theology's critique of autonomous moral theology is socioeconomic rather than cultural-anthropological, and this means that the dialogue would take place between two Western philosophical systems. Only the inter-cultural approach allows us to see the problem of ethical pluralism in its true dimension. This perspective makes it even clearer that both the encyclical *Veritatis splendor* and autonomous moral theology remain confined within their own world, that of European-American culture: it is in this world that their dispute is carried on.[10]

From a concern for praxis, Bujo presents liberation theology as critical to autonomous moral theology for failing to adequately address the question of solidarity.[11] He is critical of the same non-involvement of Christianity in the social-economic life of the faithful. He states, "Our African Christianity has not yet penetrated our modern money economy to make

8. Ibid., 145.

9. Ibid.

10. Bujo, *Foundations of an African Ethic*, 85.

11. Ibid.

it human, beneficial to all, and the glory of Africa."[12] Non-involvement of the church in the social wellbeing of the people can result in people viewing the church as an outside institution that is only concerned with its own survival. Hence, Bujo holds that Christianity should contribute to an in-depth realization of integral human development.[13]

In their mission from Christ, Christian churches must be seen to work for the transformation of life in society. The church has the mission of Christ: to proclaim good news to the poor, set captives free, to feed the hungry, heal the sick, and so on (Luke 4:14–19). It is a mission of humanization. It is in this light that we can understand the following statement by Bujo:

> Christianity is an invitation addressed to each human person and it claims that, by virtue of its full acceptance, every man or woman is offered his/her optimum chance of personal fulfillment and self-realization. To make use of this opportunity does, in no way whatsoever, imply disregard or disrespect for, and even less, a destruction of the African heritage. Genuine Christianity, apart from some of its preachers, has never done this, for it takes seriously the words of scripture (Philippians 4:8).[14]

Consequently, the elimination of oppression and poverty requires an approach that is contextual. Liberation is to come from within the community and any outside assistance can only facilitate this change from within. Christianity and the people's culture have to come into dialogue. A people's culture and traditions shape the way they respond to the Christian message. Bujo has stated: "According to its own principles, therefore, Christian ethics must integrate African culture and its values, must purify and stimulate it in order to be relevant to itself and a service to all nations, to all Christianity and humanity."[15] We should always avoid viewing Christianity and culture as different elements in the same people. It is a person who is culturally determined by the way of life of his people that becomes a Christian. You can never uproot a person from his past and from what is around him or

---

12. Bujo, *African Christian Morality at the Age of Inculturation*, 68.

13. Ibid., 69.

14. Ibid., 70–71. Phil 4:8 reads as follows: "Finally, brothers, whatever is true, whatever is honorable, whatever is just, whatever is pure, whatever is lovely, whatever is gracious, if there is any excellence and if there is anything worthy of praise, think about these things."

15. Bujo, *African Christian Morality at the Age of Inculturation*, 71.

her. It is true, as the saying goes, that you can remove a person from the village but you can never remove the village from him/her.

The same critique made against European political theology is also made against liberation theology.[16] The most notable critique is that political theology does not provide a concrete way through which society should be reordered to ensure justice and flourishing for all people. However, one can respond to such a critique by saying that it is political theorists and scientists who should formulate the ways and means for political governance. There is need for a praxis that concretely provides ways and means of doing away with systems of oppression. Some critics of liberation ethics have made the accusation that it is more political than theological.[17] Some critics can see liberation ethics as going against the separation of church and state. This separation is especially true of life in Africa where political leaders who would not want to be accountable to their people have asked church leaders to stick to church matters.[18]

ii. The Problem of Cultural Alienation in Africa

Bujo presents the cause of the major problems that afflict Africa today as having their root-cause in cultural alienation. His concern is to present an African ethics that is concerned with addressing itself to African problems: suffering, poverty, and abuse of human rights. Decisions concerning life in Africa have been made in foreign capitals regardless of what Africans have to say, especially on their economies. The International Monetary Fund and the World Bank have tried to dictate to African governments measures that should be taken to facilitate economic growth. All these have failed because they are foreign measures imposed from without with no understanding of the complexity of the concrete situations in African nations.[19]

Africa needs to devise its own ways and means to transform situations of suffering and alienation into one of humanization and total flourishing.

16. Livingston and Fiorenza, *Modern Christian Thought,* 301.

17. Ibid.

18. See the statement by the former President of Kenya, Mr. Daniel T. Moi: "The Church should not be perceived to be one of the actors in the political game. I therefore urge the Church to stick to their spiritual calling and maintain their role as a refuge for those who seek spiritual nourishment, peace and quiet" (Chege wa Gachamba, "Moi Criticizes Church Leaders," in *Nation Newspaper* [*Daily Nation*, April 26, 2000], www. nationaudio.com).

19. Bujo, *The Ethical Dimension of Community* 166–67.

A notable example of efforts coming from within Africa was the launching of "New Partnerships for African Development" (NEPAD) by Mr. Thabo Mbeki, the former president of South Africa, and others. Donor countries praised NEPAD as the way forward for African governments. NEPAD took as examples the success stories of some countries in Africa and applied them to those that have failed economically and politically. Being a brain-child of politicians, NEPAD has not been successful as previously thought because of a lack of political goodwill. The East African Newspapers reported the following on NEPAD:

> During three-days "African Forum for Envisioning Africa by African Scholars" in Nairobi last week, a section of civil society representatives and scholars said that NEPAD lacked legitimacy as it was agreed upon by African presidents and sold to Western economic powers for funding without consulting citizens, parliaments and the civil society.[20]

What is needed in many nations in Africa is a complete eradication of dehumanizing structures, which could also mean change of political and socio-economic structures that have been imported from elsewhere. A critical reflection on the African traditions and cultures should help realize societies that have their foundations on ways of living that foster African identity. Globalization in economy and politics can further the problem in Africa where international organizations, such as the World Bank and the IMF, have been known to dictate social and economic policies. The imposition of policies from outside Africa leads to cultural alienation.

The factors that have shaped modern Africa include colonialism, the missionary movement, slavery and the slave trade. Notable in this history is the cultural change that occurred with the African contact with the West. Visiting any major city in Africa today one realizes the presence of a way of life that is part African and part western. In some places in Africa, traditions and customs have been replaced with an imported way of life. People have come to identify themselves with a way of life they don't fully understand. Bujo states:

> [T]he debate on inculturation is an enormously important dimension of Africa's liberation. African poverty is not only socioeconomic. It is so total that some scholars refer to it as *anthropological poverty*. For my part, I would rather speak of a total loss of identity

20. Wambua, "Is Nepad the answer to Africa's Problems?," *The East African*, May 6 2002, http: //www. nationauadio.com.

and a total alienation, since it involves a denial of humanity to the human person, down to the cultural roots. There is no worse degree of alienation and "poverty" that affects a person more than the loss of one's cultural identity. This becomes evident, if one considers the following facts. Through their arbitrary setting up of borders, the colonial powers divided ethnic communities and created rivalry among them. In this way, the African people lost their history, traditions, artifacts, spirituality, and at times even their mother tongue; in short, all that made up their vitality and identity.[21]

The introduction of Christianity in Africa has frequently being accused of alienating Christian faithful from their culture. African alienation is clearly described by Bujo. He views Christianity to have been introduced in Africa with a feeling of superiority and even with the feeling of a certain expansionism. This was coupled with a theologically based prejudice which played a key role in the evangelization process.[22] Nevertheless, Christian churches have also historically made some major contribution in the development of the African countries. Christianity has contributed so much in the transformation of Africa. The role played by Christian churches in education and healthcare is enormous.

Despite the fact that Christianity has brought many positive things to Africa, cultural alienation until recently has also been a component part of Christianity. An example would be the foreign missionaries' idea, in the nineteenth and early twentieth centuries, to establish Christian villages where those people who became Christians would live separated from the rest of the people who were not Christians. Christian missionaries proclaimed the gospel wrapped in their various European cultures.[23]

Further, the beginning of the new century has seen the introduction of globalization mainly focusing on economic and political rationalization.[24] This has meant having one way of conducting economic business and political governance. By globalization, a new world order is implied where the west becomes like "a godfather" who shows the others the way. There is no room to be different. What Leonardo Boff says of Latin America can also be said of Africa. According to Boff:

21. Bujo, *The Ethical Dimension of Community*, 137–38.

22. Ibid., 135.

23. Hastings, *The Church in* Africa, 209–15.

24. On the strengths and weaknesses of globalized concepts of culture see Schreiter, *The New Catholicity*, 47–61.

> We have always been dependent on external centers of domina-
> tion. As a result we still have difficulty defining our identity, which
> is either rendered impossible, or found to be alienated or deeply
> divided. We have a culture of fragments, of flotsam, of something
> that once was whole. There is no escaping the fact: we are a broken
> mirror of others, violently maintained in a state of underdevelop-
> ment and thereby deprived of the necessary means to be sover-
> eigns of our own history.[25]

Cultural alienation can be understood as a phenomenon where one describes oneself from the perspective of an outsider and not from an individual person's perspective. This can also explain why economic recovery
programs made in foreign countries and imposed on Africa through the
IMF and the World Bank have failed.

The search for solutions to the problems that Africa experiences can
only successfully start from within the continent. There is need for awareness in the people that they have the power to decide what they want to be.
This is praxis. Boff describes praxis as follows:

> Praxis is the product of human reflection and will. Human beings,
> unlike animals, even the higher ones, are characterized by praxis,
> which presupposes the ability to reflect, to project, to signify, and
> to transform. Through this praxis, nature is transformed into cul-
> ture. That is to say, the logic of determination is replaced by that of
> spontaneity, and of a complex of significations and values. Culture
> is more than a mere process of adaptation of nature to human de-
> sires. It is also a language, which communicates significations and
> values.[26]

Then, one can justifiably say that culture is what gives a people their
identity. Denying a people their culture is equivalent to denying their existence. This is what colonialism did in Africa. New languages and the ban-
ning of traditional customs meant that many people were uprooted from
their culture. Unfortunately, Christian missionaries also took up what was
called a "civilizing mission" where "heathen culture" was seen as contrary
to the gospel. Just as Jesus Christ was born into a particular cultural setting,
namely Jewish, so also the gospel message should be incarnated through
intercultural dialogue. In this connection, Bujo holds that "ignoring a
people's culture may well be the first violation of human rights. In social

25. Boff, *New Evangelization*, 11.
26. Ibid., 5.

ethics, one should count as new forms of property not only the 'posses-sion of knowledge, technique and know-how' but also culture as root of the whole."²⁷

From the theology of Bujo, the solution to issues that affect Africans can be found only by returning to the roots in the traditions and cultural background of Africa. The imposition of a foreign way of life is the equiva-lent of under-development and denial of the identity of the people. We can, therefore, argue for homegrown solutions to domestic issues as the surest way to liberation.

iii. Salvation History as Liberation in Africa

In an African ethics, Christianity in Africa has to be concerned with inte-gral human development. Salvation history is only meaningful if under-stood as the history of liberation, where God is active in the lives of his people bringing spiritual, political, and socio-economic transformation. Further, the redemptive act of Jesus, his suffering, death, and resurrection, constitutes not only a spiritual liberation from sin but also liberation from the social structures that are sinful. Bujo has stated that "remembering and reenacting the deeds of Christ constitute a liberating, 'revolutionary' dy-namic which can breathe new life into a dying tradition."²⁸

Bujo's ethical method can be compared to the work of Johann Baptist Metz, Gustavo Gutiérrez and others. Bujo was educated in Europe, and therefore, German systematic theologians influenced him. This is true looking at the work of Metz and his historical understanding of the Pascal Mystery of Christ and the mystery of suffering. Bujo states:

> The Old Testament tradition is continued and extended in the New. It recounts the history of the Liberation, the *memoria lib-erationis*, began in the Old Covenant and brought now to its final consummation in the person of the Crucified One. This *memoria* is at the same time a source of energy for the future, since the self-presentation of Yahweh before Moses, which constituted the specific Old Testament ethic, took flesh and dwelt among us, and is now the criterion of the New Testament ethic, which gives a new, and liberating impetus to the old history . . . This liberation

---

27. Bujo, *The Ethical Dimension of Community*, 142.

28. Ibid., *African Theology in Its Social Context*, 88.

movement must from now on be expressed in a new experience, handed on by word of mouth from one community to another.[29]

Understanding salvation history as liberation revolutionizes history. The eschatological understanding of Jesus as Lord has impact on society. Bujo connects with Metz, who explicitly claims to have been influenced by his experience of World War II and National Socialism in Germany. Metz has noted: "the leitmotif of this biographical path is quite probably the *memoria passionis*, the remembrance of the suffering of others as a basic category of Christian discourse about God."[30] Social involvement distinguishes the historical in the political theology of Metz from historicity in some existential theologians.[31] Bujo, like Metz and others, gives warning against a "memoryless" theology. He has written:

> Johann Baptist Metz and Helmut Peukert have sharpened our awareness that our theology should not be amnestic, but anamnestic. It appears that our society is so much characterized by forgetting that it urgently needs remembering, which can lead to an anamnestic solidarity with the victims of history.[32]

The relevance of salvation history to peoples' lives can only be understood in the context of a concrete historical situation. Human suffering gives meaning to the people's yearning for redemption. The history of the Old Testament is the history of the Israelites' relationship with the God of the covenant. It is a relationship that is marred by peoples' rebellion against God through sin. Sin in the context of the Old Testament was seen as the cause of suffering. The Israelites being taken prisoners through exile was seen as a result of sin. We can postulate that the people of Israel looked at their situation of suffering and concluded that it must be as a result of their sin. In the context of suffering and alienation, they came to understand redemption by God in political as well as religious terms. The Old Testament can therefore be viewed as the story of liberation. Like Metz, Gutiérrez and others, Bujo connects the understanding of liberation in the Old Testament to the concept of salvation in the New Testament.[33]

---

29. Ibid., 89.
30. Metz, *A Passion for God,* 5.
31. Ibid., 12.
32. Bujo, *The Ethical Dimension of Community,* 139–40.
33. Bujo, *African Theology in Its Social Context,* 89.

iv. God is the God of the Poor in an African Christian Ethics

In an African ethics, God is to be understood as concerned with the plight of the poor. Theology concerns itself with the relation between God and human beings. Metz states:

> Theology, theology itself—as discourse about God—falls under the primacy of the subject, of praxis, and of alterity. Only thus is it possible to discern what is meant theologically by notions like self, existence, individuation; in short, what is meant by existence in faith.[34]

Theology, whether in political theology of Metz or Bujo's African theology, has to be concerned with the wellbeing of the people. The concern for the wellbeing of the people in a particular setting is where the theology of Bujo is similar with political and liberation theology. Liberation theology, especially in Gutiérrez, brought the poor to center stage. Gutiérrez has had a great influence in the language used in liberation theology today. He writes of the "irruption of the poor" as a vast historical event. He describes this irruption as an acknowledgement of those that have been absent in the society and the church. He clarifies that "by absent we mean of little or no significance, as well as being without the opportunity to manifest their sufferings, solidarities, projects, and hopes."[35]

The subjects of the theology of liberation are the poor people. This is clear also from what Clodovis Boff has written:

> For the theology of liberation, or, better, and more simply, for theology (all theology), liberation is taken as its subject, its raw material, or material object. In this sense, liberation is considered in all its density as a historical and political phenomenon: it's the movement of an oppressed people becoming conscious of oppression and struggling to throw off the yoke of social domination.[36]

Being subjects, the poor can reflect on their situation and come up with practical ways to reverse their situation of suffering and alienation. As Gutierrez says, "the theology of liberation—an expression of the right of the poor to 'think their faith'—is not the automatic result of this situation

34. Metz, *A Passion for God*, 24.

35. Gutiérrez, "Option for the Poor," 22. See also Sobrino, "Theology in a Suffering World," 25–30. Sobrino writes of liberation theology as "'the inbreaking' of the poor into history" (25).

36. Boff, "Society and the Kingdom," 94.

and its incarnations."[37] The theology of liberation can be said to be attentive to reading the signs of the times. It is contextual in the sense of being concerned with the poor and being critical of the systems that have led to their predicament. Nevertheless, there are instances where the poor are denied their power, by outside influence, to be subjects who have the right of deciding how to transform their situation.

Bujo connects the concerns of an African Christian ethics with liberation theology in Latin America.[38] He borrows much of the terminology he uses on liberation ethics from Gutiérrez. It is Gutiérrez who describes option for the poor as a "free commitment to the poor and oppressed."[39] He underlines that this commitment to the poor is based fundamentally on the God of our faith.[40] Gutiérrez emphasizes the deeper meaning of the term "option." He says:

> This option for the poor is not option in the sense that a Christian need not necessarily make it, any more than the love we owe every human being, without exception, is optional. It is a matter of a deep, ongoing solidarity, a voluntary daily involvement with the world of the poor. At the same time, the word option does not necessarily mean that those who make it do not already belong to the world of the poor.[41]

On the preferential option for the poor, Gutiérrez has written as follows:

> Medellin had already encouraged giving "preference to the poorest and neediest, and to those who are segregated for any reason" ("Document on Poverty," no. 9). The very term preference obviously precludes any exclusivity; it simply points to who ought to be the first—not the only—objects of our solidarity.[42]

---

37. Gutiérrez, "Option for the Poor," 23.

38. Bujo, *The Ethical Dimension of Community*, 133.

39. Gutiérrez, "Option for the Poor," 26. The poor in Africa can be seen in the peasants Ela describes thus: "The peasants today form the most miserable, exploited, oppressed, and paradoxically, undernourished class. This exploitation is unforgivable, as it is the deed of the new ruling classes and the victims are their fellow-citizens. Rural development has so far meant only the promotion of export crops in order to broaden the tax base and bring in foreign currency. The profit accrued goes to the administrative echelons rather than the rural populations" (Ela, *African Cry*, 84).

40. Gutiérrez, "Option for the Poor," 27.

41. Ibid., 26.

42. Ibid.

We need also to qualify that the preferential option for the poor does not exclude the rich, but it is a recognition of the universality of God's love. God is the God of the poor. "God can only be experienced as a liberating God if he penetrates deep into the cultural roots of the people. This is because the human person thrives on these roots in the struggle for identity."[43] In liberation theology there is a concern to avoid the danger of announcing an insubstantial God, alive only in our intellectual heads.[44] The poor are those who suffer in conditions of poverty and deprivation. Liberation theology developed as a response to inhuman situations in Latin America. Bujo understands the "option for the poor" as a commitment to the poor, fighting those factors that have made them be what they are.

Theological study should be committed to the poor. All theology in Africa has to concern itself with liberation. Bujo is critical of the lack of courage in social and church matters. He writes:

> But not only in the socio-political, even in the ecclesial field, our African theology lacks courage and boldness. It is too closely tied to the hierarchy, and it is only too obvious that many a black theologian plucks up courage to make a public declaration, only if he is assured by influential bishops of their support. Within the local church, self-criticism is a rare article and practically non-existent. The reason may well be a mistaken solidarity, but more often it is sheer careerism.[45]

In a practical way, Bujo views liberation ethics in Africa as concerned with issues of oppression, exploitation, economic misery, corruption, violence to human dignity, among others.[46] Theology has to be always concerned with the people and their well-being: "A man who does not love the brother or sister that he can see, cannot love God whom he has never seen" (1John 4:20).

Bujo is critical of an abstract theology that has no connection with reality. True theology is a theology that connects with a people's life. Bujo writes, "The professional theologian has to stay in communication with all the classes of his/her society, but he or she has to have a primary option for the poorest of the poor, the most wretched and outcast."[47] The task of theol-

---

43. Bujo, *The Ethical Dimension of Community*, 141.

44. Ibid., 133.

45. Bujo, *African Christian Morality at the Age of Inculturation*, 127.

46. Ibid.

47. Ibid., 129.

ogy is the critique of the factors that cause human suffering. Bujo holds that "theology can no longer be misunderstood as a means of livelihood, but as a training for community ministry and service, and all trace of careerism eradicated."[48] However, the aim of theology is supposedly the transformation of the society, that is, making the quality of life better especially for the poor. It is as Leonardo Boff says of liberation theology: "The principal interest of liberation theology is to generate activity on the part of the church that will aid the poor *efficaciously*. Everything must converge toward practice (love)."[49] Like Latin American theology, African theology should be a reflection upon African reality. The task of a theologian is clearly summed up by L. Boff when he states: "theological reflection is the result of an effort to understand the root problem."[50] Just as Latin American theological reflection is concerned with its Latin American reality of suffering caused by political and socio-economic injustices, so also should African theology deal with the African reality of suffering and abject poverty.

v. Eucharist as Communion with the Needy and the Oppressed

From an African worldview, Bujo suggests a more practical and culturally nuanced understanding of the Eucharistic celebration and its incarnation. For him, the Eucharistic celebration is supposed to embody "the nature of orthopraxis, in the perspective of the needs and challenges of today's Africa."[51] Bujo views the sacrament of the Eucharist as a meaningful way to understand the Christian nature of liberation. The Eucharist is the celebration that reenacts the sacrifice of Christ at Calvary. It is a celebration of the Paschal Mystery of Christ. In the Eucharist, from the teachings of the Catholic religion, Christ is present in his body and blood in the form of bread and wine. It is a celebration of Christ's presence in the lives of his people. We cannot genuinely celebrate the sacrifice of Christ and not be concerned with the suffering of our sisters and brothers. Jesus in his ministry was concerned with the welfare of the sick, the cripples, the poor, and most of all, all who needed the mercy of God.

Accordingly, Bujo holds that "the Eucharistic celebration cannot be thought of apart from life, unless it remains a superficial reality to the

---

48. Ibid.

49. Boff, "Salvation in Liberation," 4.

50. Ibid., 1.

51. Bujo, *African Christian Morality at the Age of Inculturation*, 81.

African."[52] He uses a Rahnerian Christology when he states: "Without denying that the Christ is, on account of his incarnation, one of us humans, and truly 'a piece also of this material world' (Rahner), we shall put the emphasis here on the supra-terrestrial Christ, who by his death and resurrection was established by the Father as our Proto-Ancestor."[53] He holds that the idea of Proto-Ancestor does not contradict the New Testament thought. He even goes further to call Jesus Christ "the first-born among all the ancestors."[54] Bujo holds that a sound Christology as embodied in the celebration of the Eucharist leads the Christian believers to be socially involved in the promotion of qualitative life. He is of the opinion that "to grasp this eschatological and incarnational dimension properly, means to declare a merciless struggle against the many ills which rob modern Africa of its vital force and lead its nations, slowly but surely, to a premature death."[55] Among the dehumanizing factors Bujo mentions are the numerous refugees and displaced persons in Africa, the shanty town-dwellers, and the rural poor who are so despised. To the transformation of these despicable living conditions, Bujo proposes that the institutional Church should work with basic Christian communities, denouncing the lifestyle of the affluent that is inhuman and dehumanizing. The Eucharist underscores Christ's service of all to all. According to Bujo:

> The Eucharist, which is the center of a Christian life, and at whose celebration bishop and priest preside, must make them ever more sensitive to the agonizing problems of their people. This implies that they must get rid of all clericalism, "episcopalism," "sarcedotalism" which consider the Church of Christ as a pyramid of administrative authority, minimizes the dignity of the laity, and so chokes life and vitality in the church community.[56]

Bujo also focuses on the religious life in Africa. He maintains that religious life should be so adapted to fit in the liberating process of the church. He emphasizes the importance of evangelical witness in the improving of the quality of life. Religious life should be seen as promoting the ancestral life in the community that enjoys the element of continuity.[57] He states:

52. Ibid.
53. Ibid., 82.
54. Ibid.
55. Ibid., 89.
56. Ibid., 85.
57. Ibid., 89–90.

> Promoting Africa includes promoting African religious life. In order that the religious communities transmit and encourage Proto-ancestral life in Christ in their African context, they must adopt, more and more, a specifically African life-style. It is obvious that religious communities, having migrated from overseas, will, in the course of time, adapt themselves better to this continent.[58]

Finally, the community that celebrates the Eucharist has to be in solidarity with the needy. The Christian community has an obligation to help bring about social transformation—this way the Eucharist would be understood as making it possible to realize the love of Christ in everyday life, and ultimately building a community of love. Below the community that celebrates the Eucharist is viewed to be an asset in the realization of a democratic society where the common good is shared by all people.

vi. Community Ethics and Democracy

An African communitarian ethics as proposed by Bujo has to make its contribution in the development of an African democracy in which the flourishing of all African people is ensured. The palaver, the dialogical moral norm-finding process, has a central role to play in the formulation of social and political policies in Africa.[59] Participation of all people in creating a society that caters for the well-being of all ensures peace and stability.

During the Cold War period, dictators who were maintained in power by the Soviet Union and the United States of America ran a good number of African countries. The two superpowers then were competing for supporters and were therefore prepared to pay anything to keep out their opponent in any given country in Africa. By the 1990, the Cold War had crumbled with the disintegration of the Soviet Union. Some African dictatorial regimes had no further source of revenue to govern their voiceless citizenry. This was followed by popular uprising. There was a new movement calling for democracy within Africa. Military and civil dictators could no longer ignore the cry of their people for even their donors were insisting on democracy and respect for human rights as the only way for international cooperation. Democracy was to be coupled with free markets and transparency in economic and social matters. The movement for democracy in

---

58. Ibid., 88.

59. Bujo, *Utamadunisho na Kanisa la Mazingira*, 9.

some parts of Africa can be said to have partly been successful because of foreign pressure.

One can raise the question whether democracy and capitalism as they are being developed in Africa today have an African basis or are pre-packaged goods imported from western nations without due consideration of the respective African context. Could the community ethic as presented by Bujo not be more democratic in an African context than the political systems imported and gaining root in many African countries?[60]

One cannot read Gutiérrez's critique of the theory of dependency,[61] which Bujo also shares, and not ask questions on how this reconciles with solidarity as called for by liberation and political theologies. Gutiérrez refers to solidarity of the poor people to transform their situation through the gospel, while Metz laid emphasis on the universal solidarity called for by the rich countries of the north to help the developing and very poor countries.[62] Gutiérrez's critique of the concept of dependency requires further clarification in its application in a particular context. Bujo's community ethics can be applied in an African society as a means for transforming situations of oppression to one of freedom and prosperity. Bujo's idea of communitarian ethics in Africa also needs further development. Some questions remain unanswered, such as whether the community ethics is applicable to a country like Nigeria with over 100 million people, and a historic conflict between Christians and Muslims in the north. Or how should we adapt the understanding of community in the changed circumstances in the modern nations of Africa, or even in Churches with millions of believers?

vii. Human Rights in an African Context

Further, it is important to question whether we can adopt the universal language of human rights in an African context. The issue is whether we can use the same terminology or we need express it in a language more relevant to an African setting. One may disagree with the language of human rights but not the reality that the human rights as understood today are meant to promote human wellbeing. Issues drawn from an understanding of human dignity, for example, the inviolability of innocent human life,

60. Bujo, *The Ethical Dimension of Community*, 70–79.

61. Gutiérrez, *A Theology of Liberation*, 84.

62. Metz, *Faith in History and Society*, 234–36.

rights to health, freedom of conscience, freedom of religion and expression, among others, can never be compromised without great harm being done to a people. There are some human goods or values that are trans-cultural.[63] Bujo presents African concerns regarding western thought on human rights. He has raised the question whether we can use the language of human rights in an African context just as it is in the West. Bujo states the problem of human rights as follows:

> [T]here arises the question, with regard to human rights, whether the norms they lay down are not determined by a certain philosophy and can only be understood against the background of the Western context. What is the foundation which justifies the claim to universality of the existing human rights? In my view, this claim can only be justified, when possibly all cultures enter into dialogue in order to contribute to the understanding of humanity.[64]

In the preceding statement, Bujo does not deny "human rights" as they are stipulated in such statements as the United Nations *Universal Declaration of Human Rights* and others, but raises the question of understanding the same in an African context. Bujo attempts "to explain the background of the African view of the human person, because it leads to certain concrete norms."[65] When people all over the world talk about human rights, "at the core is the concept of the dignity of the individual: being human justifies the claim to certain rights. The emphasis falls upon the individual, not upon the society; the single person should be respected as such and not on account of the relationship to others."[66] Bujo has also acknowledged the indispensability of some common values in human living all over the world. There are some basic values that are shared by all people. He holds that some common norms, values, ideals and goals bring the whole world ethically together.[67]

Considering the extent of abuses of human rights in some parts of Africa, there is need to have an ethics that advocates the rights of the

63. Cahill, "Toward Global Ethics," 324–44. Cahill states: "The public recognition of cross-cultural, even "global" values and programs is already a sort of action or practice that disposes will and emotions to solidarity" (342). See also Hollenbach, *The Common Good and Christian Ethics*. Hollenbach views a shared humanity as a basis for global values and human rights (219).

64. Bujo, *The Ethical Dimension of Community*, 143.

65. Ibid., 144.

66. Ibid.

67. Ibid., 143. See also Küng, *Global Responsibility*, xvi.

powerless and subjugated. Military and civil dictators have maimed and killed thousands of innocent people. Cases in point are the wars fought in Sierra Leone, Sudan, and Angola, among other nations with a past of political and religious conflicts. As a matter of fact, therefore, the reality expressed in the language of human rights or its equivalent is necessary. Consequently, there is a dire need of an ethics that expresses the rights of all people in a simple contextual language. An African feminist ethics would also be one way to address the question of human rights in Africa.[68]

Conclusion

Human wellbeing in Africa and elsewhere is of immediate concern. The relevance of any theology developed within an African historical and cultural foundation should be based on the consideration of situations of poverty and alienation. Bujo's African moral theology has significance in an African context because of his use of a liberation ethical method.

The significant contribution by Bujo to African theology is not just the use of liberation theological method. As analyzed in this work, Bujo also addresses social-political and economic issues affecting Africa today from a theological perspective. The relevance of African theology is to be seen in its contribution to the transformation of African societies as a whole. Nevertheless, there is more to be done in African theology especially developing theological methods that are African in origin as opposed to those adapted from outside Africa.

68. cf. "The Circle of Concerned African Women Theologians" who includes scholars like Mercy Amba Oduyoye, Musimbi R. Kanyoro, Elizabeth Amoah, among others. Their publications include *Where God Reigns* and also *Transforming Power*.

5

Human Ethics and/or Christian Ethics?
Is There a Specifically Christian Ethics?

AFRICAN ETHICS HAS BEEN discussed previously in this work as communal in nature and also as recognizing every individual human being as capable of moral discernment. Palaver was viewed as the moral-discernment process in African community ethics. Through his critical analysis of the debate about autonomous ethics and the faith ethics, Bujo opens the palaver from the confines of the community to the universal, and thus arguing for the communicable nature of moral reasoning. Bujo's understanding of autonomous ethics does not go contrary to an African community ethics. The autonomous ethics debate, according to Bujo, does not deny the contextual nature of morality. He uses autonomous ethics to show that through reason, ethical principles are related, and they are trans-cultural. The autonomous ethics debate is viewed here as relevant in an African communitarian ethics.

This chapter also explores the contribution of an African understanding of Christian morality to the western ethical theory of autonomous ethics. I analyze the autonomous ethics debate and examine how Bujo connects this debate to the context of an African human ethics. Bujo takes the argument of Christian morality as human morality and applies this to an African communitarian ethics. He emphasizes the indispensability of the individual human person in the realization of moral norms in the community. To clarify Bujo's understanding of autonomous ethics in an African context, it is necessary to consider the development of the debate in the western world especially in the works of Alfons Auer, Josef Fuchs, Klaus Demmer, Bruno Schüller, and Franz Böckle.

The question of whether Christian morality is the same as human morality has come about from the development of moral theology, and more so in the natural law tradition. The Second Vatican Council and the encyclical *Humanae Vitae* contributed in a special way to the development of the natural moral law. The debate on the autonomous nature of Christian morality is a result of the development in the natural law tradition. What is involved in the moral autonomy debate is an understanding of the fact that to be a Christian is to be human, and therefore, whatever is human in the fullest sense of the word is also Christian. The question that has been asked by moral theologians like Alfons Auer, Josef Fuchs, and Bruno Schüller, is whether Christian morality adds anything new to human morality. The answers to this question have been diverse. Klaus Demmer and Franz Böckle have tried to reconcile faith and human reason in the debate on moral autonomy and faith ethics. The advocates of faith ethics hold that Christian morality is uniquely Christian because it has as its source divine revelation and faith in Jesus Christ. This understanding of Christian morality as revealed is evident in the work of Joseph Ratzinger (whose views on the topic will be presented later in the second part of this chapter). The autonomous ethics and faith ethics debates are shaped by the premise of trying to determine the contribution of the gospel to Christian morals. Neither autonomous ethics nor faith ethics debates deny the relevance of the gospel values, but autonomous ethicians insist that gospel values can be realized through a genuine human morality.

The question about the human aspect of morality is one that is unavoidable in the making of an African ethics. We cannot talk of an African ethics, or any ethics for that matter, without being concerned with the people that share the experience, and from this experience develop some moral norms. It will be evident in this work that when we deliberate on an African ethics we are concerned with a human ethics.

A. What is Moral Autonomy?

The moral autonomy debate in Christian ethics is viewed here as an outcome of the historical development of moral theology. Although the debate by the advocates for the autonomous ethics position will be seen to emphasize that human reason is a capacity for realizing morality, this should not be construed to be a denial of the role played by Christian faith in moral discernment. "Faith and reason are in a mutually conditioning relationship."[1] The autonomous ethics debate incorporates a faith context in ethical argumentation. Some theologians who advocate moral autonomy may appear to exclude faith, but it should be emphasized that no proponent of autonomous ethics has categorically denied the role of faith in Christian morality.

Vincent MacNamara synthesizes the debate on moral autonomy and the place of faith in moral reasoning, as it has been taking place in the Roman Catholic Church. He presents the autonomous and faith ethics debates in terms of reaction versus continuity. He views an autonomous ethics as a reaction to the tradition that holds that all of Christian morality has its origin in revelation, especially in the gospels. Autonomous ethics does not deny the relevance of the gospel but it affirms reason as a source of morality. For this reason, MacNamara states:

> The moral demands by which the Christian is obliged are basically intelligible to reason as far as their content is concerned. They are no different from the demands of natural law.[2]

As stated above, it should be made clear that the debate on autonomous ethics has its foundation in St. Thomas Aquinas's teaching on the natural moral law.[3] When autonomous ethicians hold that Christian mo-

---

1. Kopfensteiner, "Globalization and the Autonomy of Moral Reasoning," 496.

2. MacNamara, *Faith and* Ethics, 37.

3. The understanding of the relation of reason and faith has its foundation in the tradition developed from Thomas Aquinas's understanding of the natural law. After describing law as "a certain ordinance of reason for the common good" (ST I-II, Q. 90 A.4), Aquinas goes ahead to show that a rational creature "has a share of the eternal reason, whereby it has a natural inclination to its proper act and end, and this participation of the eternal law in the rational creature is called the natural law" (ST I-II, Q. 91, A.2). From Aquinas, one can therefore say that the natural law is not independent of the eternal law or God's providence because human reason participates in the divine or eternal reason. The natural law can be said to have its source in the eternal law: "Therefore, all laws, insofar as they partake of right reason, are derived from eternal law" (ST I-II, Q. 93, A.3). Furthermore, Aquinas himself has affirmed that moral law has always to be reasonable. It has to be in accord with the law of nature. He categorically states that "human morals depend on their relation to reason, which is the proper principle of human acts, those morals are called good which accord with reason, and those are called bad which are discordant from reason" (ST I-II, Q. 100, A.1). This does not mean that Aquinas reduces moral issues to the domain of reason alone, but he also qualifies that "there are some matters of which man cannot judge unless helped by divine instruction, such as articles of faith" (ibid.). Ultimately, Aquinas joins the law of nature to theological virtues. Aquinas clarifies: "The things of God should be revealed to men only in proportion to their

rality is human morality, there is an understanding that all people share the same natural moral law. There is an understanding that Christians cannot escape being human. From a Christian perspective, human beings are God's creation and God offers His saving love to all people. It is in this context that James Bresnahan, S.J., states:

> [S]ince Christian ethics is the "objectification" in Jesus Christ of what every man experiences of himself in his "subjectivity," [it] does not and cannot add to human ethical self-understanding as such any material content that is, in principle, "strange" or "foreign" to man as he exists and experiences himself in this world.[4]

Bresnahan analyzes Karl Rahner's theological method which is based on the understanding of human beings as subjects, and shows the implication of this view when applied to ethics. From Rahner's understanding of people who are not in the Christian faith as "anonymous" Christians, Bresnahan further states:

> A man within the Christian community has access to a privileged articulation, in "objective" form, of this experience of "subjectivity"; he has this in the event of Jesus Christ and from the community which lives in Christ by the Spirit. Both the man outside the Christian community and the man within may have (through grace itself) accepted God's self-offer through faith, hope and love precisely in accepting his own directedness toward this offer. The former does so "anonymously," the latter in an explicitly Christian way.[5]

Notable in what Bresnahan says of Rahner's thought is the presence of God's grace in an anonymous way outside the Christian community. There

---

capacity; otherwise they might despise what was beyond their grasp, with disastrous consequences" (ST I-II, Q. 101, A.2). "The moral precepts have rational causes of their very nature; as, for instance, Thou shalt not kill, Thou shalt not steal." (ST I-II, Q. 102, A.2). Further, Aquinas distinguishes the new law from the old law: "The mystery of the redemption of the human race was fully achieved in the passion of Christ, which is why the Lord then said, *It is consummated.* Consequently, the legal precepts had to cease then entirely, their reality being fulfilled" (ST I-II, Q. 103, A.3). "But the decrees of the New Law, which chiefly consist in faith and the love of God, are rational of their very nature" (ST I-II, Q. 102, A.2). The quotations of Aquinas here are from Baumgarth and Regan, *Saint Thomas Aquinas: On Law, Morality, and Politics* and the Blackfriars Latin text and English translation, *St. Thomas Aquinas.*

4. Bresnahan, "Rahner's Christian ethics," 353.

5. Ibid. On the presence of Jesus Christ in non-Christians, see Rahner, *Foundations of Christian Faith,* 311–21.

is the realization that all people have a capacity given at creation to realize morality as those in the Christian community. However, Christians have an added advantage through the support of the community of faith. The Christian community has the resources of scripture and doctrine that in a special way embody the "objectification" of the common human experience.[6]

It should be emphasized here that the debate on moral autonomy is an outcome of the development of natural law tradition in moral theology that began with St. Thomas Aquinas. Natural law is the participation of rational reason in the eternal law. Natural law is not opposed to God, but God being its source makes it possible. Kopfensteiner and Keenan have argued that autonomous ethics should be understood in the context of the theory of the natural moral law. They have written the following:

> The thesis of an autonomous ethic in the context of faith can be legitimately understood in light of natural-law argumentation. In a natural law tradition there is the unquestioned assumption of the rationality of moral insight; moral insight is accessible to others through plausible arguments. The thesis of the autonomy of moral reasoning, then, is guided by the legitimate interest of safeguarding the communicability of moral insight. It recalls the public nature of theological discourse, opens up avenues of dialogue with other sciences, and prevents the tradition from ever falling into the temptation of sectarianism by underlining what different moral traditions have in common.[7]

Therefore, the debate on the autonomous nature of morality should not be seen as going against the tradition of the natural moral law, but as advancing it. The advocates of an autonomous ethics do not deny the role of faith in moral reasoning but recognize that it is the believer who discerns how to live out every day the call given by God. Autonomous ethics realizes the human dignity that was given by God at creation. From the perspective of God's endowment at creation, "the human person is seen as a creator, as having responsibility for himself and for the world."[8]

The emphasis on autonomous ethics does not replace the role of faith in moral reasoning but lays stress on the exalted vocation of the faithful (Vatican II).[9] The response to the God who calls is only possible when

6. McCormick, *Notes on Moral Theology*, 302.

7. Kopfensteiner and Keenan, "Moral Theology out of Western Europe," 116.

8. MacNamara, *Faith and Ethics*, 39.

9. Writing on the close association between religion and science, GS 36 states:

the human being is the subject. Morality is only possible considering the self-determination of the human subject. To this end, Demmer's statement is instructive: "Because faith is not incompatible with reason, any voluntaristic interpretation must be avoided; because it also transcends reason, however, it brings into the picture an additional component that needs to be thought out."[10]

Moral discernment by an individual Christian is made through reasoning guided by faith. Autonomous ethics avoids the separation of faith and reason. It is the whole human person who makes moral decisions. Kopfensteiner and Keenan show how moral reasoning and faith go together when they write:

> [M]oral reasoning continues to make the implications of faith transparent and, on the other hand, faith undergirds reason and provides it with a creative impulse. There is no opposition between human freedom and faith in God.[11]

From this understanding of autonomous ethics, we can understand the following conclusion:

> The theologian, then, is at the service of the Church-in-the-world. Moral theologians are not limited to intra-ecclesial discussions, but their work is meant to serve as the bridge between the *consensus fidelium* and the *consensus universalis.*[12]

The preceding statement is a mediating position between autonomy and faith ethics. In the debate between autonomous and faith ethics, there should be a focus not only on the role of faith in Christian morality but also on the relevance of Christian morality to non-Christians. An appeal to reason in moral discernment opens up Christian morality to all people. Christian morality should not be sectarian but inclusive of all human beings. The role of the theologian should be to reconcile faith and reason in moral discernment.

"Consequently, methodical research in all branches of knowledge, provided it is carried out in a truly scientific manner and does not override moral laws, can never conflict with the faith, because the things of the world and the things of faith derive from the same God," quoted from Flannery, ed., *Vatican Council II*, 935.

10. Demmer, *Shaping the Moral* Life, 25–26.

11. Kopfensteiner and Keenan, "Moral Theology out of Western Europe," 119.

12. Ibid., 111–12.

A Christian is a person who lives in the world with other people. The understanding of Christian morality as human morality opens up a room for dialogue between Christians and peoples of other faith. It is a realization that Christians share a common life with others outside the Christian Churches. According to John Macquarrie:

> [W]hat is distinctive in the Christian ethic is not its ultimate goals or its fundamental principles, for these are shared with all serious-minded people in whatever tradition they stand. The distinctive element is the special context within which the moral life is perceived. This special context includes the normative place assigned to Jesus Christ and his teaching—not, indeed, as a paradigm for external imitation, but rather as the criterion and inspiration for a style of life.[13]

The basis of the argument for autonomous ethics is the understanding that morality has to do with what is reasonable. We make decisions on the course of action we are to take basing ourselves on the knowledge we have at hand. In making a decision, one considers the goods and values that are at stake. This understanding of human action and moral agency of the human person is common to all people, Christian or non-Christians.

The moral autonomy debate understands Christian morality as fully human morality. The question that arises frequently in the debate concerns the role of faith in moral reasoning. It will emerge below in the proponents of an autonomous ethics that they tackle repeatedly not only the human capacity of realizing morality, but also the place of Christian faith in moral reasoning.

It is imperative here to consider the various proponents of the moral autonomy debate. This will prove necessary since it will make it possible to see from what perspectives these authors, including Bujo, are coming. The theologians mostly associated with developing the moral autonomy debate in Roman Catholic moral theology include Alfons Auer, Josef Fuchs, and Bruno Schüller. In a critical analysis I will consider each theologian and show how he relates and differs from the others. Later in this work, Klaus Demmer and Franz Böckle will be seen to argue that faith and reason constitute one process of moral discernment and are not opposed to each other. I will consider the contribution of Böckle and Demmer to the debate on faith and autonomous ethics after analyzing the proponents of

---

13. Macquarrie, *Three Issues in Ethics*, 89. See also McCormick, *Notes on Moral Theology*, 296.

autonomous ethics: Auer, Fuchs, and Schüller. I treat the work of each of these theologians on the moral autonomy debate, and later on analyze the work of Joseph Ratzinger and Heinz Schürmann, the advocates of the faith-ethics' position in this debate.

i. Alfons Auer

Alfons Auer is among the first theologians to contribute a great deal in the debate on the autonomous nature of Christian morality. He is associated with the idea that Christian morality is human morality. He is known to have emphasized the human element in Christian morality. Auer in a categorical way pointed out that it is the human being endowed with reason that realizes morality. In his ethics, we can say that there would be no morality without human beings. Auer states:

> [M]orality therefore aims at the optimum happiness of human beings, then ethical statements must be able to be made understandable to every human being; they must be communicable; everyone must be able to speak with others, about what constitutes the true good of human beings (*bonum humanum*)—even with those who are non-Christians. But this is only possible, however if one "takes out of play" the church and Christian faith and argues with reason. Thomas Aquinas means as much, that moral obligation comes not from an authority, but from the inner reasonableness of a moral norm.[14]

According to Auer, the human capacity for knowledge goes hand in hand with a moral responsibility. Human beings have a capacity to distinguish between what is good and bad. Auer states:

> Human rationality implies responsibility for the rationality of the world. Who is capable to bring the world nearer to its meaning

14. Auer, "Die Bedeutung des Christlichen bei der Normfindung," in *Zur Theologie der Ethik*, 208. Original text: *"[W]enn also das Sittliche auf optimal geglücktes Menschsein zielt, dann muß die ethische Aussage jedem Menschen verständlich gemacht werden können; sie muß kommunikabel sein; man muß mit jedem darüber sprechen können, was das eigenliche Gut des Menschseins (bonum humanum) ausmacht—auch mit dem, der nicht Christ ist. Dies ist aber nur möglich, wenn man Kirche und christlichen Glauben zunächst aus dem Spiel läßt und mit Vernuftgründen argumentiert. Thomas von Aquin meint ohnehin, die sittliche Verbindlichkeit komme nicht von einer Autorität, sondern von der inneren Vernünftigkeit einer sittlichen Norm"* (my translation). Cf., Auer, "Das Spannungsfeld zwischen Recht und Sittlichkeit in der Theologischen Ethik," 140–57.

and its order, is taken with this capacity in obligation. Here is the peculiarity of the source of morality.[15]

Further, moral autonomy, as presented by Auer, realizes the role of faith in moral reasoning. The fact that human beings can realize moral norms through their rational nature does not rule out the necessity of faith in Christ. Necessarily, Christian morality in Auer's understanding does not provide new moral norms but a new dimension into which morality is lived. "The Christian *proprium* lies in the 'new being' in Christ and with it the derived new horizon of meaning."[16] Like Fuchs, Auer describes the new being in Christ and the new horizon of meaning in Christian ethics in terms of motivation: "The new being and new horizon of meaning describes a new motivation power, the kernel of which is agape."[17]

Auer contributes to moral theology through his recognition of the indispensability of the personal element in morality. However, he also clearly distinguishes between a human or earthly morality and a Christian morality. Although Auer's position is similar to Fuchs's view of moral autonomy, Auer appears to emphasize the categorical difference and similarity between human morality and Christian morality. For Fuchs the difference is only in motivation but not of content. For Auer, Christian ethics is different from any other worldly ethos through what he calls "*qualitativer oder transzendenter Uberbietung*" (a qualitative or transcendent surpassing).[18] He holds that Christian morality has a religious dimension. But the religious dimension has also to be realized in the world, i.e. by human beings who are in space and time (history). Hence, Auer states:

> This religious dimension of morality must also in itself be realized however in the structures of the autonomous world; it is not assigned to a specific testing field, from which the Christian could be dispensed from the realization of human dignity.[19]

15. Auer, *Autonome Moral und Christlicher Glaube*, 36. Original text: "*Menschliche Rationalität impliziert Verantwortung für die Rationalität der Welt. Wer fähig ist, die Welt ihrem Sinn und ihrer Ordnung näherzubringen, ist mit dieser Fähigkeit in Pflicht genommen. Hier ist der eigenliche Ursprungsort des Sittlichen*" (my translation).

16. Ibid., 177. Original text: "*Das christliche Proprium liegt in dem "neuen Sein" in Christus und in dem damit erschlossen neuen Sinnhorizont*" (my translation).

17. Auer, Ibid., 178. "*Dem neuen Sein und dem neuen Sinnhorizont entspricht eine neue Kraft der Motivation, deren Kernstück die agape ist*" (my translation).

18. Ibid., 92.

19. Ibid., 27. Original text: "*Diese religiöse Dimension des Sittlichen muß sich aber in den autonom weltlichen Strukturen realisieren; es ist ihr nicht ein spezifisches Feld der*

MacNamara makes an evaluation of Auer's understanding of moral autonomy as follows:

> God did not first create the human person and then give him a code of ethical rules; he created him with reason so that he might give himself moral norms. The discovery of moral norms, therefore, is a matter of human reason. The Christian message, he says, gives no concrete ethical normativity: its ethical relevance lies in something other than material norms. Its content is "human" not "Christian." Therefore, the affirmation is true that ethics can be shared by people having different metaphysical or religious viewpoints.[20]

Auer's work on Christian morality as human morality is similar to the work of other theologians in the renewal of moral theology after Vatican II. Together with Fuchs, and other renewal moral theologians, Auer considers the nature of moral theology as it relates to all of humanity. Considering Christian morality as human morality, Auer opens Christian ethics to include all serious-minded people concerned with ethical living. However, as seen before, the interpretation of Thomas Aquinas's teaching on the natural moral law has laid the foundation for the debate on moral autonomy. This is also viewed as evident in the theology of Fuchs.

ii. Josef Fuchs

Another major contributor in the moral autonomy debate is Josef Fuchs. To show how the human element in morality should be understood, Fuchs focuses on what Vatican II has to say about being human in the world. On the right behavior in the world, Fuchs writes:

> The Council understands the world as the world of the human being: the personal individual in his dignity (also seen religiously and morally), the various inter-personal relationships, the many institutions, human society, scientific acquisitions of knowledge and technical possibilities, etc.[21]

Fuchs views morality as concerned with the realization of the human person in the world. Christian morality is not concerned with what is foreign

---

Bewährung zugewiesen, von dem aus sich der Christ gar vom Engagement für die Verwirklichung der Menschenwürde dispensieren könnte" (my translation).

20. MacNamara, *Faith and Ethics*, 44.

21. Fuchs, "Vatican II: Salvation, Personal Morality, Right Behavior," 23.

to human beings but the true nature of the human person as created by God. He shows that his understanding of the human person and morality has its foundation in the Second Vatican Council. He states:

> The Council sees a new kind of humanism at work in the contemporary attempt to resolve the great questions of mankind (GS 55). It intends to speak of a humanism which seeks to arrive at "the true and full realization of the human being" through a true "culture, i.e., the development and nurturing of the goods and values of nature" (GS 53); at the development "of the full human personality" (GS 56); at a continuous alteration of the human person "above himself" (GS 35). The human person, according to the Council, becomes the criterion for "right" behavior in humanity's world. Natural law according to the Council, includes the possibility of different cultures and therefore of different lifestyles and "moralities" (GS 53).[22]

However, Fuchs affirms that personal morality is influenced by our image of God. He notes, "The right realization of the human world is without doubt the will of its Creator and Savior."[23] But he also questions, like Schüller, whether we can refer to morality as coming from the "commanding God." He states:

> The expression "commanding God" means that God is understood as Lord, that from beyond the world God simultaneously sends commands into the categorial world and binds humanity to order and develop reality in exact accordance with commands which have been issued: human persons accept the commands and carry them out in conscientious, loving obedience.[24]

For Fuchs, autonomy in morality protects us from voluntarism. Human beings have a capacity for self-determination. He categorically holds that

22. Ibid., 24.

23. Fuchs, "Our Image of God and the Morality of Innerworldly Behavior," 28. See also Fuchs's statement: "We must, therefore, not perceive man and his world—pantheistically or mystically—as either "divine", or as a world of humans on whom a detached God externally imposes a moral law—his "will." God's creation is not man (or humanity) with his world plus God's will for man (that is, a moral order), but quite simply, humanity and its world. If we wish to speak of God's will, this is nothing else than the divine desire that man might exist and live. This implies, however, that he live as man, that he discover himself and his world as well as their latent possibilities, that he understand them, that he shape and realize himself as genuinely human, as bodily-spiritual being" (Fuchs, "Is there a Distinctively Christian Morality?," 59).

24. Fuchs, "Our Image of God and the Morality of Innerworldly Behavior," 29–30.

humans have to discover how the word of God should be realized so as to better humanity and to correspond to the task bestowed on human persons through creation itself.[25] Further, he categorically states:

> There is less talk of God's commandments as a "law" which the human discovers within his conscience, and which he has "not given to himself." Rather God has written it (Rom. 2) "into the person's heart"; the human must obey it. That is, the "law" is grounded in the "eternal, objective, and universal divine law." And that the human can recognize this . . . corresponds to the essential order of human nature . . . many principles of this order are viewed as universal and unchangeable and hence independent of historical and cultural factors.[26]

Evidently, Fuchs has contributed in a remarkable way in the development of autonomous ethics debate. He takes the debate in the context of confirming the understanding of human beings as subjects in moral reasoning. He has also recognized that Christian moral norms are inseparable from human reasoning. A Christian also uses reason in moral discernment. However, reason is not exclusively Christian. It is shared by all people, and therefore, all people can reach to the same and/or similar moral norms. Fuchs clearly describes the problem as follows:

> In recent years the question of the *proprium* of Christian norms of behavior on the basis of biblical statements has been examined very critically. In view of their genesis, are these norms independent, in that they arise from Christianity as such? Do they comprise a *distinctivum*, that is, a set of moral judgments that are only in Christianity? Do they belong to the *specificum* of what is Christian, that is, do they appertain absolutely (if not also exclusively) to Christian morality? Does the Bible itself regard them as universal norms not bound by time, or rather as answers to questions which were posed by a specific culture?[27]

Fuchs identifies Christian morality as human morality. According to his explanation, "Our reflection about the genuinely human and genuinely Christian dimensions of Christian morality derives basically from the fact that believers must translate their living faith—that is, their Christian

---

25. Ibid., 29.

26. Ibid., 32.

27. Fuchs, "Christian Morality: Biblical Orientation and Human Evaluation," 5.

intentionality—into concrete living and manifest it in their lives."[28] From his perspective there is no way to conceive Christian morality other than as human morality. Emphatically holding that Christians are human beings, Fuchs does not rule out the contribution of Christian revelation. He holds that "Christians may find help in the sources of revelation, help not only for a distinctively Christian morality, but for a genuinely human understanding of the person and of human morality."[29] Further, Fuchs categorically maintains that "The newness that Christ brings is not really a new (material) morality, but the new creature of grace and of the Kingdom of God, the man of divinely self-giving love."[30]

Evidently, Fuchs shows that the human element in Christian morality makes it relevant to all human beings. For him, the Bible has a human element. Human reason is indispensable not only in understanding the Bible but also in the realization of moral norms. He states:

> It has been pointed out that even the Decalogue should not be regarded as a direct revelation of moral behavior by God, but rather as a brief synthesis of religious prescriptions imposed on the people of Israel (first to third commandments) and of fundamental modes of societal action in Israel—parallel to those of the neighboring peoples (fourth to tenth commandments). It is indeed true that the observance of these precepts will be Israel's expression of fidelity to the covenant that God has offered to his people, and thus indicates a deep religious sense that goes beyond its apparent moral import.[31]

Fuchs, without denying God's intervention, recognizes the human element in the Decalogue. We can say that revelation by God becomes revelation only when it is expressed in human language, that is, a language that people can understand. God reveals himself to human beings, and therefore, there is need for a language human beings can understand. Morality concerns human beings, and for this reason, humanity is indispensable.

Like Auer, Fuchs makes a very important point when he affirms that it is the human person who makes morality possible. He states: "Correct human behavior in this human world is to be discovered by the partner created by the Creator, and with the aid of the human reason of the creature

28. Fuchs, "Is There A Distinctively Christian Morality?," 58.

29. Ibid., 58.

30. Ibid., 61.

31. Fuchs, "Christian Morality: Biblical Orientation and Human Evaluation," 6.

which reflects the wisdom of the Creator."[32] Human beings, according to Fuchs, have the capacity to realize morality in the world. This human capacity is God-given at creation. From Fuchs, it can be said that human reason makes morality possible. Making reference to Vatican II's *Gaudium et Spes*, Fuchs points out that "although significant things are said about responsible behavior in the world in general, and above all about particular questions in a special way, a theory of behavior is not developed."[33] He acknowledges that in the background there is another deeper moral problem, namely, that of the inner world with behavior, which is ultimately grounded in personal morality. According to the Council personal morality in its turn presupposes "that 'healing' and 'sanctifying' transformation of the human person, who, left to himself, is a sinner; this transformation is the salvation given by God as a gift that calls the human person and makes him 'good'— before God."[34]

Notably, Fuchs describes Christian morality as personal morality. He explains:

> Personal morality means the opposite of egotism that is closed in upon itself, i.e., personal morality means openness of the person as such—for God, for men, for all that is good and right; it is thus a "sacrificial gift acceptable to God" (GS 38). Personal morality is also, therefore, inner openness and readiness to work for the good of others (GS 39), to care for the right shaping of the world of man (GS 39); it is a tendency toward the correct "act and truth of life" (GS 42), a readiness to become involved for the sake of the world (GS 43), a motivation in the correct shaping of the world (GS 4). Righteousness, generosity, fidelity, chastity are like openness and readiness for right behavior, and so they are just as much moral goodness as openness and readiness for right behavior in civil, economic, international affairs, etc.[35]

According to MacNamara, Christian morality as presented by Fuchs differs from non-Christian or human morality only in terms of motivation and not the material content. In terms of motivation, the Christian sees "morality in a different light or framework from the non-Christian."[36]

---

32. Ibid., 17.

33. Fuchs, "Vatican II: Salvation, Personal Morality, Right Behavior," 19.

34. Ibid.

35. Ibid., 21–22.

36. MacNamara, *Faith and Ethics*, 42.

MacNamara evaluates Fuchs's view of Christian morality in the moral autonomy debate as follows:

> The morality of the Christian has a specific intentionality. It has a goal. It is going somewhere. He means that the basic reality for the Christian is his relationship to God and that morality is important to that relationship.[37]

However, it should be made clear that the specific Christian intentionality, according to Fuchs, does not refer to the content of Christian morality: "Christian intentionality is an element which, while pervading and completing the particular-categorial conduct, does not determine its content."[38] In Fuchs's perspective, the content of Christian morality is not distinct from that of human morality.

From the above, Fuchs comes close to presenting Christian morality and human morality as identical. He identifies Christian morality as human morality with a difference only in the motivation.

iii. Bruno Schüller

Schüller argues that there can be no separation between faith (grace) and reason in Christian morality. He points out that Christian ethics has a foundation peculiarly its own. He states: "In short, the love of God and Christ is both motive and standard for the love Christians are required to have."[39] From St. Paul he quotes "We are people who already live in the Spirit; therefore we must walk in the Spirit!" (Gal. 5:25).[40] He holds that "the linking of moral exigencies with God's saving action is characteristic of biblical ethics in its entirety."[41]

For Schüller:

---

37. Ibid. See Fuchs's statement: "Yes, of course one can point to the distinctive element of Christian morality, and it is clear that it is the decisive element of Christian morality. This distinctive element of Christian morality is that specific *Christian intentionality* which transcends and fulfills all human moral values" (Fuchs, "Human, Humanist and Christian Morality," 123).

38. Fuchs, "Is There a Distinctively Christian Morality?," 57.

39. Schüller, "The Debate on the Specific Character of a Christian Ethics: Some Remarks," 16.

40. Ibid., 17.

41. Ibid.

> The gospel is a statement about the moral goodness of God and how this goodness makes itself known to human beings who, when judged by the demands of morality, prove themselves sinners. To this extent the gospel itself already uses the language of morality.[42]

He views the Bible as exhortative in its presentation. Exhortation, for Schüller, is based on the fact that God is good and that a Christian recalling God's goodness should also do good. In this understanding, God's goodness becomes an example for the believer. Hence, Schüller states:

> The Christian acknowledges that God has shown him nothing but (moral) goodness and love. In virtue of this acknowledgement he is challenged to imitate God as his model and, like God, to show goodness (as far as he can) to everyone.[43]

But he makes a further qualification to show that human beings have the capacity to realize their moral calling. He holds, "Only if we suppose that human persons already experience themselves as called to be morally good, can God appear to them as a model to be unconditionally imitated, once they have recognized him as the absolute embodiment of moral goodness."[44] However, he also cautions against viewing exhortation as a theonomous and Christonomous moral positivism where God and Christ would be understood as constituting the concept of moral goodness. The Bible speaks the language of exhortation.[45] On the relation of the gospel (faith and grace) and law in morality, Schüller sees a solution: "an exhortation which appeals to the gospel for its basis suggests that although the fulfillment of the requirements of morality is the free and responsible act of the human beings to whom these requirements are addressed, yet it is antecedently and concomitantly a fulfillment which is a gift of God in Christ."[46]

Exhortation, according to Schüller, starts with the gospel. On biblical exhortation, Schüller states:

> Admittedly, exhortation of itself does not convey any new moral insights. But it does have or is intended to have the result that the person addressed allows its moral insights to touch him personally

42. Ibid., 19.

43. Ibid., 20.

44. Ibid., 21.

45. Ibid., 21–22.

46. Ibid., 23.

and that he hears them as a challenge to be converted, do penance, change his life, and act as he knows he ought to act.[47]

The call to moral obedience of commands is based on the authority of their moral goodness and rightness.[48] However, Schüller carefully shows the role played by faith in Christian morality:

> The thesis that for the Christian, as for everyone else, moral imperatives are identical to the natural law does not mean, in other words, that a Christian's faith cannot reveal to him an understanding of existence that simply transcends the limits of the insight otherwise available to him.[49]

Christian faith provides a new dimension (or an understanding) to morality. Like Auer and Fuchs, Schüller recognizes the role of reason in moral discernment, but unlike them (Auer and Fuchs) Schüller categorically points out the limits of reason: "Recall all the errors and confusions to which, as experience shows, people succumb who are forced to rely on natural reason alone for their grasp of the moral law."[50] For Schüller, faith gives human reason a new dimension. Therefore, from Schüller's perspective, one can say that faith provides some clarity in moral discernment, but this should not be conceived to mean that reason cannot realize morality. Schüller emphasizes that faith can never be conceived without reason.

Evidently, Schüller's view of faith and reason in Christian morality is based on an understanding of the natural law. Natural law, as in Thomas Aquinas, is not opposed to faith in God. Of great significance is the fact that in human beings natural law is a participation in the divine eternal law. Through natural law reasoning, Schüller holds: "From the theological viewpoint the requirements of morality, insofar as they are accessible in principle to natural reason, are commandments of the Creator."[51] Schüller presents faith and reason not as opposed to each other but as necessarily pointing to each other. He states:

> Therefore, if we want to compare faith and reason from a gnoseological point of view, we must compare true knowledge through faith and true knowledge through reason, or truths of faith with

47. Ibid., 25.
48. Ibid., 27.
49. Ibid., 28.
50. Ibid., 31.
51. Ibid., 37.

truths of reason. Then the relation between the two turns out to be that *fides supponit rationem et transcendit eam* [faith supposes reason and goes beyond it].[52]

Affirming that a Christian is a person with faith in God, Schüller seems to point out that there is something specific in Christian morality. Christian morality supposes faith and reason. Does faith give Christian morality a specifically Christian character? It seems in Schüller's view that Christian faith makes Christian morality have something that is unique or particularly Christian. But he also acknowledges that natural law reasoning is capable of realizing moral norms such as in the Decalogue.[53]

MacNamara makes an important analysis of Schüller's understanding of moral autonomous reasoning and its relation to faith. According to MacNamara, Schüller holds the role of Jesus in morals as maieutic or pedagogic. This role is also referred to above as parenesis or exhortation. What Jesus does is to help us to understand the demands of our own reason. Jesus does not determine but only clarifies the moral demand already determined by reason. The Christianizing of morality is not regarded as referring to content, but it refers to the horizon of meaning and final grounding which the Christian can give to his morality. For the Christian, morality is the will of God; it is the expression of his response to God.[54]

From the preceding, autonomous ethics is viewed as proceeding from an understanding of the true nature of the human person. There is recognition of the capacity of self-determination in human beings. It is only when one acts on what is coming from within that one can be said to be a responsible moral agent. Faith does not destroy reason but illuminates it. Faith transcends reason but is not opposed to it. The emphasis in the moral autonomy debate is on the capacity of human reason to realize moral norms. In the next section on faith ethics, Christian faith is viewed as making Christian morality unique.

B. Faith Ethics

Faith ethics' advocates question the reduction of Christian morality to human morality. MacNamara views the proponents of a faith ethic as concerned with historical continuity in moral theology. He says of Joseph

52. Ibid., 36.
53. Ibid., 37.
54. MacNamara, *Faith and Ethics*, 47.

Ratzinger and the biblical scholar, Heinz Schürmann, that they answer the autonomous position by saying that the Bible is an indispensable source of moral teaching and that it is possible and necessary to have recourse to it. Faith-ethics advocates see reason that is not guided by faith as prone to error. MacNamara makes faith-ethics' distrust of reason clear when he states: "Reason is not clear. It capitulates to the spirit of the times. It is not easy to distinguish what is true rationality and only the appearance of rationality."[55]

Further, faith ethics' advocates hold that the Bible is indispensable in the realization of moral norms. Faith ethics is opposed to autonomous ethics' position on the capacity of human reason to realize the same norms as in the gospel. MacNamara distinguishes the faith-ethics and autonomous ethics debates as follows:

> The autonomy movement says that there is no specific content to Christian morality, only specific motivation: the *Glaubensethik* claims specificity of content. Very much depends on how one defines "morality," "content" and "motivation" but none of the authors from either side has examined the terms.[56]

We can, therefore, say that faith ethics holds that Christian morals are specific in content and source. For faith ethics, revelation in Sacred Scriptures and tradition constitute the source of the moral norms in a direct sense. In a word, faith ethics can be said to view morality as having its source in God. Alternatively, autonomous ethics can be seen as a reaction to faith ethics' view of morality as revealed.

The faith ethics and the autonomous ethics debates represent the two approaches in Roman Catholic moral theology to the relation of faith and reason. In the previous section I have considered how autonomous ethics incorporates the reality of faith in Christian moral reasoning. Here I analyze the argument that is held by those who hold a faith-ethics as opposed to an autonomous ethics. Joseph Ratzinger and Heinz Schürmann are among the most active advocates of the faith ethics position. Ratzinger and Schürmann present the Bible in their work as the preeminent source of moral norms.

55. Ibid., 57.
56. Ibid.

i. Joseph Ratzinger

From Ratzinger's perspective, Christian morality has a special and distinctive character. He is against the view "that affirms that there is no such thing as a specifically Christian morality and that Christianity must take its norms of conduct from the anthropological insights of its time."[57] However, as seen previously, the advocates of moral autonomy also do not deny the role of faith in moral reasoning but affirm the irreplaceability of human reasoning in Christian ethics. Ratzinger is opposed to the advocates of moral autonomy of whom he says, "[T]hey point to reason as the only source of moral norms."[58] He also sees a problem in the adherents of moral autonomy because in their theory "there is no place for a church teaching authority in moral matters."[59]

Referring to martyrdom as understood in the early church and especially in the work of Ignatius of Antioch, Ratzinger holds that Christianity has something that is distinctively Christian. He states: "Christianity is a conspiracy to promote the good; the theological and moral aspects are fused inseparably, both in the word itself and deeper, in the basic concept of what Christian reality is."[60] He further adds:

> Christian praxis is nourished by the core of Christian faith, that is, the grace that appeared in Christ and that is appropriated in the sacraments of the Church. Faith's praxis depends on faith's truth.[61]

However, Fuchs differs with Ratzinger on the specificity of Christian moral norms. For Fuchs the moral demands of the Sacred Scripture can be realized through human reason. Fuchs responds to Ratzinger's view on moral norms and the Bible as follows:

> While the Bible does teach some ethical principles, the *proprium* of biblical morality does not consist of a list of exclusive norms: but on the other hand, elements that have their origin elsewhere (traditions, rational insights) can become a *specificum* of biblical morality. However, the criterion for selecting the norms that come from elsewhere is biblical faith itself.[62]

57. Ratzinger, "The Church's Teaching Authority—Faith—Morals," 49.

58. Ibid., 50–51.

59. Ibid., 51.

60. Ibid., 61.

61. Ibid., 70.

62. Fuchs, "Christian Morality: Biblical Orientation," 8.

Fuchs argues that faith ethics advocates misunderstand the position of autonomous ethics. He asserts that it is the human person as such, who is capable of experiencing and understanding (hence as *ratio*), and who actually understands and experiences.[63] Faith does not exempt one from the *conditio humana*. "Finally, 'Faith ethics' which puts its trust in understanding based on belief has until now not demonstrated how it actually arrives at a normative behavioral ethics without a healthy confidence in the *ratio* (Auer)."[64] In the understanding of human morality in the world, "natural law reasoning is the only way on which one can determine whether a revealed duty is trans-temporal or time-conditioned."[65] As it was seen in Schüller, natural law is law, a reality recognized in Scripture.

ii. Heinz Schürmann

Although he is an advocate of faith ethics, Schürmann is closer to the proponents of an autonomous ethics in the way he connects Christian morality to the Sacred Scriptures and the person of Jesus Christ. According to Schürmann, Jesus is the norm of morality. He states: "For the New Testament writers, Jesus' deeds and words provide a standard of values, an ultimate ethical norm. They are the "law of Christ" (Gal. 6:2) that has been accepted as the norm in the hearts of believers (cf. 1 Cor. 9:21)."[66] He categorically holds that the New Testament contains binding teaching on morality. Christ's teaching has "the character of ultimate precept and yields an 'accord with Christ Jesus' (Rom.15:5), the 'mind of Christ Jesus' (Phil 2:5)."[67] Schürmann affirms that "the believer is a person on whom the law of Christ has been implanted as a normative principle (cf. 1 Cor. 9:21)."[68] His argument is valid in a transcendental way.[69] He is right because he

63. Ibid., 10.

64. Ibid., 11.

65. McCormick, *Notes on Moral Theology*, 129.

66. Schürmann, "How Normative are the Values and Precepts of the New Testament?," 18.

67. Ibid.

68. Ibid.

69. Transcendental here is used in a Rahnerian context where a human person is understood as a subject who encounters the world. Rahner states, "Hence our transcendental knowledge or experience is mediated by a categorical encounter with concrete reality in our world, both the world of things and the world of persons. This is also true of the knowledge of God" (Rahner, *Foundations of Christian Faith*, 52).

recognizes a Christian as a human being who has faith in Jesus Christ. He can be said to view faith and reason as constituting an integral human person who lives in a concrete historical setting.[70] Like Demmer, Schürmann holds that faith and reason are inseparable in Christian moral reasoning.

However, Schürmann understands Christian morality as given its specificity in Jesus and the eschaton. He states:

> [T]he New Testament commandment of love draws its distinctiveness and radicality from eschatology, which provides a future-oriented motivation for the Christian life (particularly in the pre-Easter preaching of Jesus), ultimately this distinctiveness and radicality come from the fact that the eschaton has already broken through into our world with the coming of Jesus—and definitively with Jesus' death and resurrection.[71]

The words of Jesus, according to Schürmann, should be held as the ultimate ethical norms. He holds that "many of them are clearly models of conduct, that is, they are intended as paradigms."[72] The demands of the New Testament claim to be absolutely binding due to the fact of "arising from the conduct and the words of Jesus, but also to the majority of apostolic instructions and those originating in the primitive Church."[73]

As an exegete, Schürmann's views on New Testament ethics seem to be so much focused on the part of God, who commands, and the law of Christ. He appears to pay little attention to the human person who acts, not to mention human self-determination and natural moral law in Christian ethics. It is on his use of Sacred Scripture as a source of moral norms that Fuchs is critical of Schürmann. Notably, Fuchs holds that Schürmann affirms that the Bible offers concrete norms for the daily decisions of Christians living in the world today, though he gives very little that is concrete. "Schürmann's attempt represents an impressive endeavor to relate the behavioral morality of today's Christians with that of the Bible."[74]

The debate on autonomous ethics and faith ethics is concerned with the Christian realization of the moral norms. From the on-going discussion, there is recognition that the debate makes various distinctions through

---

70. Schürmann, "How Normative are the Values and Precepts of the New Testament?," 37.

71. Ibid., 21.

72. Ibid., 24.

73. Ibid., 42.

74. Fuchs, "Christian Morality: Biblical Orientation," 8.

emphasis. Autonomous ethics emphasizes reason while the advocates of the faith-ethics emphasizes faith in Christian morality. However, other participants in the debate have shown that faith and reason are realities realized in one and the same human being. Below Demmer and Böckle provide ways to resolve the problem of separating faith and reason in the debate on moral autonomy and the ethics of faith.

C. Resolution of the Problem of Autonomous and Faith Ethics Debate

There are also theologians who have tried to reconcile autonomous and faith ethics. These include Klaus Demmer and Franz Böckle who both view the autonomous and faith ethics positions as not essentially opposed to each other. Demmer and Böckle argue that faith and reason are inseparable in the Christian moral discernment process. According to Böckle, moral autonomy in human beings can only be understood from the perspective of human freedom. He holds that human freedom understood properly has to be viewed as made possible by God, while Demmer maintains that faith and reason are inseparable in Christian moral reasoning.

i. Klaus Demmer

The autonomous ethics position affirms the human capacity for moral self-determination. It recognizes human subjectivity as a capacity necessary for discernment in moral issues. Demmer notes, "The most appropriate word to convey the spirit of our time is autonomy; moral life is a function of personal self-realization."[75] The human subject in freedom is open to self-determination. In freedom, a person is open to all knowledge including the knowledge of God. This knowledge and freedom makes human self-determination possible. Autonomous ethics acknowledges the capacity for moral reasoning in human beings.

Demmer also affirms that "Christian morality is human morality brought to its perfection—so it can be understood by all people of good will."[76] The assertion here is that morality for a Christian is both Christian and human. Basically, Christians are human beings who can have something to offer to other human beings.

75. Demmer, *Shaping the Moral Life*, 22.
76. Ibid., 23.

The realization that Christian morality is human morality highlights the indispensability of the world and humanity in Christianity. Christian morality is not a sectarian morality. Autonomous ethics is concerned with showing the relevance of Christian ethics to all people in the world. Demmer has clearly noted:

> The model of an autonomous morality is concerned primarily with the problem of universal communication; it attempts to prevent Christian morality from falling into practical insignificance. While . . . an ethics of faith aims at recovering the public relevance of Christian identity and the "specificity" of a moral reason enlightened by faith.[77]

An autonomous ethics and an ethics of faith, are not in essence contradictory, but their emphasis either on faith or reason marks the distinction. However, from the on-going discussion, Demmer in his evaluation of autonomous ethics appears to be markedly different from Fuchs. Clearly, Demmer recognizes the role of reason and faith in Christian morality. He is critical of the proponents of an autonomous ethics for diminishing the role of faith, and thereby offers a different perspective from either Fuchs or Auer who view human reason as autonomous in its capacity for moral discernment. For Demmer, there is no separation of faith from reason in a human person. His contribution is a great help in avoiding the unnecessary dichotomy (or misunderstanding) of separating faith from human reason in Christian morality. Faith has a human element, and this is what Demmer calls the anthropological correlate of faith. There is no way one can separate faith from the human dimension. According to Demmer:

> The system of anthropological coordinates represents the fruit of *ratio fide illuminata* (reason enlightened by faith) and bears witness to the fact that faith truly represents an *obsequium rationi humanae consentaneum* (a respect or submission congruent with human reason).[78]

The advocates of autonomous ethics appear to come close to denying the role of faith in ethical issues. They lay emphasis on the human aspect of morality without explicitly denying the illumination brought about by Christian faith. Demmer is critical of autonomous ethics where he holds "Christian revelation is viewed first of all in the sphere of motivation, and

77. Ibid., 25.
78. Ibid.

secondly in the sphere of adding a 'Christian horizon of meaning.'"[79] In this statement, Demmer differs from Fuchs, who holds that Christian morality and human morality are not materially different in content, but only in the motivation.

According to Demmer, in a human person there is no separation of faith and reason. They complement and enhance each other. Theology has traditionally been described as faith seeking understanding, and on the other hand, we cannot deny that understanding can also seek faith. Demmer holds that faith and reason in morality point to different levels of the same process. He states that "Moral norms cannot be immediately derived from faith or put in direct correlation with faith; the two belong to different levels of discourse, each characterized by its own epistemic status."[80] He takes the argument further to say that "Scripture cannot be conceived as a handbook of moral theology, nor does it present any ethical system that could provide a ready-made answer for every area of life."[81]

Demmer is clearly critical of autonomous ethics, but he also contributes in making more nuances in the debate. He states:

> Moreover, from a theological point of view the model of autonomous morality operates on an understanding of revelation that is extrinsic and essentially sanctions secular ethics with only a Christian blessing; in addition, by concentrating exclusively on normative ethics . . . it fails to provide an accurate account of reality of human action. Moral action is not immediately defined by the categorical norms it is supposed to fulfill but by the goals and ideals it pursues.[82]

He questions how autonomous ethics understands the role of faith and revelation in morality. He views autonomous ethics as understanding faith to be secondary in a human person. He is opposed to the idea of a dichotomy of faith and reason in moral reasoning. From Demmer's perspective, Christian faith is central in moral reasoning. There is no one time when a Christian is moral discerning with faith, and other times when reason is without faith. Clearly for Demmer, faith and reason are the essential elements of Christian morality.

79. Ibid., 24.
80. Ibid., 27.
81. Ibid.
82. Ibid., 24–25.

ii. Franz Böckle

From philosophical and theological perspectives, Böckle traces the historical development of the debate on moral autonomy. He presents the autonomous ethics debate as an outcome of a historical development on the understanding of human subject through the influence of Immanuel Kant's turn to the subject. He views moral autonomy as a result of a process of Copernican change, through Kant and the philosophers of idealism who followed him. Moral autonomy was "seen as a fundamental condition of the intelligible subject. As moral autonomy, it meant the binding of the subject to the law of rational self-determination."[83] According to Böckle, "Kant is the originator of this approach in which the autonomy of nature, in the sense in which this was understood by such philosophers as Leibniz and Wolff, was abandoned in favor of the autonomy of the subject."[84] But Böckle does not use the notion of autonomy in the same way as Kant.

In the Kantian perspective, autonomy came to mean "man's possibility and task, as a rational being, of determining himself and of being in harmony with a law that he has given himself. The greatest common denominator in this modern claim to autonomy is the rejection of every kind of alien determination or heteronomy."[85] Böckle points out that "Kant saw autonomy as the determination of the transcendental (intelligible) subject, binding him to order which could only be considered by intelligence."[86] The distinction between nature and reason and between the empirical and the intelligible subject was for him of decisive importance. In man both were present: he was at the same time nature and reason.[87]

Böckle views the theological justification of moral autonomy in the context of modern philosophy. The human being has become "the subject of history by claiming autonomy."[88] Thus the human subject "is responsible for himself and is ready to accept his historical and social destiny."[89] According to Böckle, this is the product of philosophical development, as it is clear, when he states that "Nicholas of Cusa, Descartes and Kant all stressed

---

83. Böckle, *Fundamental Moral Theology*, 32.
84. Ibid., 33.
85. Ibid., 31.
86. Ibid., 34.
87. Ibid., 33.
88. Ibid., 46.
89. Ibid.

subjectivity as the real condition of knowledge of man's being in the world and in this way provided a new impetus for scientific research into that being."[90] According to Böckle, the idea of moral autonomy is inseparable from the philosophical inquiry in the search for God. Moral autonomy is as a result of this search for God, and is therefore, inseparable from God. The realization of the human being as a subject led to an understanding of God in a way that was not there before. He states:

> The discovery of autonomous subjectivity was from the very beginning overshadowed by the discussion about the traditional metaphysical concept of God. The metaphysical attempt to think about God had been based on knowledge of natural objects (This was the *via eminentiae*) . . . when Philosophers returned to man and a criticism of his knowledge, they were unable to approach God from the departure point of natural objects.[91]

God is the ground of autonomous freedom. In this line of thinking, Böckle holds that finite freedom presupposes infinite freedom. Free human subjects point to the existence of an infinitely free absolute being. Hence, Böckle states that "God's creative activity transcendentally embraces the whole categorical evolution of the world, and man and the world are borne up by the sovereign and creative freedom of God in such a way that God himself is in no sense dependent on the world."[92] God becomes the ground of the possibility of human subjectivity. "It is on this foundation that man is able fully to affirm his existence as an autonomous, moral rational being."[93] In Böckle, we can conclude, that although he advocates autonomy in human morality, there is no way morality can be conceived and not think of God. When all is said and done, God makes human freedom possible.

MacNamara views Böckle as dealing with the moral autonomy debate from the perspective of Karl Rahner's theology. Notable here is MacNamara's assertion that Böckle uses Rahner's position of an inclusivist view of Christianity. MacNamara holds that "Böckle's position is that the only true morality—the only morality worth talking about—is Christian morality. All morality is in some sense Christian."[94] This position can be seen as an

90. Ibid., 50.

91. Ibid., 49.

92. Ibid, 54.

93. Ibid.

94. Ibid., 51. MacNamara refers to Böckle's *Fundamental Moral Theology*, 223. Böckle has argued that Christianity is the fulfillment of what it is to be a human being.

outcome of Rahner's theological view on an anonymous Christianity where the power of Christ is seen as active outside the Christian Churches. From a Rahnerian perspective:

> moral knowledge without revelation is not pure natural knowledge: it is always supernatural and supernaturally modified. What appears to be purely natural acts, i.e. acts performed by someone without faith, belong to the supernatural order.[95]

Böckle's understanding of moral autonomy is similar to that of Demmer. Like Demmer, for Böckle there is no separation of human reason or freedom from faith (God). In moral discernment, human beings exercise and participate in the God-given power of reason and freedom. Without denying the human nature in moral reasoning, Böckle has affirmed morality as theonomous.

Later, Bujo will also be seen to contribute in the resolving of the problem of the autonomous and faith ethics debate. Like Demmer and Böckle, Bujo holds that faith and reason should never be viewed as separate entities in Christian morality. But unlike, Demmer and Böckle, Bujo goes a step further to show that Christianity is always lived in a particular historical and cultural context that shapes moral reasoning.

D. Bujo's African Ethic and the Moral Autonomy-Faith Ethics Debate

The theology of Bujo draws heavily from the western development in moral theology. He uses the moral autonomy debate to show that African Christian ethics is not a sectarian ethic. Through the debate on moral autonomy, he shows that African ethics has to appeal to what is reasonable. He clearly makes the connection between African ethics and the moral autonomy debate when he states:

> [O]ne may not accuse African ethics of cutting itself off from the rest of the world, or of the ethnocentric fallacy: it intends to raise its voice in the universal dimension—but it does so in the plural. It may be true to say that the claim made by natural law refers "only to the minimum presuppositions" that all human persons,

---

95. MacNamara, *Faith and Ethics*, 54.

irrespective of the culture to which they belong, ought to acknowledge, since they are included in the ethical phenomenon.[96]

He categorically advocates the indispensability of faith and the cultural heritage in morality. Like Demmer, Bujo realizes that the attempt to separate faith from reason in morality is a false problem. He has insisted that:

> Faith is a continuous dialogue with the believer and consequently with the concrete milieu in which this believer lives. That supposes historicity and communicability, and thus brings about a mutual enrichment.[97]

In this dialogue of faith and the cultural milieu, the community plays an active role in shaping meaningful moral life. "This involves effective and active participation not only in the establishing of norms but also in the positing and the application of these norms."[98]

Although Bujo acknowledges the contribution of Auer in the moral autonomy debate, his contribution goes beyond Auer. He strongly notes:

> Without Alfons Auer, the discussion of autonomous moral theology would be unthinkable. His book *Autonome Moral und christlicher Glaube*, first published in 1971, generated a worldwide debate within Catholic moral theology. Even the moral encyclical *Veritatis Splendor*, which intends to offer a corrective to Auer's position, cannot escape his influence.[99]

By locating moral reasoning in a cultural context, Bujo distinguishes himself from Auer. As it was seen previously in this work, Auer emphasized the *ratio* in the moral process.

Like Schüller, Bujo acknowledges the illumination of reason by faith in moral reasoning. He affirms the capacity of human reason to realize moral norms. It is in this context of examining the role of reason in the making of moral norms that Bujo states the following:

> Is there a revealed moral theology, such that the church alone can claim to have the truth at its disposal and to declare and confirm universal moral principles on the basis of an essence of the human person? But not all ethical wisdom that proceeds from human nature is the exclusive inheritance of the Catholic Church;

96. Bujo, *Foundations of an African Ethic*, 20.

97. Bujo, "Can Morality Be Christian in Africa?," 10.

98. Bujo, *Foundations of an African Ethic*, 24.

99. Ibid., 76.

the proponents of autonomous moral theology point out here that a "baptized" reason does not automatically add to ethical knowledge. Human reason is derived from creation, which includes all human persons without distinction, believers and unbelievers, Catholics and non-Catholics.[100]

Evidently Bujo, like the proponents of an autonomous ethics in the context of faith, follows the natural law approach. In the theology of Bujo, the human being is created in the image and likeness of God. Bujo uses the natural moral law, as developed by St. Thomas Aquinas who viewed the natural law as the participation by human beings in the eternal reason (law) of God.

Bujo maintains that the church cannot claim absolute authority in teaching based on natural law. Natural law reasoning is available to both believers and unbelievers of the Christian faith. He uses St. Thomas Aquinas's idea that human likeness to God makes the human person an ethical subject.[101] Hence, Bujo states:

> The proponents of autonomous moral theology "in the Christian context" argue here that the church's magisterium can no longer make the same claim to competence in the field of natural law as Pius XII (a claim confirmed subsequently in *Humanae vitae*). This field is accessible to reason, and the church should not disqualify the human person from making his own interpretation of the natural ethical laws, based on the *ratio*.[102]

Bujo also agrees with Fuchs on the understanding of moral autonomy. Fuchs also emphasizes the role of human reasoning in morality. He has written: "The Christian's act of faith is the human person's act of faith and is therefore always at the same time an act of human morality, the act of faith of the human person who is continually realizing himself ethically."[103] This does not mean that Fuchs denies the role of faith in the making of moral norms, but he categorically shows that it is the human person who makes moral norms possible. However, Fuchs comes close to separating reason and faith in the discernment of moral norms. We cannot separate Christian

---

100. Ibid., 77. Bujo does not deny the role of faith in moral reasoning. What he affirms is that reason is indispensable in the realization of morality. Elsewhere he has stated: "[A]n African Christocentric ethic does not of course exclude rational reflection; but to work out a theological discourse, rational reflection must be in continuous dialogue with the propositions of faith" (*African Theology in Its Social Context*, 91).

101. Bujo, *Foundations of an African Ethic*, 78.

102. Ibid.

103. Ibid. See also Fuchs, "Is There a Distinctively Christian Morality?," 121.

faith from human reasoning in the realization of morality. Alfons Auer is perhaps even less ambiguous on this point: the Christian faith exercises an integrative, challenging, and critical function vis-à-vis the "world ethos."[104]

Bujo understands moral autonomy in the sense that "human beings by reason of their intelligence can interpret the happenings they are faced with, and arrange their own moral life."[105] He argues that autonomy is:

> the methodic independence of moral reason and . . . the finality that the human person possesses in itself . . . The conjunction of the two principles *secundum rationem agere* and *secundum personam agere*. In such an autonomy there is no collision with the theonomy which gives it precisely its foundation and consistence.[106]

He is of the opinion that his work is "an attempt to demonstrate that autonomy of ethics is not a mere philosophical or theological construction, but the very exigency of a genuinely Christian faith."[107]

Categorically, Bujo presents autonomy from the perspective that human beings were created in the image and likeness of God. It is in the context of understanding human being as created in the image and likeness of God that Bujo says that there is "only one truly mortal sin which God is unable to forgive, namely the sin against the 'humanization' of humankind."[108] Autonomous ethics recognizes the dignity that God instilled in the human person. Bujo states:

> the human autonomy constituted by God's image in him/her, can never contradict the Creator's autonomy . . . The autonomy that Christian and Catholic moral theology preaches is a theonomous autonomy. This does not mean that it can always explicitly appeal to this theonomous dimension. In ethical activity not only the non-baptized but even the Christian will posit moral acts, engage in political, social and other actions without thinking explicitly of God. But the conviction of God's presence is always there, at least in an athematic way, since there is no way of eclipsing God's

---

104. Bujo, *Foundations of an African Ethic*, 78. Bujo makes reference to Auer, *Autonome Moral*, 189–97.

105. Bujo, *African Christian Morality at the Age of Inculturation*, 16.

106. Ibid.

107. Ibid. 36.

108. Ibid., 65.

transcendent activity which has as its aim to make us ever more truly human.[109]

Human nature is the result of God's creation. It is impossible to pinpoint when a human person is acting from faith and when acting from a natural way. The human person is integrally whole, body and spirit. Grace and nature are not opposed to each other—Grace elevates nature. From an autonomous perspective, "Christian morality can never be conceived as a compartment morality with a first level of natural efforts and an additional Christian event forming an upper layer."[110] Hence, Bujo holds that in moral theology faith and reason are inseparable. A human being is whole only when viewed from the perspective of faith and reason. Therefore, the human being as the subject makes morality possible and moral autonomy in Christian ethics should always be conceived in a faith context.

Conclusion

Autonomous ethics is presented here as relevant in understanding Christian morality as human morality. Theology, and especially moral theology, cannot afford to ignore an understanding of what it means to be human. Contemporary theology has realized that any theological study has to proceed from an understanding of the human being. The starting point in theology is not from "above," that is, not from beyond human existence. However, there should be an awareness of the role of faith in Christian morality, and a realization that it is the human person endowed with reason and faith that is the subject in moral discernment. Our understanding of our human nature determines how we respond to the call by God and its ethical implications.

A "faith-ethics" that holds Christian morality is revealed morality, and ignores an understanding of human capacity for realizing what is morally right or wrong would hit a dead-end. There has to be a human person who receives revelation, and consequently responds to the God who calls. Christians believe in a personal God who reveals himself personally, and requires a personal response from human beings. The Sacred Scripture, in Judeo-Christian tradition, is understood as God's revelation. However, Scripture cannot be viewed as a direct source of moral norms. There is need for interpretation. Furthermore, there is more tension in Sacred Scripture

109. Ibid., 19–20.
110. Ibid., 36.

than the autonomy and faith ethics debates acknowledges. For instance, Scripture supports mass murder of enemy tribes (cf. 1 Sam 15, the book of Joshua, Numbers 31, and Deuteronomy 20), and gives a father the right to sell his daughter into slavery (Exod 21:7). The New Testament assumes the morality of slavery (cf. St. Paul's letter to Philemon). This was assumed to be in accord with "natural" law.

Nevertheless, the autonomy debate with its emphasis on the human element of morality provides a method through which one can concretely analyze the reasonableness of Christian morality. The theory of autonomous ethics does not deny the role that faith in God plays in Christian ethics. It begins from a realization that a human being is a moral subject who is capable of responding to the call to Christian life by Christ. Moral autonomy is therefore an affirmation that it is impossible to have Christian ethics without an affirmation of human subjectivity. Autonomous ethics recognizes that the moral precepts realized through Christian faith appeal also to human reason. One cannot separate what contributes to human flourishing from what is genuinely Christian. It is from this perspective that Bujo connects an African ethics with the debate on moral autonomy in the West. An African Christian ethics should be concerned with what is genuinely human, just as the debate on moral autonomy realizes how irreplaceable to ethics is a sound understanding of human subjectivity.

Finally, it is my view that in Christian ethics there should be no separation between faith and reason. We cannot say there are times a human being is making moral discernment with faith alone, and other times when it is by reason alone. Christianity should be understood as presenting an integral understanding of human being. Created by God, human reason is a way of realizing the true meaning of human existence in the world. Reason should not be viewed as opposed to faith.

6

Veritatis Splendor as a Response to Renewal in Moral Theology

TO UNDERSTAND THE ENCYCLICAL *Veritatis Splendor*, one needs to read it in the context of the renewal of moral theology. More specifically, the encyclical is a response to the various theological developments in Roman Catholic moral theology since Vatican II. The issues addressed in the encyclical include, among others, the biblical foundation of Christian morality, the criticism of autonomous ethics, relativism, teleology, and proportionalism. The encyclical is viewed here as proposing an ethics of faith in opposition to the contemporary emphasis on moral autonomy. Some moral theologians have emphasized the autonomous nature of Christian morality. The encyclical responds to those theologians who, according to Pope John Paul II, have given a prominent place to reason in moral theology at the expense of faith and revelation. Some theologians also responded to the criticism leveled by the encyclical by insisting that no theologian has advocated the separation of faith or revelation from reason. In light of the diverse views in moral theology today, this work presents a critical reading of the encyclical and also explores the responses from various theologians to the encyclical.

This chapter begins by presenting a general overview of the encyclical which is followed by a critical analysis of the various issues mentioned or condemned by the encyclical. The evaluation of the responses of various theologians helps in the understanding of the theological environment in which the encyclical was received. Theological responses critical of the encyclical include those by European and American theologians such as

Louis Janssens, Richard McCormick, Charles Curran, William Spohn, and Bénézet Bujo who is an African theologian. However, some theologians and philosophers like Livio Melina, Germain Grisez, and John Finnis, will be seen as responding in support of the encyclical. These theologians and philosophers who support the encyclical view the condemnation of relativism and other theological trends they see as contrary to the revealed morality in the gospel as long overdue. On the other hand, those theologians critical of the encyclical, view it as somehow misunderstanding their work or as taking the side of one theological system, namely the proponents of faith ethics. Further, I argue that critically analyzing what the various theologians have to say on *Veritatis Splendor* helps in understanding the encyclical as well as the broader theological context addressed by the encyclical.

Part One: General Theological Context and Overview of the Encyclical *Veritatis Splendor*

The encyclical *Veritatis Splendor* by John Paul II deals with general moral theological issues. A good understanding of this encyclical requires an understanding of the theological context into which it evolved and into which it was received. This makes it possible to locate and understand the moral theological issues dealt with in the encyclical.

1. Veritatis Splendor *as a Response to the Renewal of Moral Theology*

Veritatis Splendor addresses the issues called for in the renewal of moral theology in the Second Vatican Council.[1] Previously in this work, I analyzed the renewal of moral theology as characterized by the use of Sacred Scripture, the understanding of the nature of Christian ethics as Christocentric, the relevance of history in moral theology, the integral nature of human activity, and the natural moral law, among other characteristics. The theological debates that have taken place after Vatican II have reflected how the renewal of moral theology has been taking place in the Roman Catholic Church. An example of these debates is the autonomous ethics debate in a faith context, and also the debate on the proportionalist and teleological nature of human action.

---

1. Vatican Council II, *Optatam Totius*, no. 16. See also Vidal, "Die 'Encyclical Veritatis Splendor' und der Weltkatechismus," 244–70.

Veritatis Splendor can therefore be said to have come about as a church response or reaction to developments in moral theology. Joseph Selling points out that:

> In the summer of 1987, John Paul II came to the decision that there was a need to address not simply the current debates that were taking place within the public forum and the church community itself, but the very foundations of morality as a theological discipline. He announced that he would write an encyclical on the topic because he felt that those foundations were being undermined by certain contemporary theories. It took six years, and if rumors could be believed several drafts, for this encyclical to be published. In it one finds not only the reflective words of the bishop of Rome but evidently as well the counter-(r) evolutionary speculations of theorists representing the more traditional school of Christian ethics.[2]

From the above, the encyclical appears to have been a response to the needs in contemporary theology, as perceived by Pope John Paul II. Besides the issues about which the encyclical is critical, the general idea of reminding theologians to avoid the various extremes that have or can come up in their work is a laudable concern. However, the reality of theological diversity in the Church or even outside the Church is a fact that no one can deny. How to embrace diversity and make good use of it in Christian ethics is a task all theologians should embrace wholeheartedly.[3]

Studying the theology of Bénézet Bujo, one cannot avoid critically studying what *Veritatis Splendor* has to say about the state of moral theology after Vatican II. Bujo deals with issues related with the renewal of moral theology. An example of the issues characterizing the renewal of moral theology, and realized in the theology of Bujo, include the use of sacred scripture, a historically conscious method, and the natural moral law tradition. Bujo locates African Christian theology in the context of the renewal

---

2. Selling, "The Context and the Arguments," 22.

3. There is no single way to categorize contemporary moral theology. Many theologians have shown that diversity is the true nature of moral theology today. For example, James Bresnahan describes the contemporary situation in ethics as follows: "This experience of our freedom as power which produces moral dilemma has precipitated a crisis in contemporary ethics. Ethical reflection is supposed to help us understand and solve moral dilemmas. Yet today ethics, including natural-law thinking in ethics, does not seem able to produce readily understandable, or at least widely acceptable, solutions to the dilemmas we face" (Bresnahan, "An Ethics of Faith," 171).

of moral theology after Vatican II. Therefore, African moral theology also falls under the trends in theology addressed by *Veritatis Splendor*.

2. *General Concerns in the Encyclical,* Veritatis Splendor[4]

It is therefore necessary to make an analysis and assessment of the main points considered in the encyclical, *Veritatis Splendor* (VS). I begin by making a critical exposition of the main points in the encyclical, and later on analyze what Bujo and other theologians have written on the encyclical. The task at hand here involves analyzing the theological issues raised, criticized or condemned by the encyclical. A consideration of the sources of *Veritatis Splendor* is also made.

The encyclical letter *Veritatis Splendor* was signed by John Paul II on August 6, 1993 and released the following October 5.[5] The encyclical is addressed to all the bishops of the Roman Catholic Church and concerns certain fundamental questions of the church's moral teaching (VS Introduction). Then the encyclical makes a statement on truth when it states that "The splendor of truth shines forth in all the works of creation and, in a special way, in man, created in the image and likeness of God (cf. Gen. 1:26)" (VS Introduction). Through its repeated reference to the truth, the encyclical shows its concern for truth in moral theology although it does not define what it means by "truth." *Veritatis Splendor* was brought about (or occasioned) by what it says is a concern for fundamental truths:

> Today, however, it seems *necessary to reflect on the whole of the Church's moral teaching,* with the precise goal of recalling certain fundamental truths of Catholic doctrine which, in the present circumstances, risk being distorted or denied . . . It is no longer a matter of limited and occasional dissent, but of an overall and systematic calling into question of traditional moral doctrine, on the basis of certain anthropological and ethical presuppositions (VS 4).

The preceding statement sums up what prompted the writing and issuing of the encyclical. However, the encyclical acknowledges a human capacity for knowledge but at the same time shows how this capacity is limited. Hence,

---

4. The edition used here of the *Veritatis Splendor* is the one by *Libreria Editrice Vaticana*.

5. McCormick, "Some Early Reactions to *Veritatis Splendor*," 481. McCormick refers to VS as published in the *Origins* 23 (1993) 297–334.

the Pope states that "Man's capacity to know the truth is also darkened, and his will to submit to it is weakened" (VS 1). If the capacity for truth in human beings is weakened, then there is need for a higher power to meet this deficiency. This seems to prepare the reader of the encyclical to consider the commandments and moral law, and ultimately, the need for grace and the role of the teaching authority of the Church's magisterium.

The encyclical was intended to correct errors in contemporary moral theology, and thereby make known the official teaching of the church on various issues. The pope states:

> The specific purpose of the present encyclical is this: to set forth, with regard to the problems being discussed, the principles of a moral teaching based upon Sacred Scripture and the living Apostolic Tradition, and at the same time to shed light on the presuppositions and consequences of the dissent which that teaching has met (VS 11).

The insistence on the importance of making use of Sacred Scripture and Tradition in moral theology is a positive point in the encyclical. Renewal in moral theology, as discussed previously, was characterized by the use of Sacred Scripture. The natural moral law tradition (although not mentioned in *Optatam Totius* 16) together with the Sacred Scriptures were important elements of the renewal of moral theology in the Roman Catholic Church.

Further, the encyclical makes an exploration of what has been going on in moral theology, and through this it makes a critical analysis on some of the controverted issues in moral theology. Acknowledging the call by Vatican II for renewal, the encyclical states:

> The Council also encouraged theologians, while respecting the methods and requirements of theological science, to look for a more appropriate way of communicating doctrine to the people of their time (VS 29).

The Pope indicates that not all developments in moral theology after the Council have been positive. The encyclical denounces most of what has been developing in moral theology as not in line with sound doctrine. Hence, the encyclical states:

> Also, an opinion is frequently heard which questions the intrinsic and unbreakable bond between faith and morality, as if membership in the Church and her internal unity were to be decided on

the basis of faith alone, while in the sphere of morality a pluralism of opinions and of kinds of behavior could be tolerated (VS 4).

The relationship between faith and morality is an issue that has generated different theological perspectives. Some theologians have come to hold that Christian ethics is totally unique because of faith in Christ, while others have maintained that Christian ethics is specifically human and therefore can be realized in a genuinely human ethics. This question on faith ethics and autonomous ethics has been discussed elsewhere in this work.

Among the theological issues considered in *Veritatis Splendor* include the use of Sacred Scripture, the role of the magisterium of the Church in moral theology, freedom and its relation to the truth, conscience, the relationship between faith and reason in morality, and the natural law. It is necessary to analyze these theological issues dealt with in the encyclical in a more specific way.

i. The use of Sacred Scripture

Vatican II recommended that morality should be nurtured by Sacred Scripture and tradition.[6] The encyclical, *Veritatis Splendor*, is commendable in its use of Scripture, and also its realization of the Christocentric nature of Christian morality.[7] It begins with the question of the young man in the gospel who asked Jesus: "Teacher, what good must I do . . ." (Matt 19:16; VS 7). The Pope takes this passage to show how faith in Christ affects the answer to the question about morality: "It is an essential and unavoidable question for the life of every man, for it is about the moral good which must be done, and about eternal life" (VS 8). The encyclical uses scripture to show the connection between grace and law in Christian moral life. The passage from Matthew is analyzed and directly applied to modern moral questions. The text is used as an example of Gospel morality, and to show the immutability of the teaching of Jesus on moral issues:

> If we therefore wish to go to the heart of the Gospels' moral teaching and grasp its profound and unchanging content, we must carefully inquire into the meaning of the question asked by the rich

6. *Optatam Totius*, 16.

7. In VS 5, the encyclical refers to *Dei Verbum*, 10, where the Second Vatican Council recommends that moral teaching should be based upon Sacred Scripture and the living Apostolic Tradition.

young man in the Gospel and, even more, the meaning of Jesus' reply, allowing ourselves to be guided by him (VS 8).

However, Sacred Scripture as presented in the encyclical is an important source of moral theology. Moral theology appeals to scripture and tradition. No theologian has denied the use of Scripture in Christian morality, but what theologians question is the method or the way to use Scripture in moral reasoning. *Veritatis Splendor*, in its use of Scripture, shows how indispensable the word of God is to moral reasoning.

The important thing to note is the encyclical's emphasis on the Word of God in the Bible, for it shows the character of moral theology after the Vatican Council II. This is true when the encyclical states: "Indeed, Sacred Scripture remains the living and fruitful source of the Church's moral doctrine" (VS 28). But it is also important to point out that no Catholic moral theologian can deny the relevance of Scripture in moral theology and yet remain a Catholic Christian moral theologian.

ii. The Teaching Role of the Magisterium

The encyclical defends the role of the church's magisterium as one of authentically interpreting the Word of God and proclaiming moral principles (VS 27).[8] In addition, the encyclical calls for the response of obedience to the magisterium of the church by theologians and other Roman Catholic Christians. Konrad Hilpert refers to this call for obedience in the encyclical when he states:

> The basic stance, which is prior to the fulfillment of the individual commandments, is obedience. There is hardly a document of the universal Church since Vatican II in which such clearly stressed obedience is demanded. In all, the concept appears almost thirty times and is thus demonstrated to be, besides "law," one of the most frequently used theological keywords of the encyclical.[9]

---

8. *Dei Verbum*, 10, points out that the magisterium of the church has a duty to "reverently preserve and faithfully expound" the word of God.

9. Hilpert, "Glanz der Wahrheit," 628. As stated in German: "Die Basishaltung, die der Erfüllung der einezelnen Gebote vorangestellt wird, ist der Gehorsam. Es dürfte kaum ein gesamtkirchliches Dokument seit dem II. Vatikanum geben, in dem so betont Gehorsam eingefordert wird; insgesamt kommt der Begriff fast dreißigmal vor und erweist sich damit neben 'Gesetz' als eines der am häufigsten gebrauchen theologischen Stichwörter der Enzyklika!"

The encyclical emphasizes the teaching role of the church magisterium. According to the encyclical, the magisterium provides authentic and absolute interpretations of the Word of God.[10] Because of this teaching authority in the Church, there is a call to obey moral principles as taught by the bishops and the Pope. However, the encyclical does not provide the method it applies in the realization of the moral norms from Sacred Scripture or tradition. The encyclical also does not show the interaction between the magisterium of the Church and moral theologians in the development of the moral teaching.[11]

The encyclical is intended to make known the teaching of the church on certain moral issues and as a result calls for assent from theologians to the church's moral teaching. Hence, the encyclical condemns some theological positions such as relativism, the denial of intrinsic evil, and proportionalism as contrary to the moral teachings of the church.

iii. Freedom

The encyclical expresses concern about moral theories that over-exalt human freedom. The encyclical's concern is: "Certain currents of modern thought have gone so far as to exalt freedom to such an extent that it becomes an absolute, which would then be the source of values" (VS 32). This concern on human freedom is valid. However, the encyclical does not deny human freedom but it shows that human freedom is coupled with

---

10. It is worth mentioning here Hoose's view that magisterial authority in the church varies depending on its link between revelation, fidelity to the lived faith of the church (tradition), and the teachings in question ("Authority in the Church," 113–14).

11. One can question whether the magisterium of the church is subject to a normal human learning and listening process. To understand the meaning of the magisterial tradition in the church, from which *Veritatis Splendor* has its source, Richard McCormick's views are helpful. McCormick describes how the contemporary understanding of the magisterium came about. He notes that since the 1830s the magisterium has been presented in a very juridical way, and this understanding reached its climax in the encyclical *Humani Generis* under Pius XII. He states: "The focus that went into its (magisterium) making . . . produced a notion of magisterium with the following three characteristics [emphasis mine]: (1) an undue distinction between the teaching and learning function in the Church, with a consequent unique emphasis on the right to teach—and relatively little on the duty to learn and the sources of learning in the Church; (2) an undue identification of the teaching function with a single group in the Church, the hierarchy; (3) an undue isolation of a single aspect of teaching, the judgmental, the decisive, the 'final word'" (McCormick, *The Critical Calling*, 19). See also the letter of sixty theologians of Quebec, "Lettre ouverte aux évêques du Québec," 14–15.

responsible moral action. There is an awareness in the encyclical that from a Christian perspective, God makes human freedom itself possible. The encyclical is critical of the tendency to view human freedom as absolute (this is a modern tendency), and thus denying the human dependency on God as the creator. However, to deny human freedom as a reality in human existence would also be a denial of the gift of God to humanity. Human freedom, made possible by God, should never be seen as standing in opposition to God. From the book of Genesis, human beings are made in the image and likeness of God (Gen 1:26–27).[12] For this reason, we can say that humans have a power of self-determination. When this power of self-determination is taken away, it is referred to as coercion or control by an external force, and thereby moral responsibility is excluded. A major issue arising from *Veritatis Splendor* is: how do freedom of conscience and external authority interact in human conduct? It is good to emphasize that to be a moral agent, a human being must have the freedom of choice.

The encyclical moves on to show the intimate connection between freedom and truth. It is opposed to what it calls some tendencies of separating freedom and truth. "Despite their variety, these tendencies are at one in lessening or even denying the dependence of freedom on truth" (VS 34). The Pope does not tell us who is separating freedom from truth, but emphasizes the adherence to the truth.[13] *Veritatis Splendor* expresses the magisterium's concern, notably the implication of over-emphasizing individual freedom in moral theology at the expense of the social or communal life in Christian living. Basically, human freedom should always be geared toward the pursuit of truth.

Further, the encyclical connects truth to the moral law. The encyclical also expresses disappointment with some theologians for separating freedom from the law. The pope has stated:

> The alleged conflict between freedom and law is forcefully brought
> up once again today with regard to the natural law, and particu-
> larly with regard to nature. Debates about nature and freedom

12. Referring to GS 24, and VS 13, presents the commandment of love of neighbor as the "precise expression of the singular dignity of the human person."

13. VS 34 calls for people to seek the truth and adhere to it. Reference here is made to Second Vatican Council, *Dignitatis Humanae* (Declaration on Religious Freedom), 2, which declares in part: "The Council further declares that the right to religious freedom is based on the very dignity of the human person as known through the revealed word of God and by reason itself. This right of the human person to religious freedom must be given such recognition in the constitutional order of society as will make it a civil right."

have always marked the history of moral reflection; they grew especially heated at the time of the Renaissance and the Reformation . . . The penchant for empirical observation, the procedures of scientific objectification, technological progress and certain forms of liberalism have led to these two terms being set in opposition, as if a dialectic, if not absolute conflict, between freedom and nature were characteristic of the structure of human history . . . In this context even moral facts, despite their specificity, are frequently treated as if they were statistically verifiable data, patterns of behavior which can be subject to observation or explained exclusively in categories of psychosocial processes (VS 46).

Freedom has always to do with self-determination of an individual person, that is, the ability to pursue the good. This self-determination includes realization of the right or the true moral norms. On the other hand, the separation of freedom from truth spells disaster in morality. The separation of truth and freedom in morality would mean a contradiction because freedom implies a capacity for knowing what is right and what is wrong. Freedom is coupled with responsibility. To act responsibly, a human person is entitled to seek knowledge. Freedom and knowledge are inseparable in responsible moral action. "The Pope is concerned that freedom uncoupled from truth will lead to a 'moral autonomy' (VS 35). Such a moral autonomy, it is feared would not only have an 'absolute sovereignty' but would also deny the existence of a Divine Revelation that contains 'a specific and determined moral content' which is 'universally valid and permanent'" (VS 37).[14] Moral autonomy is concerned with the fact that an individual human being has the capacity of moral determination. Autonomous ethics, as understood in this work, advocates the possibility of realization of morality by human beings through reason. Moral norms are important, but without the moral agent who acts from the heart, they remain in a book in a distant library or archive. Basically, human beings' capacity for knowledge and freedom of choice is the foundation of moral action.

Nonetheless, *Veritatis Splendor* holds that human beings are free, but it connects this freedom with the commandments: "The man is certainly free, inasmuch as he can understand and accept God's commands" (VS 35).[15] The Pope questions the absolutization of human freedom, but on the other

14. Donfried, "The Use of Scripture in Veritatis Splendor," 48.

15. It should be noted here that the encyclical refers to Thomas Aquinas on the new law as the grace of the Holy Spirit given through faith in Christ (*Summa Theologiae*, I-II, q. 106, a. 1).

hand, it is questionable whether there would be individual moral respon-sibility without the individual having the capacity for self-determination. The pope says, "These doctrines would grant to individuals or social groups the right to determine what is good or evil" (VS 35). The question that would remain is who decides for whom what is right or wrong. It is true to say that even the commandments of God or Sacred Scripture do not address all moral dilemmas people find themselves in, not to mention cir-cumstances and all the concrete factors that go into any decision making. Human freedom is a determinant factor in morality.

iv. Conscience

In human action is expressed the human capacity for self-determination. Freedom of conscience makes responsible human action possible.[16] The reality of conscience and freedom are understandable only when viewed as constitutive of human moral reasoning and action. On human conscience, the encyclical expresses the following concern: "The individual conscience is accorded the status of a supreme tribunal of moral judgment which hands down categorical and infallible decisions about good and evil" (VS 32), and "Such an outlook is quite congenial to an individualist ethic, wherein each individual is faced with his own truth, different from the truth of others. Taken to its extreme consequences, this individualism leads to a denial of the very idea of human nature" (VS 32). And then, an individualist ethics would "end up, if not with an outright denial of universal human values, at least with a relativistic conception of morality" (VS 33). The encyclical does not deny the reality of freedom of conscience: what it emphasizes is that Christian morality has a communal or social dimension, and that Christian morality is realized through divine revelation. An individual conscience can be erroneous, and therefore, individual human beings have a respon-sibility to the formation of their consciences by seeking to overcome igno-rance by knowledge.[17]

For the encyclical, formation of conscience is realized through listening to the word of God and the teaching tradition of the Church's

16. GS 17 states: "Since human freedom has been weakened by sin it is only by the help of God's grace that man can give his actions their full and proper relationship to God. Before the judgment seat of God an account of his own life will be rendered to each one according as he has done either good or evil."

17. On the human responsibility to seek the truth always, VS refers to Second Vatican Council, *Dignitatis Humanae* (Declaration on Religious Freedom), 2.

magisterium. Basically, the formation of conscience is an individual and communal responsibility. Traditionally in the Roman Catholic Church, the formation of conscience has always been given a central place in the lives of the Christian faithful. Formation of conscience does not mean coercion but some sort of moral education or spiritual growth. Formation of conscience is a task that shows an individual person's responsibility to conduct the affairs of one's life.

The encyclical's warning against relativism and individualism is a valid concern. The communal or social nature of human beings is indispensable. Individuality and community are correlative terms. You cannot have one without the other. An ethic that emphasizes individuality and ignores the community dimension of morality is defective. The same can be said of a communal ethic that ignores the individual aspect of morality. Morality is made possible by the personal dimension of human beings which in turn is realized in the social perspective. Without doubt, there is the subjective and the objective pole in morality. An individual Christian is always a member of a community of faith.

v. The relationship between Faith and Reason in Morality

The encyclical supports the faith-ethics position and is opposed to an autonomous ethics. The Pope emphasizes the role of faith in ethical matters and shows that reason alone is prone to error (VS 36). *Veritatis Splendor* acknowledges the desire to foster dialogue in modern culture, where human rational nature is emphasized to show the communicable nature of Christian moral norms.

However, *Veritatis Splendor* clarifies that Christian morality is not solely based on human reason, but that it has its source in divine revelation (VS 36). In the theological work of the advocates of an autonomous ethics, faith and reason go hand in hand in Christian moral reasoning. But some advocates of an autonomous ethics have also emphasized reason in such a way that they have left faith in the periphery of Christian morals.

In an explicit way, the encyclical condemns the advocates of an "erroneous concept of autonomy" (VS 37).[18] Alternatively, the encyclical shows that "a rightful autonomy is due to every man, as well as to the human

18. Alfons Auer sparked the debate on moral autonomy in the Roman Catholic Church through his book, *Autonome Moral und christlicher Glaube.*

community"(VS 38).[19] The encyclical uses Vatican II to show that what it presents is a proper understanding of autonomy: "[T]he council warns against a false concept of the autonomy of earthly realities, one which would maintain that created things are not dependent on God and that man can use them without reference to their creator" (VS 39).[20] Further, Pope John Paul II argues that "obedience to God is not, as some would believe, a heteronomy, as if the moral life were subject to the will of something all-powerful, absolute, extraneous to man and intolerant of his freedom" (VS 41). The encyclical holds that "if a heteronomy of morality were to mean a denial of man's self-determination or imposition of norms unrelated to his good, this would be in contradiction to the Revelation of the Covenant and of the redemptive Incarnation" (VS 41). In the preceding, the encyclical seems to be basing itself on a transcendental or an existential premise where God is viewed as embodying the true realization of human existence as subject. In self-determination, human beings exercise the capacity given by God at creation, and therefore human freedom should be understood as made possible by God. However, the advocates of an autonomous ethics also share with the encyclical the understanding that the capacity of human self-determination makes morality possible. Nonetheless, it should be clarified that the encyclical is critical of the proponents of an autonomous ethics for presenting Christian morality as based on human freedom and not adequately showing the role played by divine revelation.

Connected with the debate about autonomous and faith ethics are the proponents of the distinction between an ethical order and an order of salvation.[21] According to the encyclical, there is no separation between an ethical order and an order of salvation. The Pope's view is that Christian moral life should be identified with the journey of salvation. Evidently, the encyclical condemns the advocates of separation between an ethical order and order of salvation. It raises questions on the separation of the ethical order from the order of salvation. The Pope holds that the separation of an ethical order and an order of salvation is erroneous and contrary to Catholic doctrine. This separation is viewed by the Pope as a denial that there exists "in Divine Revelation, a specific and determined moral content, uni-

19. The Pope also acknowledges that the rational nature of human beings makes it possible to have understandable and communicable moral norms (VS 36). Reference is made here to GS 40 and 43. See also Thomas Aquinas, *Summa Theologiae*, I-II, q. 71, a. 6.

20. See GS 36.

21. See Fuchs, "Moral Truths—Truths of Salvation?," 48–67.

versally valid and permanent" (VS 37). The separation of an ethical order from the order of salvation, further limits the word of God to proposing an exhortation, a generic paranesis, while "the autonomous reason alone would then have the task of completing with normative directives which are truly 'objective,' that is, adapted to the concrete historical situation" (VS 37).[22] The separation of an ethical order and an order of salvation, according to the encyclical, is a misunderstanding of morality as understood in the Roman Catholic Tradition.

vi. Natural Moral Law

The interpretation of the natural moral law has shaped much of moral theology after Vatican II. The condemnation of moral autonomy and some contemporary moral theological developments, in *Veritatis Splendor*, is based on an interpretation of the natural law.[23] The Pope writes: "[T]he natural law is nothing other than the light of understanding infused in us by God, whereby we understand what must be done and what must be avoided. God gave this light and this law to man at creation" (VS 40). However, there are numerous interpretations on the meaning of the natural moral law.[24] The use of the natural moral law in the encyclical connects it to the moral theological debate on the renewal of moral theology coming after the Second Vatican Council. In regard to renewal moral theologians, the encyclical states:

> As a result, some ethicists, professionally engaged in the study of human realities and behavior, can be tempted to take as the

22. Note the encyclical does not make any reference in footnote or otherwise, either from Vatican II or other papal encyclicals, when it condemns the separation of an ethical order from an order of salvation.

23. The encyclical understands the natural law as it is presented by Thomas Aquinas. In VS 12, the pope refers to *Summa Theologie*, I-II, q. 91, a. 2. The encyclical also makes reference to the Second Vatican Ecumenical Council, GS 41.

24. For an evaluation of *Veritatis Splendor* and the natural law, see Lash, "Crisis and Tradition in Veritatis Splendor," 22–28. Lash positively evaluates the encyclical's use of natural law as follows: "Weaving in Aquinas' classic definition of 'natural law' as nothing other than the light of understanding infused in us by God, whereby we understand what must be done and what must be avoided, and presenting the commandments as not a 'minimum limit' but rather as 'the first necessary step on the journey towards freedom,' the Pope integrates precepts and counsels into a single story of the human journey, enabled, drawn and coaxed by God, through holiness towards eternal life" (23). See also the article by Smith, "Natural Law and Personalism in Veritatis Splendor," 67–84.

standard for their discipline and even for its operative norms the results of statistical study of concrete human behavior patterns and the opinions about morality encountered in the majority of people (VS 46).

Moral theology cannot ignore developments in other fields of human and social sciences. However, as the encyclical cautions (VS 46), Christian morality should not be limited to "statistical study of concrete human behavior," but it should also focus on human self-realization in God. However, the encyclical does not explicitly rule out the necessity of research in moral theology. Besides Sacred Scripture and tradition, moral theology makes use of the findings of social and human sciences. Moral theology after Vatican II has realized that it has a wider audience, and therefore it needs methods that present Christian morality as applicable to all human beings. Natural moral law has contributed in a tremendous way by presenting Christian morality, not as a sectarian ethic, but one that is human and Christian at the same time. All people share reason, and therefore, moral theologians appealing to reason demonstrate the communicable nature of Christian morality, and reason also safeguard it from sectarianism. The natural moral law tradition is one of the major ways that Christian morality has been presented as reasonable and as having something to offer to all people. A shared humanity is a basis for shared values and goals.

vii. The relation between Morality and Law in *Veritatis Splendor*

The encyclical presents Christian morality is to be understood in the context of obedience to the law or the commandments. To show the connection between morality and law, the Pope appeals to the text in the gospel of Matthew (19:16–26). This text is used by the encyclical to show that for one to be saved, observance of the commandments is vital. Further, the encyclical uses the same gospel passage to show the intricate relationship between morality and law. The encyclical, therefore, understands morality in terms of obedience to the law.[25]

Nevertheless, the encyclical can be understood in a way that equates Christian morality with obedience to the commandments of God.

25. See O'Connell, *Principles for a Catholic Morality*. O'Connell states: "The law of the Spirit, the law of the Christian's new being, is an inner law. It is not a law imposed by God on unwilling humankind. Rather, it is, if we may put it this way, the result of intimate communication between the heart of a loving God and the heart of the believing human person" (146).

According to the encyclical, God's will is knowable through the commandments. "The commandments thus represent the basic condition for love of neighbor; at the same time they are the proof of that love. They are the first necessary step on the journey towards freedom" (VS 13). According to the encyclical, God has already given what human beings need to know about morality through his commandments. Thus, the Pope writes: "Man's genuine moral autonomy in no way means the rejection but rather the acceptance of the moral law, of God's command: "The Lord God gave this command to the man . . . (Gen. 2:16)" (VS 41).

Considering the encyclical's emphasis on the commandments and the moral law, one cannot avoid to be concerned whether the encyclical is recommending a return to the moral theology before the renewal. Before the renewal, manuals of moral theology had a legalistic view of morality. A typical example of moral theology's emphasis on law, before the renewal, would be Bernard Häring's "Law of Christ," but this is markedly different from his "Free and Faithful in Christ" which was written after Vatican II.[26] There is a notable difference between the manuals before and those after Vatican II. Before the renewal, most of the manuals of moral theology laid emphasis on the moral law and not the human person who performed a particular act. A moral act was determined to be good or bad depending on whether a moral law had been fulfilled or broken. Manuals had as their primary focus the formation of future priests who would hear confessions. They were meant to help confessors understand the weight of the sins, which were confessed in kind and number, in order to give the right penance. Is the encyclical recommending a return to manualist moral theology in its emphasis of the law? Realistically, the time of the manuals is past and pluralism in theology is a reality that has taken root in contemporary theology. There is no one way or method in the study of moral theology.

Consequently, the commandments are just one aspect of the Christian life. In a more concrete way, Christianity is not a religion of just meeting some requirements. Jesus invited his followers to go beyond the commandments. Christianity should not just emphasize the letter of the law but also the spirit of the law. The encyclical emphasizes the commandments: "Jesus refers to the two commandments of love of God and love of neighbor (cf. LK. 10:25–27), and reminds him that only by observing them will he have eternal life: "Do this, and you will live" (LK. 10:28)" (VS 14). Undeniably, the motivation in Christian living is the love of God and neighbor. But to

26. Häring, *Free and Faithful in Christ*. Also by Häring, *The Law of Christ*, 3 vols.

reduce morality to the observance of the law (commandments) leads to a minimalist ethics of requirements. Therefore, understanding the relationship between God and humanity as love shows the depths and boundlessness of Christian living. Commandments may not have answers to some situations Christians might find themselves in, but love always acts as a guide to proper decisions and actions.

It is notable that the encyclical raises important theological issues. The Pope emphasizes the role of Sacred Scripture as the source of moral theology. Although it is not my concern here, the near-equation of revelation and Scripture's teaching is problematic. There are very concrete commands in Scripture to conquer the Promised Land and drive out and kill its inhabitants (cf. Deuteronomy 20 and Numbers 31). These were very influential in the early and late medieval Christian practice as evidenced in the Crusades.[27] Considering all the tension in the Bible can we say there is a revealed morality? Nevertheless, the encyclical is not the final word but it should be seen as a call to engage further in the moral theological debate in the contemporary world. In the encyclical, it is undeniable that many contemporary moral theologica! positions that have been developing since the renewal are condemned or questioned. Hence, it is necessary to analyze the responses of various theologians to the issues dealt with in the encyclical.

Part Two: Theological Response to *Veritatis Splendor*

Having analyzed the various issues addressed in the encyclical, *Veritatis Splendor*, in the previous section, I proceed here with a study of the various theological responses to the encyclical. The respondents to the encyclical either support or oppose it. After presenting Bujo's response to the encyclical, I present the arguments of the theologians who support the encyclical and later the theologians who are opposed to the encyclical.

---

27. Cf. Lefebure, *Revelation, the Religions, and Violence*. Lefebure writes: "The manifold ways that interpretations of revelation have supported violence demand a critical appropriation of the Scriptures and the Christian tradition itself" (2).

1. Bujo's Critical Analysis of Veritatis Splendor

Bujo, like Louis Janssens[28] and others, has analyzed the encyclical from the perspective of Thomas Aquinas's teaching on the natural law.[29] The pope also uses Aquinas in the encyclical (VS).[30] In its use of Aquinas, the encyclical differs from other theological interpretations or readings of Aquinas. As in Janssens and McCormick, Bujo also uses Aquinas's theology to show how *Veritatis Splendor* differs from the position of Aquinas. The responses to the encyclical by Janssens and McCormick are treated in the next section.

Bujo's theology is among the theological positions questioned by the encyclical, *Veritatis Splendor*. Previously, I presented Bujo's view of moral autonomy in an African perspective. Bujo's theology is concerned with a concrete consideration of moral issues. He is critical of theological perspectives that tend to generalize moral issues without due consideration of particular circumstances as well as cultural and historical background. Even without mention, Bujo's theology comes into direct confrontation with *Veritatis Splendor* where truth, freedom, and moral norms appear to be predetermined issues by the moral magisterium of the Church. Bujo's perspective is clear when he writes the following:

> Some critics of the autonomous moral theology have suggested the need for an ethics of faith. As the entire discussion in the 1970s showed, the accusation made by these critics missed the point, since the proponents of an autonomous moral theology did not in the least deny the *proprium christianum* in moral theology; their concern was only to avoid a fundamentalistic perspective, a "fallacy of faith" in moral theology. The encyclical *Veritatis Splendor* likewise gives the impression of having misunderstood the fundamental thesis of the autonomous moral theology which it criticizes.[31]

Bujo advocates an autonomous ethics in the context of faith. He views the autonomous ethics debate as making a positive contribution to the realization of moral theology. He views the autonomous ethics debate as a development in the teaching on the natural moral law. He holds that the adherents of the autonomous ethics debate in no way support the separation

28. See Janssens, "Teleology and Proportionality," 99–113.

29. On Thomas Aquinas's teaching on natural law, see *Summa Theologiae* ST I-II, Q. 90 to Q. 94.

30. See VS 36, where the encyclical refers to St. Thomas Aquinas, ST I-II, q. 71, a. 6.

31. Bujo, *Foundations of African Ethic*, 80.

of faith and reason in moral discernment. Therefore, he views the encyclical as exaggerating the moral autonomy position when the encyclical says that they (autonomous ethicians) remove faith in morality or separate freedom from truth. He states:

> As for its critique of autonomy, one sometimes has the impression that the encyclical exaggerates its points and thereby misses the mark. Few moral theologians would agree that there are tendencies which "despite their variety are at one in lessening or even denying *the dependence of freedom on truth*" (VS 34).[32]

Further, Bujo also questions whether "there are actually any Catholic moral theologians who deny the fact that the natural moral law has God as its author, and that man, by the use of reason, participates in the eternal law, which it is not for him to establish" (VS 36).[33] Hence the general conclusion or feeling of many moral theologians, according to Bujo is as follows:

> The proponents of autonomous moral theology see in this critique more than a simple misunderstanding but rather an unjust criticism when the encyclical says: "Hence obedience to God is not, as some would believe, a heteronomy as if the moral life were subject to the will of something all-powerful, absolute, extraneous to man and intolerant of his freedom" (VS 41).[34]

Fundamentally, according to Bujo, the advocates of autonomous ethics were strongly influenced by St. Thomas Aquinas's view that "the human person is *capax Dei*." Basing himself on Aquinas's understanding of the nature of the human person, Bujo holds that "This 'capacity for God' enables the human person to transcend himself and discover the ultimate ground of his being transcendentally in God."[35] *Capax Dei* makes it possible for human beings to be involved in a "dynamic process in which he expresses his orientation to God."[36] In being morally responsible, human beings realize their true nature created by God. This perspective is based on the understanding of the human person as created in the image and likeness of God. Bujo's view on human morality has its source in the Bible, where the image of God is realized to be present in all human beings. Bujo sums this up when

---

32. Ibid., 81
33. Ibid.
34. Ibid.
35. Ibid.
36. Ibid., 82.

he writes that "one can become like God only by acting freely, autonomously, and creatively; this does not in any way abolish the theonomy."[37] Human reason has a mandate to explore the truths in the world, including ethical truths. Bujo understands moral autonomy in the context of the realization of the splendor of creation in human beings. Notable in the theory of moral autonomy is the recognition of the human power of self-determination and creativity. God, who is the creator of human beings and all that exists, makes human freedom possible. Hence, moral autonomy cannot denounce the involvement of God in human ethics.

However, Bujo does not disagree with the encyclical's teaching on morality but he suggests that there is need for some qualification or further elaboration. He states: "When the encyclical speaks of the 'universality' of moral norms (VS 51ff.), moral theologians will not disagree, provided that this is meant in the sense of general principles—since it is always true that 'One must do good and avoid evil,' 'You shall be just,' and so on."[38] It could be said that the encyclical wants to provide a simple answer to some theological developments that have taken so much time to take the shape they have today. There is no simple answer. Theologians have used the theology and philosophy of Thomas Aquinas, which has come to have several nuances over time, as well as other theological traditions.

On the debate on moral norms, Bujo says the following on Thomas Aquinas: "The moral theologian will, however, join Thomas Aquinas at this point in adding that the validity of these general principles does not always find the same expression in *praxis*. The more concretely one must act, the more difficult it becomes to translate general principles into action. This is clear from STh I-II q. 94 a.4, where Thomas distinguishes between 'speculative reason' and 'practical reason.'"[39] Aquinas acknowledged that the natural law is realized in concrete and particular instances. Bujo writes: "Thus Thomas's position is that, while the natural law is one and the same for all persons when considered 'in general terms,' there are certain individual points, 'presenting as it were consequences drawn from the fundamental principles' (STh I-II q. 94 a. 4), which are not the same in all contexts."[40] From Aquinas's perspective, Bujo is critical of *Veritatis Splendor* when it

---

37. Ibid. Cf. Böckle, *Fundamental Moral Theology*, 182–87.

38. Bujo, *Foundations of an African Ethic*, 82.

39. Ibid.

40. Ibid., 83.

insists "on the immutability of the natural law."[41] Bujo's theology and analysis of *Veritatis Splendor* is based on the natural law tradition in the Roman Catholic Church. This is evident, for example, when Bujo makes reference to Fuchs in the following statement: "The individual norms concerning prohibitions, as well as the theory of the *intrinsic malum* as such—even though this is traditional, and is taught in the Church—are justified only by the natural law, which means by human reflection. But human reflection cannot absolutely exclude erroneous thinking."[42] Using natural moral law reasoning, according to Bujo, should be contextualized in a concrete historical and cultural setting.

Evidently, the encyclical is aware of varying cultural contexts but insists that truth goes beyond cultural limitations (VS 53). Bujo points out that "*Veritatis splendor* employs a western doctrine of natural law; but the precepts deduced from this doctrine are based on human reason, which does not necessarily exclude errors."[43] But the western natural law doctrine is not the only method that can be used in moral theology. Bujo has suggested an intercultural approach to moral issues. Through an intercultural approach (or method), various theological traditions can dialogue, and thereby enrich each other. This leads to a more historical understanding of the natural law.

From the above, *Veritatis Splendor* appears to be confined to moral theology in the West. All other theologies are not given due consideration. There is an assumption that moral norms are the same all over the world. This is true when one looks at *Veritatis Splendor* on issues such as truth, freedom, and the commandments, among others. These demonstrate the encyclical's nostalgia for a return to scholastic theology, where truth was certain and the only thing the theologian was expected to do was to devise how to defend the truth. In an attempt to unify theological developments,

---

41. Ibid.

42. Ibid. When Bujo holds that intrinsic evil as taught by the church is known only through the natural law, he makes reference to Fuchs, "*Die sittliche Handlung: das intrinsece malum*," 177–93. See also Haldane, "From Law to Virtue and Back Again," 27–40. Commenting on *Veritatis Splendor*, Haldane states: "The main concern throughout is to show that a proper understanding of human agency implies that certain kinds of actions are intrinsically bad (*intrinsic malum*) and not such as can be justified by a pre-established fundamental option, good motives (*causis bonis*) or by a specific intention to produce beneficial outcomes" (34).

43. Bujo, *Foundations of an African Ethic*, 83.

diversity is easily done away with in the theological categories that the encyclical stipulates.

As an alternative, Bujo has suggested "Only the inter-cultural approach allows us to see the problem of ethical pluralism in its true dimensions. This perspective makes it even clearer that both the encyclical *Veritatis Splendor* and autonomous moral theology remain confined within their own world, that of European-American culture: it is in this world that their dispute is carried on."[44] *Veritatis Splendor* fails to realize, according to Bujo, that "it is not a dispute about pluralism within one and the same system, but rather about accepting that differing modes of thought endeavor to interpret one and the same fundamental principle of the gospel and to put it into practice."[45] The encyclical fails "since it asserts a priori a claim to universality *in moralibus*."[46] The gospel of Jesus Christ has been used variously by different Christian denominations and also theologians to reach to different but related theological and ethical conclusions (some of which have been horrendous).

In Bujo's analysis of *Veritatis Splendor*, the pope's words might have taken on greater significance if he had urged moral theologians not to assert the absolute validity of their own views but to listen to the voices of other cultures too. This would have taken up a discussion that, for example, Latin American liberation theology has sought with regard to autonomous moral theology. In an attempt to emphasize the universality of the magisterium of the church, the encyclical forgets that universality has to be understood in particular cultural and historical settings. An African Christian or theologian can be justified in feeling that the encyclical does not address African issues. This feeling is categorically stated by Bujo when he writes: "Although it addresses the bishops of the whole world (see VS 5), it operates within the categories of Western philosophy and ethics and addresses problems that are an urgent concern for the Western world."[47] The encyclical in its use of the natural moral law reasoning should go beyond the western philosophy, and in this way be inclusive of other traditions. Pluralism is an enriching element in theological study.

However, Bujo also points out the positive contribution of the encyclical in its use of Sacred Scripture. He does not go in depth in analyzing how

44. Ibid., 85.
45. Ibid., 83.
46. Ibid.
47. Ibid., 84.

Scripture is used in the encyclical. He states: "By starting with the example of the rich young man (Matt 19:16), the encyclical operates on two levels of ethical argumentation. On the one hand, it refers to the Ten Commandments (Matt 19:17–19); on the other hand, it emphasizes the words of Jesus which urge the rich young man to go beyond the observance of the commandments (see VS 6–27)."[48] This would be seen to come into conflict with other theologians who argue that *Veritatis Splendor* does not use the passage from Matthew in an accurate way.[49]

In a precise way, Bujo has critically analyzed *Veritatis Splendor* from the perspective of Thomas Aquinas's natural law teaching. He suggests that the natural moral law reasoning should incorporate an inter-cultural method as a way to embrace pluralism and the use of Sacred Scripture. According to Bujo, an inter-cultural method in moral theology realizes that moral reasoning takes place in concrete historical and cultural context.

2. Other Theological Responses to Veritatis Splendor

In addition, it is necessary to explore other theological responses to *Veritatis Splendor,* and the reasons theologians have given in support of or as critique of the encyclical. Some theological issues in the encyclical, and to which theologians variously respond include: authority of the magisterium of the Church, freedom, truth, conscience, moral autonomy, the use of Sacred Scripture, intrinsic evil, proportionalism, relativism, revealed morality, and the relation between morality and law.

Some theologians supported the encyclical and saw it as a document long overdue coming from the Pope. Their opinion was that some theological works, over the years, are contrary to what is Christian and, therefore, warrant a condemnation. Other theologians saw the encyclical as one-sided in its critique of the theological developments associated with them. These theologians somehow felt the encyclical was condemning theological positions associated with them. The theologians critical of *Veritatis Splendor* are

---

48. Ibid. 81.

49. Cf. Demmer, *Shaping the Moral Life.* Demmer states: "Scripture cannot be conceived as a handbook of moral theology, nor does it present any ethical system that could provide a ready-made answer for every area of life" (27). The use of Sacred Scripture in moral theology, especially after Vatican II, is a major concern of renewal moral theologians. Later in this section, a critical analysis of the use of Sacred Scripture in VS is made through a review of the work of William C. Spohn.

viewed here as making a response to the encyclical, and also as clarifying theological positions associated with their work.

The division of the section below into two parts corresponds with the theologians who support the encyclical's condemnations of various positions in contemporary moral theology and further the theologians who have expressed concern about the encyclical's condemnations. In my research it emerged that there are more theologians who are opposed to *Veritatis Splendor's* condemnations than those in support of the encyclical. For this reason, the section on the theologians opposed to the encyclical is more extensive than the one on those who support it. Livio Melina, Germain Grisez, and John Finnis are the theologians who support the encyclical. Among the theologians critical of the encyclical include: Richard McCormick, Louis Janssens, Charles Curran, and William C. Spohn. McCormick is critical of the way the encyclical condemns proportionalism. Janssens presents teleology as having its foundation in Thomas Aquinas, and for this reason views the encyclical's criticism of teleological thinking as a criticism of the same natural law method used in the encyclical and other church teachings on morality. On the other hand, Curran is critical of the presentation of Christian morality in a legalistic way in *Veritatis Splendor*. And Spohn is critical of the way Sacred Scripture is used in the encyclical.

A. Theologians in Support of *Veritatis Splendor*

Veritatis Splendor can be praised as a coming to awareness by the magisterium of the Roman Catholic Church on the issues being debated in contemporary moral theology. Whether the encyclical is critical of the majority of the theological debates is not the main point, but one can say that there is an awareness of many controverted issues that remain open to further theological inquiry. The encyclical represents the Church authority's participation and expression of caution in the debates, and presents what is the Church's official position on various issues concerning fundamental moral theology.

The theologians in support of the encyclical considered here include the Italian theologian, Livio Melina, Germain Grisez, and John Finnis. These theologians support the Pope on issues concerning (i) the relation of freedom and truth, (ii) conscience, (iii) the role of revelation and faith in Christian morality, and (iv) the intrinsically evil acts.

i. Livio Melina

Melina points out the contribution of *Veritatis Splendor* in moral theology. He views the encyclical as calling theologians to participate fully in the renewal of moral theology called for by Vatican Council II in *Optatam totius* (no. 16).[50] He views the encyclical as providing guidance to theologians, and thereby stimulating renewal in light of Vatican Council II. He has written: "The encyclical also offers positive directions for carrying on the work of renewing moral theology by exploring new paths that can overcome the limits found in the more recent tradition and in its insufficient revision."[51]

Melina notes that the encyclical is concerned with the "breaking of the bond between freedom and truth and of that between faith and morals" (no. 4).[52] He locates this in the crisis of postmodernity where he says there is no link between "reason and universal and permanent truth, [postmodernity] abandons freedom to subjectivist arbitrariness."[53] He takes the argument further to maintain that "the rupture between faith and morality gives legitimacy to a pluralism of (contradictory) ethical views."[54] Of great significance for Melina is that *Veritatis Splendor* gives us "precious indications for deepening moral theology and giving it its theological and philosophical foundations."[55]

ii. Germain Grisez

According to Grisez, the purpose of the encyclical is to correct errors in moral theologians and in the Christian faithful, and to show that truth should be safeguarded in moral teaching. He states:

> The encyclical does not deal with specific kinds of acts, such as contraception or abortion, homosexual behavior or adultery. Rather, it examines and finds wanting dissenting views that attempt to find a way around some or all of the precepts which exclude those or other acts as always wrong.[57]

50. Melina, *Sharing in Christ's Virtues*, 2.

51. Ibid., 3.

52. Ibid.

53. Ibid.

54. Ibid., 4.

55. Ibid., 5.

Grisez points out that the Pope, in his criticism of dissent, categorically holds that "faith includes specific moral requirements."[56] He clearly holds that the natural law in no way contradicts God's revelation but that the two go together. Grisez states: "The encyclical points out that God has communicated the same moral requirements both as a natural law, by giving human persons understanding of what is right and wrong, and as revealed truth."[57] He lauds the Pope's charge that a mistaken view treats conscience "as a creative decision rather than as a judgment following from moral truth."[58]

Grisez views the encyclical as a masterpiece by the Pope showing the true and right way in Roman Catholic moral theology. The Pope's intention, according to Grisez, is to correct the dissenters who "circumvent traditional teaching by flatly denying that the precepts forbidding certain kinds of acts as intrinsically evil really are exceptionless."[59] Grisez holds the main teaching of the encyclical is the intrinsic evil of some acts forbidden in the traditional teaching of the Roman Catholic Church. He differs with the proportionalists or consequentialists when he says they hold that morality is determined by considering "the actual circumstances, the greater or the lesser good or lesser evil which it might bring about."[60] However, Grisez points out that the Pope teaches, "that the exceptionlessness of the relevant norms is a revealed truth—that is, a truth demanding from every Catholic the assent of faith."[61] Grisez concludes that dissenting theologians should either "admit that they are mistaken, to admit that they do not believe God's word, or to claim that the Pope is grossly misinterpreting the Bible."[62]

iii. John Finnis

Another theologian who supports *Veritatis Splendor* wholeheartedly is John Finnis. For Finnis the focus of the encyclical is on action and specifically on intrinsically evil acts. On the theologians who are condemned in the encyclical, Finnis says "they overlook the relevant exceptionless norm which the

56. Ibid., 2.
57. Ibid.
58. Ibid., 4.
59. Ibid.
60. Ibid.,
61. Ibid., 7.
62. Ibid.

Church's tradition, authoritatively interpreting revelation, has constantly and most firmly taught as truth to be held by every Catholic: it is always wrong to choose to kill the innocent, whatever the circumstances."[63] He views proportionalists' teaching as unreasonable. He writes: "Proportionalism's appeal to 'proportionate reasons' identifiable neither by reason nor by Catholic faith points everyone to decisions of 'conscience' grounded in whatever one *feels* appropriate, all things considered."[64] He finds the encyclical as coming at an opportune time reminding theologians and Catholic faithful of the truth. He states: "The encyclical's reaffirmation that there are intrinsically evil acts, exceptionless specific moral norms and inviolable human rights is philosophically defensible and manifestly necessary to preserve the moral substance of Christian faith."[65]

For Melina, Grisez, and Finnis, *Veritatis Splendor* is "kind of a voice crying out in the wilderness" for theologians to return to the right path. These three theologians focus on acts rather than the person performing those acts. Their work seems to be a throwback to the manuals of moral theology where lists of sins and corresponding penances that a confessor was to administer in the sacrament of reconciliation were clearly stipulated. From the work of Melina, Grisez, and Finnis, the encyclical is a call to reform theology, and most of all to repair the damage that has been done over the years by showing the errors of contemporary moral theology. The call to theological objectivity in the encyclical can be seen as an awareness that despite all the theological diversity in the world today, there are still some areas of agreement. However, in the following section some of the theologians meant to be corrected by the encyclical will be seen to defend the validity of the positions they have taken, and show that the encyclical somehow exaggerates or misunderstands their theological positions.

B. Theologians Critical of *Veritatis Splendor*

The theologians dealt with here should not be viewed as totally opposed to the encyclical, but as trying to nuance the various theological positions

---

63. Finnis, "Beyond the Encyclical," 70. It is worth mentioning here the contradiction in the Sacred Scripture on the requirement not to kill the innocent. While Exod 20:13 says, "You shall not murder," 1 Sam 15:3 states, "Now go and attack Amalek, and utterly destroy all that they have; do not spare them, but kill both man and woman, child and infant, ox and sheep, camel and donkey." Cf. Deut 20.

64. Finnis, "Beyond the Encyclical," 71. See also Pinches, *Theology and Action*, 59–86.

65. Finnis, "Beyond the Encyclical," 74.

associated with them and condemned in the encyclical. Suffice it to say that theologians critical of the encyclical also have some positive evaluation of the encyclical.

In its editorial, *Commonweal*, summarizes the issues *Veritatis Splendor* condemns as follows:

> The errors include: making freedom an absolute; according conscience the status of a supreme tribunal; granting reason complete sovereignty; making a sharp distinction between the ethical order and the order of salvation; pitting law against freedom; dividing the unity of the person; denying the universality and immutability of natural law; elevating a "fundamental option for the good" above concrete moral choices; denying a distinction between mortal and venial sins.[66]

From the statement above, the encyclical was intended to show that human beings need revealed morality in order to realize their ultimate end. Human beings are the recipients of God's revelation. When the encyclical refers to revealed morality, there should be a clarifying point that the revealed morality is realized through the rational nature in human beings. For this reason, the encyclical has also to affirm the undeniable requirement of human reason, not to mention conscience in morality. Christian morality presupposes a rational nature created by God. To suggest a dichotomy between the revealed morality and a genuine human morality is untenable. God is the creator of human beings as well as the source of revelation. No Catholic theologian has openly supported the extreme forms of dualities condemned by the encyclical, such as the separation of freedom from truth or even relativism.

Many theologians view in *Veritatis Splendor* a shift in the theology of John Paul II. Selling notes that John Paul II is a "personalist" (phenomenologist), and that *Veritatis Splendor* is different from his earlier works especially on social ethics. For this reason the authorship of *Veritatis Splendor* is seen to point to multiple authors. Some theologians, like Selling, have suggested that the nature of the encyclical implies someone familiar with terms like autonomous ethics, theonomy, paranesis, ontic evil or physicalism and biologism.[67] This is seen to clearly point to someone or some people versed with trends or tendencies or currents of thought in theologies coming up in the West for decades in the past. Hence, Selling points out that the en-

---

66. "Editorial," 4.

67. Selling, "Context and Arguments of *Veritatis Splendor*," 26.

cyclical makes a "reinterpretation of the theory of the sources of morality: object, intention and circumstances."[68]

However, the theologians critical of the encyclical also see some positive points in the document. Lisa Sowle Cahill supports the positive aspects in the encyclical. She begins by saying that a "Lasting contribution of *Splendor Veritatis* [sic] is its affirmation of objectivity in moral thinking, against relativism and the absolutization of personal choice. The encyclical places . . . moral theology in a faith context, both to maintain the connection between the moral life and religious commitment, and to assert the authority of the magisterium over theological interpretation."[69] This is also true of Richard McCormick who commends the encyclical on some issues while he also disagrees with others.[70]

Contemporary moral theology is characterized by diversity of opinions and methods. The encyclical points out the dangers of the various theological positions. However, some theologians will be seen in this section, to indicate that the encyclical somehow exaggerates some theological positions to the extreme. For instance, there is a general claim that there are no moral theologians who advocates relativism in moral issues. It is with an acknowledgement of diversity in contemporary moral theology that I limit myself here to the critical evaluation of the encyclical by four theologians: Louis Janssens, Richard McCormick, Charles Curran, and William Spohn.

i. Louis Janssens: Teleology

Besides McCormick's critical analysis of the issues in the encyclical, Louis Janssens adds another view in his analysis of the encyclical from the perspective of the work of Thomas Aquinas. According to Janssens, there is no way the magisterium can use the theology of St. Thomas Aquinas and not be subject to teleology and proportionalism. Writing on teleology and proportionalism in the thinking of Thomas Aquinas, Janssens states:

> In its approach to the moral analysis of human action, the encyclical frequently refers to texts of St. Thomas. Thomas takes as his point of departure the inner act of the will, the principle of each

---

68. Ibid., 34.

69. Cahill, "Veritatis Splendor," 15.

70. McCormick, "*Veritatis Splendor* and Moral Theology," 9.

moral act, and he emphasizes the priority of the end, the specific object of the will.[71]

One can say from the above passage that teleology and proportionalism are present in the work of Aquinas. Therefore, when the encyclical refers to Aquinas it seems to appeal, in a way, to proportionalism and teleological thinking in morality. Nevertheless, the encyclical condemns proportionalism and teleological thinking.

The theology of Thomas Aquinas is concerned with humanity coming forth from God and returning back to God (*exitus et reditus*). In this return, the consideration of the end and means to that end is unavoidable. In connection to the final end and proportionality, Janssens states:

> According to St. Thomas, moral theology must first deal with the final end of human life and only after this can it deal with those things by which persons achieve this end, for it is from the end that one determines those things that are oriented toward that end (S.T., I-II, q. 1, *Introductio*). Clearly, this is a teleological perspective.[72]

The rightness and the wrongness of an act is determined by its contribution or hindering the realization of the final end. Janssens states:

> The object of an action is a real good (*vere bonum*) when it stands in the right relationship (*proportio, ordinatio, commensuratio*) with the demands of love; it is only an apparent good (*bonum apparens*) if it stands in contradiction (*repugnantia, contrarietas, exclusio*) with love.[73]

From Aquinas, Janssens holds that:

> Human persons not only apprehend the reality of the end, they also have a comprehensive understanding of the end and the relationship between the end and that which needs to be done in order to achieve it *(cognoscitur ratio finis et proportio eius quod ordinatur in finem ad ipsum . . . proportio actus ad finem)*. What is more, in contemplating an end, a person may consider not only the end itself but also that which must be done in order to achieve

---

71. Janssens, Janssens, "Teleology and Proportionality," 102.

72. Ibid., 103.

73. Ibid., 103–4.

that end, and only then decide whether one wants to perform the action (S.T., I-II, q. 6, a. 2).[74]

From Aquinas, the relation between the end and the means can be understood in the context of teleology and proportionality. The means should always be proportionate to the end. Therefore, for the Church to recommend the theology of Aquinas as a standard appears to be an acceptance of the teleological and proportionate nature of human morality (although this is what the encyclical is teaching against). Hence, Janssens states:

> Thomas, therefore, arrives at the moral judgment of particular actions teleologically. From this it follows that whatever is done in order to achieve a goal (*ea quae sunt ad finem*) must be proportionate to that goal and thus must not be in contradiction to the moral value that is present in the goal itself.[75]

The rightness and the wrongness of an act is determined by its contribution or hindering of the realization of the final end, and also by the means chosen. "The object of an action must be described in such a way that it can be determined whether it is in accord with reason and is therefore *conveniens* or *inconveniens*."[76] For example, on whether stealing is to be viewed as intrinsically evil, one has to consider the circumstance, intention, and object. Janssens notes that "On the basis of a goal-directed right to private property, Thomas concludes that in a situation of extreme need (*urgens, extrema necessitas*) one may take that which one needs from another's property when there is no other means to guarantee that which is needed to sustain one's life."[77]

Janssens makes an important contribution by showing how *Veritatis Splendor* makes use of the work of St. Thomas Aquinas. As I previously emphasized, Roman Catholic moral theological tradition was/is influenced in a tremendous way by the theology and philosophy of Thomas Aquinas. However, there are many interpretations of the work of Aquinas. Hence, Janssens makes a good contribution in his analysis of how the encyclical uses Aquinas's work. This is also true in Richard McCormick's analysis of the encyclical.

---

74. Ibid., 102–3.

75. Ibid., 106.

76. Ibid., 105.

77. Ibid., 108–9.

ii. Richard McCormick: Proportionalism and Intrinsic Evil

McCormick notes that the encyclical is written in a very technical language. For this reason, the readers of the encyclical need some training to understand what has been going on in moral theology. The encyclical is addressed to the Roman Catholic bishops in the world. Some commentators on the encyclical have wondered whether all bishops whom the encyclical addresses can grasp the issues dealt with in the encyclical, for example, the distinction between the ethical order and the order of salvation.

The commendable point, according to McCormick, is the encyclical's Christocentric presentation in chapter one. Of importance also to moral theologians is "the ringing rejection of the false dichotomies identified by John Paul II: between autonomy and theonomy, freedom and law, conscience and truth, etc. These extreme positions dead-end in relativism, subjectivism and individualism, and all of us repudiate such pathologies. But many theologians will protest that their work has nothing to do with these deviations."[78]

McCormick sees a problem in Chapter Two of *Veritatis Splendor*. He writes: "In its key second chapter, *Veritatis Splendor* is dense and technical. The Pope has joined an in-house conversation among moral theologians. To deal with the encyclical adequately, one has to plow into some heavy theological literature and language."[79] Among the repudiated issues in the encyclical are: proportionalism, teleology, relativism, and the controversy of intrinsic evil. McCormick finds the encyclical lacking because it judges some acts just by their objects without considering the circumstances and the intention of the moral agent. He states: "Equivalently, the Pope is saying that certain actions are morally wrong from the object (*ex objecto*) independently of circumstances."[80] He further clarifies that "The key problem is: What objects should be characterized as morally wrong and on what criteria? Of course, hidden in this question is the further one: What is to count as pertaining to the object? That is often decided by an independent ethical judgment about what one thinks is morally right or wrong in certain areas."[81]

---

78. Ibid.
79. Ibid.
80. Ibid.
81. Ibid.

Nevertheless, the encyclical is concerned with moral theology in the Roman Catholic Church. It is meant to give direction to bishops who as teachers in the Church ought to give guidelines to theologians and Christian faithful. To exercise his teaching role in the Church, the Pope highlights the importance of sound teaching based on Sacred Scripture as well the Sacred Tradition in the Church. However, he also condemns some recent theological concepts such as proportionalism, relativism, and the separation of truth from freedom, as not faithful to the Sacred Scripture and Tradition. On the condemnation of proportionalism in the encyclical, McCormick holds that the encyclical does not accurately describe what proportionalism is all about. What the so-called proportionalists have in common "is the insistence that causing certain disvalues (nonmoral, premoral evils) in our conduct does not by that very fact make the action morally wrong, as certain traditional formulations supposed. The action becomes morally wrong when, all things considered, there is not a proportionate reason in the act justifying the disvalue."[82]

As a theologian, McCormick feels that while the encyclical has some positive points, it also has somehow misunderstood some theological positions on issues such as proportionalism and intrinsic evil. McCormick notes:

> Later, in No. 81, we read: "If acts are intrinsically evil, a good intention or particular circumstances can diminish their evil, but they cannot remove it." In brief, the encyclical repeatedly states of proportionalism that it attempts to justify morally wrong actions by a good intention. This, I regret to say, is a misrepresentation.

Further, referring to the encyclical, McCormick presents the problem by those who are for and against proportionalism as follows:

> In the past, some have objected that certain actions are (and have been taught by the magisterium to be) morally wrong *ex objecto* (from the object). But the proportionalist, it is asserted, does not and cannot say this since he or she insists on looking at all dimensions of the act before saying it is morally wrong. The acts in question are contraception, masturbation, etc.[83]

---

82. Ibid. See also Vacek, "Proportionalism," 287–314. And also Hoose, *Proportionalism*, 69–95.

83. Ibid.

According to McCormick, an action cannot be judged morally wrong simply by looking at the material happening, or at its object in a very narrow and restricted sense. The object, the circumstances, and the intention of the acting person should be considered in evaluating whether an action is moral or immoral. McCormick gives an example:

> [A] theft is not simply "taking another's property," but doing so "against the reasonable will of the owner." This latter addition has two characteristics in the tradition. 1) It is considered as essential to the object. 2) It excludes any possible exceptions. Why? Because if a person is in extreme difficulty and needs food, the owner is not reasonably unwilling that his food be taken.[84]

The encyclical does not distinguish between proportionalism and the intrinsic evil controversy. Referring to the Pope's words in the encyclical, McCormick states:

> He cites as an objection to proportionalist tendencies the notion that some acts are intrinsically evil from their object. I believe all proportionalists would admit this *if the object is broadly understood as including all the morally relevant circumstances.*[85]

McCormick clarifies the position taken by the proportionalists concerning how to consider the morality of an act. He states:

> [W]e must look at all dimensions (morally relevant circumstances) before we know what the action is and whether it should be said to be "contrary to the commands of the divine and natural law."[86]

Finally, McCormick's response can be said to provide an important analysis of the issues dealt with in the encyclical. His critical evaluation of the encyclical is summed up here by his view of the encyclical's condemnation of proportionalism as based on a misunderstanding of what proportionalism is all about. However, McCormick's response to the encyclical is an important contribution in understanding the encyclical as well as some of the issues in contemporary moral theology such as proportionalism. Janssens's contribution, in his analysis of the encyclical from a teleological

---

84. Ibid.

85. Ibid.

86. Ibid. For a philosophical exposition on the background arguments in *Veritatis Splendor*, see also MacIntyre, "How Can We Learn What *Veritatis Splendor* Has to Teach?" MacIntyre argues that the encyclical uses a Thomistic understanding of the natural law, especially in its teaching on intrinsic evil (176).

perspective, is related to McCormick's critical analysis of the encyclical from the perspective of proportionalism

iii. Charles Curran: Moral Law

Curran views the encyclical as intending to show the role of the magisterium of the church in moral teaching. He points out that in the encyclical moral theologians "are called to be an example of loyal assent, both internal and external, to the magisterium's teaching (n.106–117)."[87] However, he is opposed to the encyclical's presentation of Christian morality as realized through obedience to the commandments of God. He is critical of the encyclical's emphasis on morality as law. He states:

> The first objection comes from the moral model which the pope proposes in *Veritatis Splendor*. Here John Paul II understands morality primarily on the basis of a legal model. Such an approach, which characterized the manuals of moral theology in vogue until very recent times, sees morality primarily in terms of obedience to the law or the commandments of God.[88]

Presenting moral issues in a legal framework goes against the understanding of morality from a Christocentric perspective, where morality should be seen as a response to the God who calls people in love to follow him. From a Thomistic perspective, Curran expresses concern over a legalistic understanding of morality. He writes:

> Thomas Aquinas did not follow a legal model, but rather a teleological model, based on what is the ultimate end of human beings. For Aquinas, the ultimate end of human beings is happiness, and actions are good if they bring one to that end and evil if they prevent one's arriving at that end.[89]

The preceding statement by Curran compares to the position taken by Louis Janssens on the use of the work of Thomas Aquinas by the encyclical, as previously noted. However, Curran questions the encyclical's legal model. According to Curran, "*Veritatis Splendor* thus gives the impression that it is describing the model for moral theology in general."[90]

87. Curran, "*Veritatis Splendor*," 226–27.

88. Ibid., 230.

89. Ibid., 231.

90. Ibid.

Basically, Christian morality goes beyond observing the command-ments. The legal model, according to Curran, is contrary to the Catholic tradition. He writes:

> The Catholic tradition as illustrated in Thomas Aquinas has al-ways insisted on an intrinsic morality. For Aquinas something is commanded because it is good. For Aquinas the ultimate end of human beings is happiness. Morality involves what is good for me as a person and ultimately makes me flourish. There is no opposi-tion between freedom and moral obligation, because the moral obligation is based on what is good for the individual.94

However, the preceding statement by Curran seems to need further clarifi-cation. He limits morality to the good of the individual, whereas morality has a communal or a social dimension. Nevertheless, he makes an impor-tant contribution by pointing out that morality is not founded on "com-mands" but on the personal capacity to realize what is right or wrong.

Ultimately, the legal model of moral reasoning in the encyclical can be seen to further support the Church's firmness in defending universal and unchanging moral norms (VS 96). The legal model is evident when the encyclical emphasizes the commandments, instead of intrinsic morality. "The major thrust of the encyclical insists on universal, immutable moral commandments which prohibit always and without exception intrinsically evil acts."[91] Curran notes that the Pope never cites the fifth commandment, "Thou shalt not kill," because of the many variations surrounding this com-mandment. For example, the manuals only forbid "direct killing of the innocent on one's own authority," and allowed indirect killing; killing in self-defense or in war, and capital punishment.[92]

Evidently, the encyclical is critical of contemporary moral theology. "*Veritatis Splendor* strongly disagrees with and condemns many of the developments in Catholic moral theology since Vatican II and stands op-posed to the revisionist moral theology in general."[93] Curran further views the encyclical as a part of a theological system that wants to replace other

91. Ibid., 232. See also Donfried, "The Use of Scripture in Veritatis Splendor." Com-menting on the use of Matt 19:16–22 in VS Donfried asks whether Jesus had in mind the universal and unchanging norms (VS 96) when he referred to the commandments. He states; "The broad generalizations in this section of *Veritatis Splendor* go far beyond what is said in the Matthean pericope or what can responsibly be attributed to Paul" (56).

92. Curran, "*Veritatis Splendor*," 232.

93. Ibid., 233. See also Oppenheimer, "Some Anglican Comments on *Veritatis Splendor*," 35–37.

theological systems. According to Curran, however, *Veritatis Splendor* should not occupy any privileged position but it should present its case in a convincing way and be open to criticism and disagreements as any other theological system. He states:

> The pope explicitly denies any intention "to impose upon the faithful any particular theological system, still less a philosophical one" (n.29). However, in reality John Paul II strongly reasserts the nineteenth and twentieth century Neo-Scholasticism of the manuals of moral theology within his more personalistic framework.[94]

From Curran's perspective, one can say that reducing Christian morality to the observance of commandments or moral law has the danger of making it a minimalist ethics. To be a Christian means to be a new creation or a new being in Christ. It is an integral way of life. The commandments or even the moral norms are relevant to Christian life, but they are not the only aspect of Christianity. We should never forget that a Christian person encounters new situations every day. Some situations are not dealt with in the moral law or the commandments, and therefore, require a response coming from the "new being in Christ." The gospels or the Bible provide basic principles that need to be applied to Christian living. Experience in the world provides an important tool in interpretation and decision-making in everyday life.

From the responses of McCormick, Janssens, and Curran, one can say that the issues dealt with in the encyclical are controversial, but are at the same time, indispensable in contemporary moral theology. However, the three theologians dealt with above, have been seen to question the position of the encyclical on issues in contemporary moral theology. On the other hand, some issues raised in the encyclical are helpful to contemporary moral theology. In addition, Spohn critically sheds some light through his analysis on the encyclical's use of Sacred Scripture.

iv. William C. Spohn: The Use of Sacred Scripture

Just as contemporary moral theologians have used Scripture in their work, so also the encyclical begins with an extensive use of the gospel story among other scriptural references. Spohn commends *Veritatis Splendor*

---

94. Curran, "*Veritatis Splendor*," 226. See also McBrien, "Teaching the Truth," 1004–5.

for its use of Sacred Scripture. He acknowledges the undoubtable place of Sacred Scripture in moral theology. He states:

> Examining the contours of moral theology's method will complement the historical map. Most writers in Christian ethics today would agree that there are four sources for moral reflection: Scripture, tradition, moral philosophy, and the empirical data relevant to the issue under consideration. Each of them makes an indispensable contribution.

Spohn does not question the encyclical's use of Sacred Scripture in general but whether it makes the right interpretation of the scriptural passages it references. The encyclical uses several texts from the Bible. These texts are applied in the encyclical to show that the points made are based on the Bible. The word of God is an authoritative way of showing the relevance of moral teaching and its agreement with the bigger picture of God's revelation. However, the question of method in the use of scripture is an important one that always requires consideration in any theological study.

Spohn is concerned with the theological method used in *Veritatis Splendor*. Unfortunately, the encyclical does not explain the method it applies in its use of Sacred Scripture. Spohn raises concern over the methodology and the context of the encyclical in its use of Sacred Scripture. On the use of Sacred Scripture in moral theology, he writes:

> The major obstacle to appealing to Scripture for moral argument is its apparent irrelevance to today's burning question. Can this collection of ancient texts from diverse cultures offer moral guidance on nuclear weapons, economic justice, or the new status of women? Clearly Scripture would have little to offer on these current issues if one restricts moral guidance to particular concrete moral rules of behavior. However, when ethics is expanded beyond rules and principles to encompass one's fundamental vision of what is worthwhile in life, the shape of one's character, the moral qualities of virtue and vice, and the humane quality of social practices and institutions, then Scripture can play a more extensive role in moral guidance. Biblical events like Exodus become paradigms for action; psalms are seen to shape the deeper emotions of the heart; and narratives reveal the character of God and intimate a faithful response.[95]

---

95 Spohn, "Morality on the way of Discipleship," 87.

Nevertheless, it is a controversial issue to use Sacred Scripture as a direct and literal source of moral norms. Scripture requires critical reading and interpretation in order to avoid a naïve fundamentalism. In a critical way, Spohn raises concern on whether the encyclical reads Matthew 19 in its context. He writes:

> The chapter focuses on what four different classes of persons must do to enter the Reign of God: the married, those who do not marry, children, and the rich. In context, therefore, the rich young man is not "Everyman," but a representative of the rich and their particular impediments to discipleship.101

The law and the commandments have a new meaning when viewed from the perspective of faith in God. The grace of God is necessary to lead to a moral life, and commandments are one way to respond to the God who calls people to union of love with him.

Sacred Scripture has a universal nature in the sense that it has something to offer to all people in the world, but it should always be immanent to context and always open to interpretation. Interpretation involves the reading of a text. However, one can question Spohn's view that *Veritatis Splendor* misinterprets Sacred Scripture because, in my view, a text can have as many interpretations as there are readers. Alternatively, there is no one method of scriptural interpretation. Although, it is not my concern here, contemporary literary styles range from deconstruction, structural analysis, to the reader-response method. Historical criticism as a method, though not the only method, helps scholars to locate texts in their historical contexts. Sacred Scripture is always open to interpretation, but it is imperative to realize that a particular context always influences the reading of a text.

Notable is the fact that Spohn acknowledges that tradition also shapes the way Scripture is used, especially in ethics. He states:

> Tradition and ethics will shape the selection of Scripture in any theological argument; it is virtually impossible to proceed *sola scriptura*. Biblical material is likely to be interpreted through commitments rooted in the author's tradition in order to yield applications consistent with the tradition. Or ethics may be the controlling factor: the model of ethics which is assumed in the application phase will enlist particular doctrinal and ecclesiological themes of the tradition to select and interpret Scripture.96

96 Ibid., 89. See also the statement by Collins when he refers to the use of Sacred

According to Spohn, it is people who make an interpretation of a text, and therefore every passage derives its meaning from broader convictions and assumptions. He holds that central theological themes and methodological commitments make it possible to understand the selected texts. Further, he argues that a biblical text is used in certain way because of a people's basic notions of God, humanity and the world, christological commitments, the relation of sin and grace (or grace and nature), and models of Christian community.[97] *Veritatis Splendor* also does not escape the influence of tradition in Roman Catholic moral theology. Ultimately, Sacred Scripture and tradition are inseparable in the moral teaching of the Church.

Nevertheless, one cannot avoid questioning the criterion used in the selection of the Scriptural texts in *Veritatis Splendor*. Spohn is particularly concerned whether the historical context is considered in the encyclical. "The process of selection inevitably raises the correlative question: What canonical texts, genres, or historical periods are left out?"[98] He notes that in the first chapter of *Veritatis Splendor*, the Gospels of Matthew and John predominate. "What is missing from this set? OT narratives, wisdom literature and prophetic material are mostly absent, The Gospels of Mark and Luke,

---

Scripture in moral theology before Vatican II. He states: "To the extent that it was used at all, the Bible was generally introduced into moral theology in one of two ways. Sometimes appeal was made to a scriptural passage, taken out of its biblical context, in order to provide a biblical warrant for or a scriptural confirmation in support of a moral judgment which had been essentially elaborated by means of a merely rational process. Sometimes the Scriptures were used as a principle of organization in the exposition of moral theology" (Collins, *Christian Morality*, 1–2).

97 Spohn, "Morality on the way of Discipleship," 87–88. Scripture cannot be used to justify any ethical teaching regardless of its source. One should not read in a particular text issues that text is not addressing. For example, Donfried is critical of VS's use of Scripture because he views the use of Sacred Scripture to justify the teaching on intrinsic evil as an "over-use," that is, making Scripture address issues it was not meant to address. He gives as an example the Pope's use of Scripture in VS to counter the theologians who oppose the church's teaching on intrinsic evil. He states: "*Romans 3:8*. This text is linked 'to contraceptive practices whereby the conjugal act is intentionally rendered infertile' (VS 80) . . . This becomes a fundamental text in the attack on proportionalism (VS 78ff.) and the text is understood to mean that 'no evil done with a good intention can be excused' (VS 78). On the contrary, it is asserted, the 'moral quality of human acting is dependent on this fidelity to the commandments' (VS 82). This is not at all what Paul has in mind as he is attempting to defend his teaching on justification from false criticism. Rather than linking the righteousness of God with covenant law, Paul is actually breaking the link between righteousness and law; it is this 'danger' that leads some to falsely accuse him of antinomianism" (Donfried, "The Use of Scripture in Veritatis Splendor," 51).

98 Spohn, "Morality on the way of Discipleship," 87.

which present different images of Jesus and of morality, are peripheral at best."[99]

Besides questioning the method in *Veritatis Splendor's* use of scripture, Spohn also questions the theological method used. Spohn wants to know the theological process followed in the encyclical to reach the conclusions presented in the document. Further, he states:

> Turning to the encyclical, we can inquire how it makes these methodological options concerning biblical material and coordinates them with the other sources of moral theology. Since the argument focuses on a particular disputed question, the empirical situation influences the choice of biblical material. The encyclical makes empirical claims about certain attitudes in the Church and secular society concerning truth, freedom, conscience, moral norms etc; however, no data are offered to substantiate or analyze these assertions.[100]

From Spohn, we can conclude that Sacred Scripture is an indispensable source and resource for moral theology. Sacred Scripture and tradition go hand in hand in any study of moral theology. This is coupled with the use of reason in moral issues as evidenced in the natural law tradition. However, just as faith and reason go hand in hand in Christian moral reasoning, so also we cannot separate Sacred Scripture from human reason in the moral discernment process. Nevertheless, the use of Scripture needs to be qualified because naïve fundamentalism cannot be reconciled with any sound theological investigation. One cannot, as such, take moral norms directly from the Sacred Scripture because there is always need for reasonable interpretation.

Conclusion

Veritatis Splendor is an important response of the magisterium of the Roman Catholic Church to the developments in moral theology after Vatican II. The encyclical condemns various trends in moral theology associated with several theologians. However, the encyclical raises some positive concerns in contemporary moral theology such as the problem of relativism, the use of Sacred Scripture in moral theology, the relation between morality and law, freedom and truth, among others.

99 Ibid., 90.

100. Ibid., 88.

This work critically analyzes the various responses to the encyclical from moral theologians. Bujo suggests that the encyclical would be more powerful if it employed an intercultural method rather than limiting itself to the western natural moral law tradition. Some theologians, like Grisez, Finnis, and Melina, support the encyclical wholeheartedly as a voice of clarity in an otherwise confused world of contemporary moral theology. Spohn, on his part, was viewed as questioning the interpretation of Sacred Scripture in *Veritatis Splendor*. Other theologians like McCormick, Janssens, and Curran, are featured as questioning the way the encyclical has dealt with issues in moral theology. These theologians question the encyclical's understanding and condemnation of proportionalism, teleological thinking, and the understanding of moral law. In their response to the encyclical, Bujo, McCormick, Janssens, and Curran, take recourse to the theology of St. Thomas Aquinas. The Pope in *Veritatis Splendor* also refers to St. Thomas Aquinas to show that the encyclical is faithful to the tradition.

However, the encyclical should not be viewed as a final word in contemporary moral theology. Neither is the encyclical in this work viewed as a solution to all the problems in contemporary moral theology. Diversity in contemporary moral theology should be viewed as a positive aspect, an acknowledgement that all people, no matter what their cultural and historical background maybe, have something to contribute to the development of moral theology. Diversity should be seen as a realization of the true nature of being "catholic" or universal. Though the church is one, she has many members who have different cultural and historical backgrounds.

Although the encyclical addresses moral issues after Vatican II, there are issues that the encyclical leaves unanswered. The first issue I observe the encyclical does not address is cultural pluralism in the Roman Catholic Church. The encyclical emphasizes the Word of God as the source of moral norms, however, interpretation of Sacred Scripture takes place in a historical and a cultural setting. The encyclical seems to advocate that the moral teaching of the Church magisterium has a universal nature. But in the world today, diversity is an undeniable reality, and evidence drawn from concrete experience is helpful in the realization of moral norms. Any people's culture and history shapes their interpretation of the gospels and Christian living. In the Synod of Africa, Pope John Paul II emphasized the importance of the inculturation of the gospel in the evangelization of Africa.[101]

---

101 John Paul II, *The Church in Africa*, 41–56.

The second issue the encyclical does not address, but I think it should have, is the role of moral theologians in the official teaching of the moral magisterium of the Church. The call for obedience to the teaching of the magisterium is not enough but there is need of more dialogue on moral issues. This dialogue would be beneficial as a learning and listening process in the formulation of the teaching of the magisterium. This dialogue should include theologians and other members of the Church, and thereby enable the magisterium reconcile different theological positions. Again, the universality of the Roman Catholic Church suggests that there is a way to realize unity in diversity. The universality of the Church should enable the magisterium to accommodate diversity in moral thought. But diversity should not necessarily imply disunity but a higher level of unity, one in many and many in one.

Bibliography

1. Works by Bénézet Bujo

Bujo, Bénézet. *African Christian Morality at the Age of Inculturation.* Nairobi: St. Paul, 1990.

———. *African Theology in its Social Context.* Maryknoll, NY: Orbis, 1992.

———. *Die Begründung des Sittlichen: Zur Frage des Eudämonismus bei Thomas von Aquin.* Münich: Schoningh, 1984.

———. "Can Morality be Christian in Africa?" *African Christian Studies* 4 (1988) 5–39.

———. "A Christocentric Ethic for Black Africa." *Theology Digest* 30, no. 2 (1982) 143–46.

———. *The Ethical Dimension of Community: The African Model and the Dialogue between North and South.* Nairobi: Pauline, 1998.

———. "Feminist Theology in Africa." *Theology Digest* 36, no. 1 (1989) 25–30.

———. *Foundations of an African Ethic: Beyond the Universal Claims of Western Morality.* New York: Herder and Herder, 2001.

———. *Les Dix Commandments pour quoi faire?* Kinshasa: Saint Paul Afrique, 1980.

———. *Moralautonomie und Normenfindung bei Thomas von Aquino: Unter Einbeziehung der neutestamentlichen Kommentare.* Münich: Schöningh, 1977.

———. "Polygamy in Africa: A Pastoral Approach." *Theology Digest* 32, no. 3 (1985) 230–34.

———. "Solidarity and Freedom: Christian Ethic in Africa." *Theology Digest* 44, no. 1 (1997) 48–50.

———. *Utamandunisho na Kanisa La Mazingira.* Nairobi: Pauline, 1999.

2. Works by other Authors

Amoah, Elizabeth, ed. *Where God Reigns: Reflection on Women in God's World.* Accra, Ghana: Sam-Woode, 1997.

Appiah, Kwame Anthony. *In My Father's House: Africa in the Philosophy of Culture.* New York: Oxford University Press, 1992.

Apel, Karl-Otto. *The Response of Discourse Ethics to the Moral Challenge of the Human Situation as Such and Especially Today.* Leuven, Belgium: Peeters, 2001.

Aquinas, St. Thomas. *Summa Theologiae*. I-II, Q. 90–105. In *Saint Thomas Aquinas: On Law, Morality, and Politics*, edited by William P. Baumgarth, 11–35. Indianapolis: Hackett, 1988.

Arntz, Joseph. "Natural Law and Its History." *Concilium* 5 (1965) 39–57.

Auer, Alfons. *Autonome Moral und christlicher Glaube*. Dusseldorf: Patmos, 1971.

———. *Autonome Moral und christlicher Glaube: Zweite um einen Nachtrag Erweiterte Auflage*. Düsseldorf: Patmos, 1984.

———. *Die Bedeuting des Christlichen bei der Normfindung*. Zur Theologie der Ethik. Freiburg: Herder, 1995.

———. "Das Spannungsfeld zwischen Recht und Sittlichkeit in der Theologischen Ethik." In *Recht und Sittlichkeit, Studien zur Theologischen Ethik*, edited by Johannes Gründel, 140–157. Freiburg: Herder, 1982.

Beemer, Theo. "The Interpretation of Moral Theology." *Concilium* 5 (1969) 62–72.

Benhabib, Seyla. "Afterword: Communicative Ethics and Current Controversies in Practical Philosophy." In *The Communicative Ethics Controversy*, edited by Seyla Benhabib and Fred Dallmayr, 330–69. Cambridge, MA: MIT, 1990.

Berg, Todd M. Vanden. "Culture, Christianity, and Witchcraft in a West African Context." In *The Changing Face of Christianity: Africa, West, and the World*, edited by Lamin Sanneh and Joel A. Carpenter, 45–62. New York: Oxford University Press, 2005.

Böckle, Franz. *Fundamental Moral Theology*. Translated by N. D. Smith. New York: Pueblo, 1980.

———. "Nature as the Basis of Morality." In *Readings in Moral Theology No. 7: Natural Law and Theology*, edited by Charles Curran and Richard A. McCormick, 392–412. New York: Paulist, 1991.

Boff, Clodovis. "Society and the Kingdom: A Dialogue between a Theologian, a Christian Activist, and a Parish Priest." In *Salvation and Liberation: In Search of Balance between Faith and Politics*, edited by Leonardo Boff and Clodovis Boff, and translated from Portuguese by Robert R. Barr, 67–116. Maryknoll, New York: Orbis, 1984.

Boff, Leonardo. *New Evangelization: Good News to the Poor*. Translated by Robert R. Barr. Maryknoll, NY: Orbis, 1991.

———. "Salvation in Liberation: The Theological Meaning of Socio-historical Liberation." In *Salvation and Liberation: In Search of a Balance between Faith and Politics*, 1–13. Maryknoll, NY: Orbis, 1984.

Boyle, John P. "Faith and Christian Ethics in Rahner and Lonergan." *Thought* 50 (1975) 247–65.

Brackley, Dean, and Thomas L. Schubeck. "Moral Theology in Latin America." *Theological Studies* 63 (2002) 123–60.

Bresnahan, James. "An Ethics of Faith." In *An Introduction to the Themes and Foundations of Karl Rahner's Theology: A World of Grace*, edited by Leo J. O'Donovan, 169–84. Washington, DC: Georgetown University Press, 1995.

———. "Rahner's Christian Ethics." *America* 123 (1970) 351–54.

———. "Rahner's Ethics: Critical Natural Law Theory in Relation to Contemporary Ethical Methodology." *Journal of Religion* 56 (1976) 36–60.

Cahill, Lisa Sowle. "Toward Global Ethics." *Theological Studies* 63 (2002) 324–44.

———. "Veritatis Splendor." *Commonweal* 120 (1993) 15.

Chege wa Gachamba. "Moi Criticizes Church Leaders." *Nation Newspaper*. Nairobi: Nation Group, April 26, 2000, www.nationaudio.com (accessed April 26, 2000).

Cicero. *De Republica*, III. Translated by John Salmond. *Jurisprudence*, 22–23. London: Sweet & Maxwell, 1930.

Coetzee, Peter H. "Particularity in Morality and its Relation to Community." In *The African Philosophy Reader*, edited by P. H. Coetzee and A. P. J. Roux, 273–86. 2nd ed. New York: Routledge, 2003.

Collins, Raymond F. *Christian Morality: Biblical Foundations*. Notre Dame, Indiana: University of Notre Dame Press, 1986.

Connell, Francis. *Outlines of Moral Theology*. Milwaukee: Bruce, 1953.

Curran, Charles. "Absolute Norms in Moral Theology." In *Norm and Context in Christian Ethics*, edited by Gene H. Outka et al., 139–73. New York: Scribner's Sons, 1968.

———. "Veritatis Splendor: A Revisionist Perspective." In *Veritatis Splendor: American Responses*, edited by Michael E. Allsop and John J. O'Keefe, 224–43. Kansas City: Sheed & Ward, 1995.

Davis, Henry. *Moral and Pastoral Theology*. Vol. 1. New York: Sheed and Ward, 1935.

Demmer, Klaus. *Shaping the Moral Life: An Approach to Moral Theology*. Edited by James Keenan. Translated by Robert Dell'Oro. Foreword by Thomas Kopfensteiner. Washington, DC: Georgetown University Press, 2000.

Dirks, Walter. "How Can I Know What God Wants of Me?" *Cross Currents* 5 (1955) 76–92.

Donders, Joseph G. *Non-Bourgeois Theology: An African Experience of Jesus*. Maryknoll, NY: Orbis, 1985.

Donfried, Karl P. "The Use of Scripture in *Veritatis Splendor*." In *Ecumenical Ventures in Ethics: Protestants Engage Pope John Paul II's Moral Encyclicals*, edited by Reinhard Hütter and Theodor Dieter, 38–59. Grand Rapids: Eerdmans, 1998.

Dubay, Thomas. "The State of Moral Theology." *Theological Studies* 35 (1974) 482–506.

"Editorial." *Commonweal*, 23 October 1993, p. 4.

Egbulen, Nwaka Chris. *The Power of Africentric Celebrations: Inspirations from the Zairean Liturgy*. New York: Crossroads, 1996.

Ela, Jean-Marc. *African Cry*. Translated by Robert Barr. New York: Orbis, 1986.

———. *My Faith As an African*. Translated by John Pairman Brown and Susan Perry. Maryknoll, NY: Orbis, 1988.

Finnis, John. "Beyond the Encyclical." In *Considering Veritatis Splendor, Considering Veritatis Splendor*, edited by John Wilkins, 69–76. Cleveland: Pilgrim, 1994.

Flannery, Austin, ed. *Vatican Council II: The Conciliar and Post-Conciliar Documents*. 2 vols. in 1. Dublin: Dominican, 1988.

Ford, John C., and Gerald Kelly. *Contemporary Moral Theology*. Vol. 1. Westminster, Maryland: Newman, 1958.

Fuchs, Josef. *Christian Ethics in a Secular Arena*. Translated by Bernard Hoose and Brian McNeil. Washington, DC: Georgetown University Press, 1987.

———. *Christian Morality: The Word Becomes Flesh*. Trans. Brian McNeil. Washington, DC: Georgetown University Press, 1987.

———. *Human Values and Christian Morality*. Translated by M. H. Heelan et al. Dublin: Gill and MacMillan, 1970.

———. *Personal Responsibility and Christian Morality*. Translated by William Cleves et al. Washington, DC: Georgetown University Press, 1983.

———. "Die sittliche Handlung: das intrinsic malum." In *Moraltheologie im Abseits? Antwort auf die Enzyklika "Veritatis Splendor,"* edited by Dietmar Mieth, 177–93. Freiburg: Herder, 1994.

Gadamer, Hans-Georg. "The Universality of the Hermeneutical Problem." In *The Hermeneutic Tradition: From Ast to Ricouer*, edited by Gayle L. Ormiston and Alan D. Schrift, 147–58. Albany: State University of New York, 1990.

———. "Truth and Method." In *The Hermeneutic Tradition: From Ast to Ricoeur*, edited by Gayle L. Ormiston and Alan D. Schrift, 198–212. Albany: State University of New York, 1990.

Gallagher, John A. *Time Past, Time Future: A Historical Study of Catholic Moral Theology.* New York: Paulist, 1990.

Gewirth, Alan. *Human Rights: Essays on Justification and Application.* Chicago: University of Chicago Press, 1982.

Grisez, Germain. "Revelation versus Dissent." In *Considering Veritatis Splendor*, edited by John Wilkins, 1–8. Cleveland: Pilgrim, 1994.

Gründel, Johannes. "Natural Law (Moral)." In *Sacramentum Mundi: An Encyclopedia of Theology*, edited by Karl Rahner, 4:157–62. London: Burns & Oates, 1968–1970.

Gutiérrez, Gustavo. *A Theology of Liberation: History, Politics and Salvation.* Translated by Sister Caridad and John Eagleson. New York: Orbis, 1981.

———. "Option for the Poor." In *Systematic Theology: Perspectives from Liberation Theology: Readings from Mysterium Liberationis*, edited by Jon Sobrino and Ignacio Ellacuría, 22–37. New York: Maryknoll, 1996.

Haldane, John. "From Law to Virtue and back again: On Veritatis Splendor." In *The Bible in Ethics*, 27–40. Sheffield: Sheffield Academic, 1995.

Hallen, Barry. *A Short History of African Philosophy.* Bloomington: Indiana University Press, 2002.

Häring, Bernard. "Dynamism and Continuity in a Personalistic Approach to Natural Law." In *Norm and Context in Christian Ethics*, edited by Gene H. Outka and Paul Ramsey, 199–231. New York: Scribner's Sons, 1968.

———. *Free and Faithful in Christ.* Vol. 1. New York: Seabury, 1978.

———. *The Law of Christ.* 3 vols. Translated by Edwin G. Kasper. Westminster, MD: Newman, 1961–1966.

Hastings, Adrian. *African Catholicism: Essays in Discovery.* London: SCM, 1989.

———. *The Church in Africa: 1450–1950.* Oxford: Clarendon, 1994.

Hilpert, Konrad. "Glanz Der Wahrheit: Licht und Schatten: Eine Analyse de Neuen Moralenzyklika." *Herder Korrespondenz: Monatshefte für Gessellschaft und Religion* 12, no. 47 (1993) 623–30.

Hollenbach, David. *The Common Good and Christian Ethics.* Cambridge: Cambridge University Press, 2002.

Hoose, Bernard. "Authority in the Church." In *Theological Studies* 63 (2002) 107–22.

———. *Proportionalism: The American Debate and its European Roots.* Washington, DC: Georgetown University Press, 1987.

Hopkins, Dwight N. *Black Theology USA and South Africa.* Maryknoll, NY: Orbis, 1989.

Hordern, William. "Natural Law." In *The Westminster Dictionary of Theology*, edited by Alan Richardson, 392–93. Philadelphia: Westminster, 1983.

Hountonji, Paulin J. *African Philosophy: Myth and Reality.* Bloomington: Indiana University Press, 1976.

Hughes, Gerald J. *Authority in Morals: An Essay in Christian Ethics.* London: Heythrop, 1984.

Imbo, Samuel Oluoch. *An Introduction to African Philosophy.* New York: Rowman & Littlefield, 1998.

Isichei, Elizabeth. *A History of Christianity in Africa: From Antiquity to the Present*. Grand Rapids: Eerdmans, 1995.

Janssens, Louis. "Teleology and Proportionality: Thoughts about the Encyclical *Veritatis Splendor*." In *The Splendor of Accuracy: An Examination of the Assertions Made by Veritatis Splendor*, edited by Joseph A. Selling and Jan Hans, 99–113. Grand Rapids: Eerdmans, 1995.

Jassy, Marie-France Perrin. *Basic Community in the African Churches*. Translated by Sister Jeanne Marie Lyons. Maryknoll, NY: Orbis, 1973.

John Paul II. *The Church in Africa: Post-Synodal Apostolic Exhortation*. Nairobi: Pauline, 1995.

———. *Veritatis Splendor*. Vatican City: Libreria Editrice Vaticana, 1993.

Kant, Immanuel. *Groundwork of the Metaphysics of Morals*. Translated and edited by Mary Gregor. New York: Cambridge University Press, 1998.

Kenyatta, Jomo. *Facing Mount Kenya: The Tribal Life of the Kikuyu*. New York: Vintage, 1962.

Kirk-Greene, Anthony H. M. "'Mutumin Kirki': The Concept of the Good Man in Hausa." In *African Philosophy: An Anthology*, edited by Emmanuel Chukwudi Eze, 121–29. Malden, MA: Blackwell, 1998.

Kirwen, M. C. *The Missionary and the Diviner: Contending Theologies of Christian and African Religions*. Maryknoll, NY: Orbis, 1987.

Kobler, John F. *Vatican II and Phenomenology: Reflections on the Life-World of the Church*. Dordrecht: Nijhoff, 1985.

Kopfensteiner, Thomas R. "Globalization and the Autonomy of Moral Reasoning: An Essay in Fundamental Moral Theology." *Theological Studies* 54 (1993) 485–511.

Kopfensteiner, Thomas, and James Keenan. "Moral Theology out of Western Europe." *Theological Studies*, 59 (1998) 107–35.

Küng, Hans. *Global Responsibility: In Search of a New World Ethic*. London: SCM, 1991.

Küng, Hans, et al. *Christianity and World Religions: Paths of Dialogue with Islam, Hinduism and Buddhism*. Translated by P. Heinegg. Maryknoll, NY: Orbis, 1993

Lash, Nicholas. "Crisis and Tradition in *Veritatis Splendor*." *Studies in Christian Ethics* 7 (1994) 22–28.

Lefebure, Leo D. *Revelation, the Religions, and Violence*. Maryknoll, NY: Orbis, 2000.

"Lettre Ouverte aux évèques du Québec." *L'Eglise Canadienne* 27 (1994) 14–15.

Lindfors, Bernth, et al., eds. "Interview with Chinua Achebe." In *Palaver: Interviews with Five African Writers in Texas*, 5–12. Austin: University of Texas Press, 1972.

Little, David. "Religion, Human Rights, and Secularism: Preliminary Clarifications and Some Islamic, Jewish, and Christian Responses." In *Humanity Before God: Contemporary Faces of Jewish, Christian, and Islamic Ethics*, edited by William Schweiker et al., 256–83. Minneapolis: Fortress, 2006.

Livingston, James C., and Francis Schüssler Fiorenza. *Modern Christian Thought*. Vol. 2, *The Twentieth Century*. Upper Saddle River, NJ: Prentice-Hall, 1997.

Lottin, Odon. *Morale Fondamentale*. Tournai, Belgium: Desclée, 1954.

MacIntyre, Alasdair. "How Can We Learn What *Veritatis Splendor* Has to Teach?" *Thomist* 58 (1994) 171–95.

MacNamara, Vincent. *Faith and Ethics: Recent Roman Catholicism*. Washington, DC: Georgetown University Press, 1985.

Macquarrie, John. "Rethinking Natural Law." In *Readings in Moral Theology*, edited by Charles Curran and Richard McCormick, 2:121–45. New York: Paulist, 1980.

———. *Three Issues in Ethics*. New York: Harper & Row, 1970.

Maddox, Gregory H. "African Theology and the Search for the Universal." In *East African Expressions of Christianity*, edited by Thomas Spear and Isaria N. Kimambo, 25–36. Nairobi: EAEP, 1999.

Magesa, Laurenti. *African Religion: The Moral Traditions of Abundant Life*. Maryknoll, NY: Orbis, 1997.

———. "Christ's Spirit as Empowerment of the Church-as-Family." In *The Model of "Church-as-Family": Meeting the African Challenge*, edited by Patrick Ryan, 19–35. Nairobi: CUEA, 1999.

Mahoney, John. *The Making of Moral Theology: A Study of the Roman Catholic Tradition*. Oxford: Clarendon, 1987.

Manus, Ukachukwu Chr. "African Christologies: The Center-piece of African Christian Theology." *Zeitschrift für Missionswissenschaft und Religioniswissenschaft* 1 (1998) 3–23.

Martey, Emmanuel. *African Theology: Inculturation and Liberation*. New York: Orbis, 1993.

Matthews, Donald H. *Honoring the Ancestors: An African Cultural Interpretation of Black Religion and Literature*. New York: Oxford University Press, 1998.

Mbiti, John S. *Introduction to African Religion*. London: Heinemann, 1975.

McBrien, Richard P. "Teaching the Truth." *Christian Century*, Oct. 20, 1993, pp. 1004–5.

McCool, Gerald A. *From Unity to Pluralism: The Internal Evolution of Thomism*. New York: Fordham University Press, 1989.

McCormick, Richard A. *Notes on Moral Theology: 1965 through 1980*. Washington, DC: University Press of America, 1981.

———. *The Critical Calling: Reflections on Moral Dilemmas since Vatican II*. Washington, DC: Georgetown University Press, 1989.

———. "Some Early Reactions to *Veritatis Splendor*." *Theological Studies* 55 (1994) 481–506.

———. "*Veritatis Splendor* and Moral Theology." *America* 169, no. 13 (1993) 8–11.

McHugh, John A., and Charles J. Callan. *Moral Theology: A Complete Course Based on St. Thomas and the Best Modern Authorities*. Vol. 1. New York: Wagner, 1958.

Meditz, Sandra. *Zaire: A Country Study*. 4th ed. Washington, DC: American University, 1994.

Melina, Livio. *Sharing in Christ's Virtues: For a Renewal of Moral Theology in Light of Veritatis Splendor*. Translated by William E. May. Washington, DC, Catholic University of America Press, 2001.

Mendieta, Eduardo. *The Adventures of Transcendental Philosophy: Karl-Otto Apel's Discourse Ethics*. New York: Rowman & Littlefield, 2002.

Metz, Johann Baptist. *A Passion for God: The Mystical-Political Dimension of Christianity*. Translated by J. Matthew Ashley. New York: Paulist, 1998.

———. *Faith in History and Society: Toward a Practical Fundamental Theology*. Translated by David Smith. New York: Crossroad, 1980.

Mieth, Dietmar. "Universal Values or a Specific Ethic? Whither Moral Theology." *Concilium: In Search of Universal Values*, edited by Karl-Josef Kuschel and Dietmar Mieth, 147–53. London: SCM, 2001.

Moore, Gareth. "Some Remarks on the Use of Scripture in *Veritatis Splendor*." In *The Splendor of Accuracy: An Examination of the Assertions Made by Veritatis Splendor*, edited by Joseph A. Selling and Jan Jans, 71–98. Grand Rapids: Eerdmans, 1995.

Mudimbe, V. Y. *Parables and Fables: Exegesis, Textuality, and Politics in Central Africa.* Madison: University of Wisconsin Press, 1991.

Mugambi, J. N. K. *African Christian Theology: An Introduction.* Nairobi: Heinemann, 1989.

Mushete, A. Ngindu. "The History of Theology in Africa: From Polemics to Critical Irenics." In *African Theology en Route: Papers from the Pan-African Conference of Third World Theologians*, edited by Kofi Appiah-Kubi and Sergio Torres, 23–35. Maryknoll, NY: Orbis, 1979.

Muzorewa, Gwiyai H. *The Origins and Development of African Theology.* Maryknoll, NY: Orbis, 1985.

Muya, Juvénal Ilunga. "Bénézet Bujo: The Awakening of a Systematic and Authentically African Thought." In *African Theology in the 21st Century*, edited by Bénézet Bujo and Juvénal Ilunga Muya, 1:107–49. Nairobi: Paulines, 2003.

Njoku, Francis O. C. *Essays in African Philosophy, Thought & Theology.* Enugu, Lagos, Nigeria: Claretan Institute of Philosophy Nkede Owerri, 2002.

Novak, Michael. *Free Persons and the Common Good.* New York: Madison, 1989.

Nyamiti, Charles. "African Christologies Today." In *Faces of Jesus in Africa*, edited by Robert Schreiter, 3–23. Maryknoll, NY: Orbis, 1991.

———. "Some Items on African Family Ecclesiology." In *The Model of "Church-as-Family": Meeting the African Challenge*, edited by Patrick Ryan, 1–18. Nairobi: Catholic University of Eastern Africa, 1999.

O'Connell, Timothy. *Principles for a Catholic Morality.* San Francisco: Harper & Row, 1990.

O'Meara, Thomas F. *Thomas Aquinas: Theologian.* Notre Dame, IN: University of Notre Dame Press, 1997.

O'Neil, William. "African Moral Theology." *Theological Studies* 62 (2001) 122–39.

Oppenheimer, Helen. "Some Anglican Comments on Veritatis Splendor." *Studies in Christian Ethics* 7 (1994) 35–37.

p'Bitek, Okot. *African Religion in Western Scholarship.* Nairobi: East African Literature Bureau, 1970.

Ozankom, Claude. "Oscar Bimwenyi: End of Discussion on the Possibility of African Theology." In *African Theology in the 21st Century: The Contribution of the Pioneers*, edited by Bénézet Bujo and Juvénal Ilunga Muya, 1:95–106. Nairobi: Paulines, 2003.

Pegis, Anton C. *Introduction to St. Thomas Aquinas, The Summa Theologiae; The Summa Contra Gentiles*, edited by Anton Pegis, 609–50. New York: McGraw-Hill, 1948.

Pinches, Charles R. *Theology and Action: After Theory in Christian Ethics.* Grand Rapids: Eerdmans, 2002.

Pinckaers, Servais. "The Use of Scripture and the Renewal of Moral Theology: The Catechism and *Veritatis Splendor*." *Thomist* 59 (1995) 1–19.

Porter, Jean. *Moral Action and Christian Ethics.* Cambridge: Cambridge University Press, 1995.

Rahner, Karl. *Foundations of Christian Faith: An Introduction to the Idea of Christianity.* Translated by William V. Dych. New York: Crossroad, 1982.

Rahner, Karl. *Theological Investigations.* Vol. 14. London, 1976.

Ratzinger, Joseph. "The Church's Teaching Authority—Faith—Morals." Translated by Graham Harrison. In *Principles of Christian Morality*, edited by Heinz Schürmann et al., 47–73. San Francisco: Ignatius, 1986.

Rorty, Richard. *Contingency, Irony, and Solidarity.* Cambridge: Cambridge University Press, 1989.

Schreiter, Robert J. "The Impact of Vatican II." In *The Twentieth Century: A Theological Overview,* edited by Gregory Baum, 158–72. Maryknoll, NY: Orbis, 1999.

———. *The New Catholicity: Theology between the Global and the Local.* Maryknoll, NY: Orbis, 1997.

Schüller, Bruno. "Can Moral Theology Ignore Natural Law?" *Theology Digest* 15 (1967) 94–99.

———. *Wholly Human: Essays on the Theory and Language of Morality.* Translated by Peter Heinnegg. Washington, DC: Georgetown University Press, 1986.

Schürmann, Heinz. "How Normative Are the Values and Precepts of the New Testament?" Translated by Graham Harrison. In *Principles of Christian Morality,* 11–44. San Francisco: Ignatius, 1986.

Selling, Joseph A. "The Context and the Arguments of *Veritatis Splendor.*" In *The Splendor of Accuracy: An Examination of the Assertions Made by Veritatis Splendor,* edited by J. A. Selling and Jan Jans, 11–70. Grand Rapids: Eerdmans, 1994.

Shorter, Alyward. *African Christian Theology—Adaptation or Incarnation?* New York: Orbis, 1977.

Slater, Thomas. *A Manual of Moral Theology.* Vol. 1. New York: Benzinger, 1908.

Smith, Janet E. "Natural Law and Personalism in *Veritatis Splendor.*" In *Readings in Moral Theology No. 10: John Paul II and Theology,* edited by Charles E. Curran and Richard A. McCormick, 67–84. New York: Paulist, 1998.

Sobrino, Jon. "Theology in a Suffering World." *Theology Digest* 41, no. 1 (1994) 25–30.

Spohn, William C. "Morality on the way of Discipleship: The Use of Scripture in *Veritatis Splendor.*" In *Veritatis Splendor: American Responses,* edited by Michael E. Allsopp and John O'Keefe, 83–105. New York: Sheed & Ward, 1995.

Sundermeir, Theo. *The Individual and Community in African Traditional Religions.* Hamburg: Lit, 1998.

Tanner, Kathryn. *Theories of Culture: A New Agenda for Theology.* Guides to Theological Inquiry. Minneapolis: Fortress, 1997.

Tempels, Placide. *Bantu Philosophy.* Translated by Colin King. Paris: Présence Africaine, 1959.

The Canon Law Society of Great Britain and Ireland. *The Code of Canon Law.* London: Collins, 1983.

Thiong'o, Ngugi wa. *Decolonising the Mind: The Politics of Language in African Literature.* Nairobi: Heinemann Kenya, 1986.

Thomas, Linda E. *Under the Canopy: Ritual Process and Spiritual Resilience in South Africa.* Columbia: University of South Carolina Press, 1999.

Uduyoye, Mercy Amba. *Hearing and Knowing: The Theological Reflections on Christianity in Africa.* Maryknoll, NY: Orbis, 1986.

———. *Transforming Power: Women in the Household of God.* Accra, Ghana: Sam-Woode, 1997.

Vacek, Edward. "Proportionalism: One View of the Debate." In *Theological Studies* 46 (1985) 287–314.

Vähäkangas, Mika. *In Search of Foundations for African Catholicism: Charles Nyamiti's Theological Methodology.* Leiden: Brill, 1999.

Vidal, Marciano. "Die Enzyklika 'Veritatis Splendor' und der Weltkatechismus: Die Restauration des Neuthomismus in der katholischen Morallehre." In *Moraltheologie im Abseits? Antwort auf die Enzyklika Veritatis Splendor*, edited by Dietmar Mieth, 244–70. Freiburg: Herder, 1994.

Wambua, Sammy. "Is NEPAD the answer to Africa's Problems?" *The East African Newspaper*. Nairobi: Nation Group, May 6 2002.

Wiredu, Kwasi. *Cultural Universals and Particulars: An African Perspective*. Bloomington: Indiana University Press, 1996.

Lightning Source UK Ltd.
Milton Keynes UK
UKOW06f1246030916

282093UK00002B/342/P